OFFICIAL TOU

Short Breaks

Information at your fingertips

This pocket guide is aimed at holidaymakers who are looking for short break ideas and accommodation special offers. You will find a selection of hotels, B&Bs, self-catering holiday homes, and camping and caravan parks in England that offer short breaks, special promotions or theme breaks in 2007. Please check special offer details with the accommodation before confirming a reservation.

Star ratings

Establishments are awarded a rating of one to five stars based on a combination of quality of facilities and services provided. The more stars, the higher the quality and the greater the range of facilities and level of service.

The process to arrive at a star rating is very thorough to ensure that when you book accommodation you can be confident it will meet your expectations. Enjoy England professional assessors visit establishments annually and work to strict criteria to rate the available facilities and service.

A quality score is awarded for every aspect of the experience. For hotels and B&B accommodation this includes the comfort of the bed, the quality of the breakfast and dinner and, most importantly, the cleanliness. For self-catering properties the assessors also take into consideration the layout and design of the accommodation, the ease of use of all appliances, the range and quality of the kitchen equipment, and the variety and presentation of the visitor information provided. The warmth of welcome and the level of care that each establishment offers its guests are noted, and places that go the extra mile to make every stay a special one will be rewarded with high scores for quality.

All the national assessing bodies (VisitBritain, VisitScotland, Visit Wales and the AA) now operate to a common set of standards for rating each category of accommodation, giving holidaymakers and travellers a clear guide on exactly what to expect at each level. An explanation of the star ratings is given below:

Ratings made easy

★	Simple, practical, no frills
★★	Well presented and well run
★★★	Good level of quality and comfort
★★★★	Excellent standard throughout
★★★★★	Exceptional with a degree of luxury

No stars? Some accommodations are waiting to be assessed under new standards scheme.

For full details of Enjoy England's Quality assessment schemes go online at **enjoyengland.com/quality**

Gold and Silver Awards

The Enjoy England awards are highly prized by proprietors and are only given to hotels and bed and breakfast accommodation offering the highest level of quality within their star rating, particularly in areas of housekeeping, service and hospitality, bedrooms, bathrooms and food.

National Accessible Scheme

Establishments with a National Accessible Scheme rating provide access and facilities for guests with special visual, hearing and mobility needs.

Designators explained

Hotel	A minimum of six bedrooms, but more likely to have more than 20.
Small Hotel	A maximum of 20 bedrooms and likely to be more personally run.
Country House Hotel	Set in ample grounds or gardens, in a rural or semi-rural location, with the emphasis on peace and quiet.
Metro Hotel	In a city or town-centre location offering full hotel services but no dinner. Located within easy walking distance of a number of places to eat. Can be of any size.
Guest Accommodation	Encompassing a wide range of establishments from one room B&Bs to larger properties which may offer dinner and hold an alcohol licence.
B&B	Accommodating no more than six people, the owners of these establishments welcome you into their own home as a special guest.
Guest House	Generally comprising more than three rooms. Dinner is unlikely to be available (if it is, it will need to be booked in advance). May be licensed.
Farmhouse	B&B, and sometimes dinner, but always on a farm.
Restaurant with Rooms	A licensed restaurant is the main business but there will be a small number of bedrooms, with all the facilities you would expect, and breakfast the following morning.
Inn	Pub with rooms, and many with restaurants, too.
Self Catering	Chose from cosy country cottages, smart town-centre apartments, seaside villas, grand country houses for large family gatherings, and even quirky conversions of windmills, railway carriages and lighthouses. Most take bookings by the week, generally from a Friday or Saturday, but short breaks are increasingly offered, particularly outside the main season.
Serviced apartments	City-centre serviced apartments are an excellent alternative to hotel accommodation, offering hotel services such as daily cleaning, room service, concierge and business centre services, but with a kitchen and lounge area that allow you to eat and relax when you chose. A telephone and internet access tend to be standard. Prices are generally based on the property, so they often represent excellent value for families and larger groups. Serviced apartments tend to accept bookings for any length of period, and many are operated by agencies whose in-depth knowledge and choice of properties makes searching easier at busy times.
Camping Park*	These sites only have pitches available for tents.
Touring Park*	If you are planning to travel with your own caravan, motor home or tent, then look out for a Touring Park.
Holiday Park*	If you want to hire a caravan holiday home for a short break or longer holiday, or are looking to buy your own holiday home, a Holiday Park is the right choice. They range from small, rural sites to large parks with all the added extras such as a pool.

* Many parks will offer a combination of these designators

How to use this guide

Each accommodation entry contains information that proprietors provide regional tourist partners (except for ratings and awards).

AMBLESIDE

Rothay Manor
Rothay Bridge, Ambleside, Cumbria, LA22 0EH

★★★ Hotel
SILVER AWARD

T:	+44 (0) 15394 33605
E:	hotel@rothaymanor.co.uk
W:	rothaymanor.co.uk

Bedrooms:	19 • B&B per room per night (single) £80-£120; (double) £135-£170 • Credit/debit cards; cash/cheques accepted
Open:	Year round except Christmas and New Year
Description:	This Regency country-house hotel stands in its own grounds a short walk from the centre of Ambleside and the head of Lake Windermere. The hotel is renowned for the relaxed, comfortable, friendly atmosphere and excellent food and wine. Free use of nearby leisure centre. Closed 3-26 January.
Offers:	Special short-break rates available. Special-interest holidays October-May: antiques, music, painting, gardening, walking, bridge and Lake District heritage.
Facilities:	

1 Postal town
2 Establishment name
3 Establishment address (or booking address if self catering)
4 Enjoy England Quality star rating and designator
5 Gold or Silver Award where applicable
6 Telephone, email and website address – note that web addresses are shown without the prefix www.
7 Accommodation details, prices and details of when establishment is open
8 At-a-glance facility symbols (for key see facing page)
9 Accessible rating where applicable
10 Cyclists/Walkers Welcome where applicable

Please note that sample entry is for illustration purposes only.
Not all symbols shown will apply necessarily to this establishment.

Key to symbols

Rooms/units

- ⊁ Non-smoking rooms/units available
- ▣ Microwave
- ☕ Tea/coffee facilities in room
- ☎ Phone in all bedrooms
- 🛏 Cots available
- ▦ Central heating
- 📺 Colour TV
- ▭ Video player
- ▭ DVD player
- 🛏 Four-poster bed available
- ▯ Freezer
- ▪ Dishwasher
- 🪮 Hairdryer in all bedrooms
- ℮ Internet
- ∥ Daily servicing of unit

General

- ◐ Night porter
- P Parking on site
- ☏ Public phone
- ⚹ Children welcome (minimum age shown in brackets or check with accommodation)
- 🪑 Highchairs
- 🍷 Licensed bar
- 🚌 Coach parties welcome
- ✕ Restaurant
- 🛍 Shop on site
- 🎵 Evening entertainment
- ✿ Garden/patio
- 🐾 Pets welcome
- ⌂ Lounge
- ▭ Linen provided
- ▭ Linen available for hire
- ▭ Washing machine or laundry
- ▯ Lifts
- ▮ Shower on site
- ⚙ Calor Gas/Camping Gaz purchase/exchange service
- ▯ Chemical toilet disposal point
- WP Motor home waste disposal point
- ⊙ Electric shaver points

Leisure

- ➘ Swimming pool – outdoor
- ➚ Swimming pool – indoor
- U Riding/pony trekking nearby
- ⚲ Tennis court(s)
- ⚫ Games room
- 🎣 Fishing nearby
- ▶ Golf nearby
- 🚲 Cycle hire nearby
- 🤸 Gym/fitness room

Mobility Symbols

Typically suitable for a person with sufficient mobility to climb a flight of steps but who would benefit from fixtures and fittings to aid balance.

Typically suitable for a person with restricted walking ability and for those who may need to use a wheelchair some of the time and can negotiate a maximum of three steps.

Typically suitable for a person who depends on the use of a wheelchair and transfers to and from the wheelchair in a seated position. This person may be an independent traveller.

Typically suitable for a person who depends on the use of a wheelchair in a seated position. This person also requires personal/mechanical assistance to aid transfer (eg carer, hoist).

Visual Impairment Symbols

Typically provides key additional services and facilities to meet the needs of visually impaired guests.

Typically provides a higher level of additional services and facilities to meet the needs of visually impaired guests.

Hearing Impairment Symbols

Typically provides key additional services and facilities to meet the needs of guests with a hearing impairment.

Typically provides a higher level of additional services and facilities to meet the needs of guests with a hearing impairment.

Cyclists Welcome and Walkers Welcome

Participants actively encourage cycling and walking by providing clean up areas for washing or drying off, help with special meal arrangements, maps and books to look up for cycling and walking routes.

BERKSHIRE

NEWBURY

East End Farm ♦♦♦♦ Guest Accommodation
East End, Newbury, Berkshire, RG20 0AB

T:	+44 (0) 1635 254895
E:	mp@eastendfarm.co.uk
W:	eastendfarm.co.uk
Rooms:	2 • B&B per room per night (single) £35-£40; (double) £60-£70 • Cash/cheques, euros accepted
Open:	Year round
Description:	Five miles south of Newbury, in an Area of Outstanding Natural Beauty, this small, working farm will give you a warm welcome. Accommodation is in a beautifully converted barn. Choice of breakfasts with home-made and local produce. Ideal base for country lovers or stopover for business or travel.
Offers:	Packages available for riders, walkers and cyclists, including stabling/grazing, meals and luggage drop-off service.
Facilities:	

WINDSOR

Royal Adelaide Hotel ★★★ Hotel
46 Kings Road, Windsor, SL4 2AG

T:	+44 (0) 1753 863916
E:	royaladelaide@meridianleisure.com
W:	meridianleisure.com
Rooms:	42 • B&B per room per night (single) £50-£105; (double) £79-£125 • Credit/debit cards; cash/cheques, euros accepted
Open:	Year round
Description:	In the heart of the town centre and a walk to Windsor Castle. This beautiful Georgian property offers interior-designed, en suite, air-conditioned accommodation with flat-screen TVs, satellite channels, and high-speed WI-FI Internet. Outstanding, award-winning executive chef. Free car parking.
Offers:	Legoland packages including overnight accommodation, full English breakfast, dinner (optional) and Legoland tickets. Licensed for registry marriages for up to 120.
Facilities:	

WINDSOR

Runnymede Hotel & Spa ★★★★ Hotel
Windsor Road, Egham, TW20 0AG   SILVER AWARD

T:	+44 (0) 1784 436171
E:	info@runnymedehotel.com
W:	runnymedehotel.com
Rooms:	180 • B&B per room per night (single) £96-£247.95; (double) £158-£314.90 • Credit/debit cards; cash/cheques accepted
Open:	Year round
Description:	Overlooking the Thames at Bell-Weir Lock, a privately owned, modern hotel set in 12 acres of landscaped gardens. Extensive state-of-the-art spa and beauty facilities including 18m indoor pool and five outdoor tennis courts. Ideal for the wealth of local tourist attractions. On A308, off M25 jct 13.
Offers:	Please call for details of health breaks, Legoland packages and other special promotions.
Facilities:	

BERKSHIRE

WINDSOR

Stirrups Country House Hotel
Maidens Green, Bracknell, RG42 6LD

★★★ Hotel
SILVER AWARD

T:	+44 (0) 1344 882284
E:	reception@stirrupshotel.co.uk
W:	stirrupshotel.co.uk
Rooms:	30 • B&B per room per night (double) £90-£140 • Credit/debit cards; cash/cheques accepted
Open:	Year round
Description:	Stirrups, with its Tudor origins, is located between Bracknell, Ascot and Windsor and is perfect for visits to Legoland Windsor (three miles). Round off your day by relaxing in the oak-beamed bar by the inglenook fire prior to dinner.
Offers:	Weekend breaks from £95 per room B&B; DB&B from £55 per person per night. Legoland breaks from £190 B&B including two-day tickets.
Facilities:	

BRISTOL

The Bowl Inn and Lilies Restaurant
16 Church Road, Almondsbury, Bristol, BS32 4DT

★★ Hotel

T:	+44 (0) 1454 612757
E:	reception@thebowlinn.co.uk
W:	thebowlinn.co.uk
Rooms:	13 • B&B per room per night (single) £48.50-£87.50; (double) £76-£97.50 • Credit/debit cards; cash/cheques accepted
Open:	Year round
Description:	Whether travelling on business or just taking a leisurely break, you will find all the comforts of modern life housed in this historic 12thC village inn. Real ales, fine wines, extensive bar fayre and a la carte restaurant. Five minutes jct 16, M5.
Offers:	Friday-Sunday inclusive weekend break – three nights (single) £140; (double) £220.
Facilities:	

BRISTOL

The Town and Country Lodge
Bridgwater Road, Bristol, BS13 8AG

★★★ Hotel

T:	+44 (0) 1275 392441
E:	reservations@tclodge.co.uk
W:	tclodge.co.uk
Rooms:	36 • B&B per room per night (single) £65-£70.50; (double) £65-£87 • Credit/debit cards; cash/cheques accepted
Open:	Year round
Description:	Highly comfortable hotel offering genuine value for money. Splendid, rural location on the A38 but only three miles from central Bristol and handy for airport, Bath, Weston and all major, local attractions. Excellent restaurant offering international cuisine with a la carte and set menus.
Offers:	Stay Friday and Saturday night and get 50% discount on the Sunday night (including bank holiday weekends).
Facilities:	

BUCKINGHAMSHIRE

AMERSHAM

Chiltern Cottages ★★★★Self Catering
Chiltern Cottages, Hill Farm Lane, Chalfont St Giles, HP8 4NT

T:	+44 (0) 1275 392441
W:	chilterncottages.org
Units:	1 • Sleeps 8 • Low season £1,000; high season £1,000-£1,400 • Cash/cheques accepted
Open:	Year round
Description:	This fine 15thC residence, in the heart of Amersham old town, boasts a large dining room with 16thC wall paintings, a fully equipped kitchen, comfortable, high-quality living room and a four-poster bed in the master bedroom. Free car parking. Approximately one mile from Underground station.
Offers:	Short-break bookings permitted two months before start date. Price: weekly rate less 10% per day not used.
Facilities:	

BUCKINGHAM

Huntsmill Holidays ★★★★Self Catering
Huntsmill Holidays, Huntsmill Farm, Buckingham, MK18 5ND

T:	+44 (0) 1280 704852
W:	huntsmill.com
Units:	6 • Sleeps up to 9 • Low season £225-£500; high season £300-£600 • Credit/debit cards; cash/cheques, euros accepted
Open:	Year round
Description:	Courtyard of traditional stone, timber and slate barns, imaginatively converted from sheds and sties, offering a high standard of accommodation. Set on a working farm in a quiet location. Large gardens with easy access to footpaths. Close to Silverstone and many National Trust properties.
Offers:	Additional rooms may be added from B&B on special room-only rate.
Facilities:	

CHALFONT ST GILES

The Ivy House ★★★★Inn
London Road, Chalfont St Giles, Buckinghamshire, HP8 4RS

T:	+44 (0) 1494 872184
E:	enquiries@theivyhouse-bucks.co.uk
W:	theivyhouse-bucks.co.uk
Rooms:	5 • Single £75; double £95 • Credit/debit cards; cash/cheques accepted
Open:	Year round
Description:	A beautiful, 18thC, brick and flint inn situated in the Chilterns. This is a family-run business, and top-quality food plays a key role alongside award-winning beers. Over the past 10 years the team has earned a well-deserved reputation, resulting in it being voted National Freehouse of the Year 2006.
Offers:	Two-night weekend breaks available at £120 (single) and £150 (double).
Facilities:	

MILTON KEYNES

Swan Revived Hotel ★★Hotel
High Street, Newport Pagnell, MK16 8AR

T:	+44 (0) 1908 610565
E:	info@swanrevived.co.uk
W:	swanrevived.co.uk
Rooms:	42 • B&B per room per night (single) £58-£85; (double) £74-£95 • Credit/debit cards; cash/cheques accepted
Open:	Year round
Description:	Just 10 minutes' drive from the centre of Milton Keynes, this hotel is a delightful mixture of the modern and traditional. Comfortable guest rooms, all tastefully decorated and well equipped, two bars, and a lovely oak-panelled dining room offering an extensive a la carte menu. Civil marriages and wedding receptions catered for.
Offers:	Murder Mystery evenings. Four-poster bedroom.
Facilities:	

BUCKINGHAMSHIRE

CAMBRIDGE

Highfield Farm ★★★★★Touring & Camping Park
Long Road, Comberton, Cambridge, CB3 7DG

T:	+44 (0) 1223 262308
E:	enquiries@highfieldfarmtouringpark.co.uk
W:	highfieldfarmtouringpark.co.uk
Pitches:	Touring: 120; touring caravans: 60; motor caravans: 60; tents: 60 • Per night (caravan and motor caravan) £9.75-£13.50; (tent) £9.25-£13.25 • Cash/cheques; euros accepted
Open:	From April to October
Description:	A popular, family-run park with excellent facilities close to the university city of Cambridge and Imperial War Museum, Duxford. Ideally situated for touring East Anglia. Please view website for further information.
Offers:	Low season rate for senior citizens – 10% discount for stay of three nights or longer.
Facilities:	

CHATTERIS

Cross Keys Inn ★Hotel
12-16 Market Hill, Chatteris, Cambridgeshire, PE16 6BA

T:	+44 (0) 1354 693036
E:	thefens@crosskeyshotel.fsnet.co.uk
W:	crosskeyshotel.net
Rooms:	12 • B&B per room per night (single) £25-£48; (double) £36-£68 • Credit/debit cards; cash/cheques, euros accepted
Open:	Year round except Christmas
Description:	This Grade II Listed Elizabethan coaching inn, built around 1540, sits in the town centre. A la carte menu and bar meals every day. Real ale, fine wine and food. Friendly atmosphere, oak-beamed lounge with log fires. Ideal for touring the Fens.
Offers:	Buy one, get one free – weekends only – includes Friday, Saturday or Sunday. Evening meals must be taken in the hotel. Includes a complimentary bottle of house wine.
Facilities:	

CAMBRIDGESHIRE

9

CAMBRIDGESHIRE

HUNTINGDON

The George Hotel & Brasserie
High Street, Buckden, St Neots, PE19 5XA

★★★Hotel
SILVER AWARD

T:	+44 (0) 1480 812300
E:	mail@thegeorgebuckden.com
W:	thegeorgebuckden.com
Rooms:	12 • B&B per room per night from (single) £80-£130; (double) £100-£130 • Credit/debit cards; cash/cheques accepted
Open:	Year round
Description:	Completely refurbished, The George re-opened in March 2004 and has been changed into a modern brasserie and wine bar (open for breakfast, lunch and dinner to non-residents). Beautifully designed bedrooms individually characterised by their namesake of a famous George and equipped with facilities expected by today's traveller.
Offers:	Special weekend breaks available throughout the year.
Facilities:	

WISBECH

Crown Lodge
Downham Road, Outwell, Wisbech, Norfolk, PE14 8SE

★★Hotel

T:	+44 (0) 1945 773391
E:	reception@thecrownlodgehotel.co.uk
W:	thecrownlodgehotel.co.uk
Rooms:	10 • B&B per room per night (single) £62; (double) £84 Credit/debit cards; cash/cheques accepted
Open:	Year round except Christmas and New Year
Description:	This privately run hotel enjoys a picturesque location on the banks of Well Creek in the village of Outwell, a short drive from Wisbech and Downham Market. The best local produce is freshly prepared to provide meals with imagination or simplicity. All public areas are climate controlled. Wireless Internet offered free of charge.
Offers:	Weekend breaks – two nights 10% discount; three nights for the price of two.
Facilities:	

WYTON

Wyton Lakes Holiday Park
Banks End, Wyton, Huntingdon, Cambridgeshire, PE28 2AA

★★★★Holiday Park

T:	+44 (0) 1480 412715
E:	loupeter@supanet.com
W:	wytonlakes.com
Pitches:	Touring: 40; touring caravans: 40; motor caravans: 10; tents: 10 • Per night (caravan and motor caravan) from £13.50; (tent) from £10 • Cash/cheques accepted
Open:	From April to October
Description:	Adults-only park. Some pitches beside the on-site carp and coarse-fishing lakes. River frontage. Close to local amenities.
Offers:	A 10% discount on all bookings seven nights or more paid in full on arrival. Seven days' fishing for the price of six.
Facilities:	

CHESHIRE

CHESTER

Chester Brooklands ★★★Guest Accommodation
8 Newton Lane, Chester, CH2 3RB

T:	+44 (0) 1244 348856
E:	enquiries@chester-bandb.com
W:	chester-bandb.com
Rooms:	4 • B&B per room per night (single) £42-£80; (double) £50-£95 • Credit/debit cards; cash/cheques, euros accepted
Open:	Year round except Christmas and New Year
Description:	Large bedrooms offering king, double, single and twin beds. Large en suite to every room with power shower. WI-FI Internet access available. Non-smoking establishment. Well located for railway station, Chester races, Cheshire Oaks and city centre.
Offers:	Stay two nights or more at £25 per person based on twin room accommodation for two full-paying adults (excluding Friday and Saturday).
Facilities:	

CHESTER

Curzon Hotel ★★Hotel
52-54 Hough Green, Chester, Cheshire, CH4 8JQ

T:	+44 (0) 1244 678581
E:	curzon.chester@virgin.net
W:	curzonhotel.co.uk
Rooms:	16 • B&B per room per night (single) £65-£85; (double) £90-£120 • Credit/debit cards; cash/cheques accepted
Open:	Year round except Christmas and New Year
Description:	The Curzon is a family-run, Victorian townhouse hotel. Unwind in the lounge bar and sample our excellent cuisine in the splendid restaurant. Sleep peacefully in one of the individually designed guest rooms. There is ample private parking, and it is within easy reach of the city centre.
Offers:	Deva Break – any two nights' DB&B £60 per person per night. Winter Warmers (from November) – third night's DB&B half price. Special breaks their forte.
Facilities:	

CHESTER

Mitchell's of Chester ★★★★★Guest Accommodation
28 Hough Green, Chester, CH4 8JQ SILVER AWARD

T:	+44 (0) 1244 679004
E:	mitoches@dialstart.net
W:	mitchellsofchester.com
Rooms:	7 • B&B per room per night (single) £40-£50; (double) £65-£75 • Credit/debit cards; cash/cheques accepted
Open:	Year round except Christmas
Description:	Highly recommended in good guides. Relax in this tastefully restored Victorian residence set in compact, landscaped gardens. All rooms are en suite and have hospitality tray, TV, radio broadband, hairdryer and many other comforts. Easy walk to city, golf club and racecourse, and on bus route.
Offers:	Discount of 25% off Sunday when taken continuously with two other nights, or 10% off the third night and onwards.
Facilities:	

CHESHIRE

MACCLESFIELD

Ryles Arms ★★★★Inn
Hollin Lane, Sutton, Macclesfield, SK11 0NN

T:	+44 (0) 1260 252244
E:	info@rylesarms.com
W:	rylesarms.com
Rooms:	5 • B&B per person per night (single) £65; (double) £83 • Credit/debit cards; cash/cheques, euros accepted
Open:	Year round
Description:	Traditional country inn with award-winning restaurant and en suite accommodation along the Gritstone Trail, amid breathtaking scenery. Quality cuisine using local produce. Rural setting, only three miles from town. Popular with business travellers and walkers. Close to Manchester Airport, Derbyshire and the Peak District. Free wireless broadband.
Offers:	Short-break rates and walking packages. Please contact us for current available offers.
Facilities:	

WILMSLOW

Stanneylands Hotel ★★★★Hotel
Stanneylands Road, Wilmslow, Cheshire, SK9 4EY
SILVER AWARD

T:	+44 (0) 1625 525225
E:	enquiries@stanneylandshotel.co.uk
W:	primahotels.co.uk
Rooms:	31 • B&B per room per night (single) £65-£110; (double) £90-£140 • Credit/debit cards; cash/cheques accepted
Open:	Year round
Description:	Exclusive country-house hotel set in several acres of beautiful gardens. All rooms en suite with satellite TV, radio, trouser-press and telephone. Rosettes for fine cuisine, in addition to many awards for excellence. Ideal base for exploring Cheshire and the Peak District. Twenty minutes from Manchester city centre and three miles from airport.
Offers:	Park and fly – £65 per person sharing (room only) including 15 days' free car parking, courtesy coach to airport 0800-2300.
Facilities:	

CORNWALL

BODMIN

Bedknobs B&B ♦♦♦♦Guest Accommodation
Polgwyn, Castle Street, Bodmin, PL31 2DX
SILVER AWARD

T:	+44 (0) 1208 77553
E:	gill@bedknobs.co.uk
W:	bedknobs.co.uk
Rooms:	3 • B&B per room per night (single) £50-£75; (double) £60-£90 • Credit/debit cards; cash/cheques accepted
Open:	Year round
Description:	An elegant, Victorian villa nestling in woodland gardens, all within easy reach of Bodmin town centre. Ideal for business or pleasure. Relax in spacious, en suite rooms with all the extras you need for a comfortable stay. Award-winning B&B where you will experience the pleasures of sustainable living.
Offers:	1 November-28 February: weekend winter breaks – stay two nights, third free. Also, discounted mid-week breaks.
Facilities:	

CORNWALL

BOSCASTLE

Wellington Hotel
★★Hotel — SILVER AWARD
The Harbour, Boscastle, Cornwall, PL35 0AQ

T:	+44 (0) 1840 250202
E:	info@boscastle-wellington.com
W:	boscastle-wellington.com
Rooms:	15 • B&B per room per night (single) £40-£45; (double) £80-£130 • Credit/debit cards; cash/cheques accepted
Open:	Year round
Description:	Listed 16thC coaching inn in the Elizabethan harbour of Boscastle. Fantastic, fine dining restaurant. Traditional pub with Cornish ales, home-cooked food and log fire. Ten acres of private woodland walks and close to coastal path. Ideal location for discovering Cornwall. Recently refurbished after the Boscastle floods.
Offers:	Special breaks available throughout year. A 10% discount for four or more nights; 15% discount for seven or more nights.
Facilities:	

BUDE

Harefield Cottage
★★★★B&B — SILVER AWARD
Upton, Bude, Cornwall, EX23 0LY

T:	+44 (0) 1288 352350
E:	sales@coast-countryside.co.uk
W:	coast-countryside.co.uk
Rooms:	3 • B&B per room per night (single) £30; (double) £50 Credit/debit cards; cash/cheques accepted
Open:	Year round
Description:	Stone-built cottage with outstanding views. Luxurious and spacious en suite bedrooms, king-size beds and four-poster available. Home cooking our speciality. All diets catered for. Personal attention assured at all times. Only 250 yards from the coastal footpath. One mile downhill to the National Cycle network. Hot tub available.
Offers:	Special three-night breaks including DB&B and packed lunch – £130; with walking – £150.
Facilities:	

BUDE

Ivyleaf Combe
★★★★Self Catering
Ivyleaf Combe, Ivyleaf Hill, Stratton, EX23 9LD

T:	+44 (0) 1288 321323
W:	ivyleafcombe.com
Units:	10 • Sleeps from 4-6 • Low season £295-£335; high season £645-£810 • Cash/cheques accepted
Open:	Year round
Description:	Discover this superbly appointed selection of lodges in a tranquil and beautiful setting. These spacious and contemporary lodges offer the perfect place in which to unwind and relax. All have their own deck/patio, and some have hot tubs. Large, safe play area. Ivyleaf Combe is perfect for that romantic break or the family holiday.
Offers:	Three-/four-night stays available. Romantic break packages in lodges with four-poster bed and hot tub.
Facilities:	

CORNWALL

BUDE

Kings Hill Meadow ♦♦♦♦♦ Guest Accommodation
Bagbury Road, Bude, EX23 8SR

T:	+44 (0) 1288 355004
E:	kingshillmeadow@btinternet.com
W:	kingshillmeadow.co.uk
Rooms:	5 • B&B per room per night (single) £30-£50; (double) £50-£80 • Credit/debit cards; cash/cheques accepted
Open:	Year round
Description:	Luxuriously appointed B&B, set in three acres overlooking Bude nature reserve. All are en suite rooms and equipped to the highest standards. Peaceful location, yet five minutes' walk from Bude town and its beautiful beaches, and ideally located to explore Devon and Cornwall. Ample parking and storage for the sports enthusiast.
Offers:	Discounts on stays of four or more days (excluding Saturday). Special price, low season breaks available – phone for details.
Facilities:	

BUDE

The Falcon Hotel ★★★ Hotel
Breakwater Road, Bude, Cornwall, EX23 8SD
SILVER AWARD

T:	+44 (0) 1288 352005
E:	reception@falconhotel.com
W:	falconhotel.com
Rooms:	29 • B&B per room per night (single) £55-£75; (double) £110-£140 • Credit/debit cards; cash/cheques accepted
Open:	Year round except Christmas
Description:	Overlooking Bude Canal, with beautiful walled gardens and a short walk to beaches and shops, this hotel has one of the most attractive positions in Cornwall. The well-appointed bedrooms have luxurious bathrooms, and Sky TV. The bar meals are very popular in the Coachmans Bar as is the a la carte and fresh fish menu in Tennyson's Restaurant.
Offers:	Special three-day B&B breaks available all year.
Facilities:	

CALLINGTON

Hampton Manor ♦♦♦ Guest Accommodation
Alston, Callington, Cornwall, PL17 8LX

T:	+44 (0) 1579 370494
E:	hamptonmanor@supanet.com
W:	hamptonmanor.co.uk
Rooms:	6 • B&B per room per night (single) £29.95-£39.95; (double) £59.90-£69.90 • Cash/cheques accepted
Open:	Year round
Description:	Small, Victorian country-house hotel set in 2.50 acres amid tranquil countryside bordering Devon. High-quality accommodation, personal service and home-cooked food (diets catered for). Thirty minutes' drive from north and south coasts, historic Plymouth, Dartmoor and Bodmin Moor.
Offers:	Romantic packages, activity weekends for bridge players, walkers, ornithologists etc. Discounts for groups and long stays.
Facilities:	

CORNWALL

FALMOUTH

Green Lawns Hotel
★★★ Hotel
SILVER AWARD

Western Terrace, Falmouth, Cornwall, TR11 4QJ

T:	+44 (0) 1326 312734
E:	info@greenlawnshotel.com
W:	greenlawnshotel.com
Rooms:	39 • B&B per room per night (single) £55-£105; (double) £100-£180 • Credit/debit cards; cash/cheques accepted
Open:	Year round except Christmas
Description:	Elegant, chateau-style hotel in prize-winning gardens with views across Falmouth Bay. Distinguished by its ivy exterior, the hotel is between the main beaches and town centre. The Green Lawns offers the perfect holiday setting or business retreat. It is privately owned and renowned for friendly hospitality and professional service.
Offers:	Special terms on DB&B based on two people sharing a twin/double for 3/5/7 nights. Spring and autumn breaks.
Facilities:	

HELSTONE

Mayrose Farm
★★★ Self Catering

Mayrose Farm, Camelford, PL32 9RN

T:	+44 (0) 1326 312734
W:	mayrosefarmcottages.co.uk
Units:	6 • Sleeps from 1-6 • Low season £285-£500; high season £682-£915 • Credit/debit cards; cash/cheques accepted
Open:	Year round
Description:	Off quiet country lane, Cornish-stone farm cottages overlooking 18 acres of fields with views down picturesque Allen Valley. Cosy whitewashed interiors, some log-burners. Linen and towels provided. Heated outdoor pool, friendly farm animals for the children. Close to coast and moor. In low season various courses available – please enquire.
Offers:	Ideal for family reunions, group holidays etc. Catering help available. Short breaks available October-March. Alternative therapy courses in autumn.
Facilities:	

LANREATH-BY-LOOE

Bocaddon Farm
★★★★ B&B

Looe, Cornwall, PL13 2PG

T:	+44 (0) 1503 220192
E:	holidays@bocaddon.com
W:	bocaddon.com
Rooms:	2 • B&B per room per night (double) £56-£60 • Credit/debit cards; cash/cheques accepted
Open:	Year round except Christmas and New Year
Description:	Hidden in the centre of our dairy farm, yet within easy reach of beautiful parts of Cornwall. Enjoy the comfort of a lovely, old stone farmhouse along with the luxury of recently converted, en suite bedrooms. Swim in the indoor, heated pool, then indulge yourself in a really good farmhouse breakfast.
Offers:	Discounts for stays of three or more nights.
Facilities:	

CORNWALL

LANREATH-BY-LOOE

The Old Rectory ★★★ Self Catering
The Old Rectory, Lanreath, Looe, PL13 2NU

T:	+44 (0) 1503 220192
W:	oldrectory-lanreath.co.uk
Units:	6 • Sleeps 2-8 • Low season £180-£345; high season £385-£830 • Credit/debit cards; cash/cheques accepted
Open:	Year round
Description:	Gracious, Georgian mansion with spacious, fully-equipped apartments reflecting the elegance of the period. Large, beautiful, secluded gardens with heated, outdoor pool. Picturesque, tranquil village in breathtaking countryside, minutes from pretty fishing villages and beaches. Superb stately homes and lovely gardens to visit. Excellent village shop two miles. On-site parking.
Offers:	Weekend and mid-week short breaks available (excluding June-September). Please telephone for further information.
Facilities:	

LAUNCESTON

Lower Dutson Farm ★★★ Self Catering
Lower Dutson Farm, Dutson, Launceston, PL15 9SP

T:	+44 (0) 1503 220192
W:	farm-cottage.co.uk
Units:	2 • Sleeps from 2-8 • Low season £185-£350; high season £380-£620 • Cash/cheques accepted
Open:	Year round
Description:	Watch for the kingfisher when relaxing or fishing by the lake or Tamar Valley riverside. Get up late and enjoy lunch at Homeleigh Garden Centre (400m). Two miles from historic Launceston with its Norman castle. Central for coasts, beaches, moors, National Trust houses and gardens.
Offers:	Free coarse fishing on lake and River Tamar (trout, salmon and grayling) for two people per cottage.
Facilities:	

LOOE

Hannafore Point Hotel ★★★ Hotel
Marine Drive, Looe, Cornwall, PL13 2DG

T:	+44 (0) 1503 263273
E:	stay@hannaforepointhotel.com
W:	hannaforepointhotel.com
Rooms:	37 • B&B per room per night (single) £37-£73; (double) £74-£146 • Credit/debit cards; cash/cheques accepted
Open:	Year round
Description:	A warm welcome awaits you. Set in picturesque Cornish village with spectacular, panoramic sea views. Superb home-cooked food. Varied dining options featuring quality local produce and fresh fish. The terrace is a popular rendezvous for cream teas or cocktails alike. Extensive leisure facilities.
Offers:	Special-event packages. Extensive range of conference and business facilities. Weddings and special occasions. Christmas and New Year celebrations.
Facilities:	

LOOE

Little Larnick Farm ♦♦♦♦ Guest Accommodation
Pelynt, Looe, PL13 2NB   SILVER AWARD

T:	+44 (0) 1503 262837
E:	littlelarnick@btclick.com
W:	littlelarnick.co.uk
Rooms:	6 • B&B per room per night (double) £52-£62 • Credit/debit cards; cash/cheques accepted
Open:	Year round except Christmas
Description:	A 200-acre farm in the beautiful West Looe River valley. The farmhouse and recently converted barn offer peaceful and relaxing, character, en suite accommodation, including a barn suite and ground-floor bedroom. Wonderful walks from the door. Drying room available.
Offers:	'Winter Warmer' breaks November-March.
Facilities:	

LOSTWITHIEL

Lanwithan Cottages ★★★★ Self Catering
Lanwithan Cottages, Lerryn Road, Lostwithiel, PL22 0LA

T:	+44 (0) 1503 262837
E:	info@lanwithancottages.co.uk
W:	lanwithancottages.co.uk
Units:	8 • Sleeps from 1-6 • Low season £200 • Cash/cheques, euros accepted
Open:	Year round
Description:	Charming selection of Georgian estate cottages nestling in the Fowey Valley with two delightful waterside properties. Cottages with leaded-light windows, crackling log fires, four-poster bed and glass-topped well. Parkland, river frontage and boat. Woodland and riverside walks from your garden gate. Come and relax and soak up the Cornish atmosphere.
Offers:	Short breaks out of season. Reduced green fees. Pets accepted in some cottages. Canoe trips available with safety boat.
Facilities:	

LOSTWITHIEL

Lostwithiel Hotel Golf & Country Club ★★★ Hotel
Lower Polscoe, Lostwithiel, Cornwall, PL22 0HQ

T:	+44 (0) 1208 873550
E:	reception@golf-hotel.co.uk
W:	golf-hotel.co.uk
Rooms:	27 • B&B per room per night (single) £35-£54; (double) £70-£108 • Credit/debit cards; cash/cheques accepted
Open:	Year round
Description:	Charming hotel in the heart of Cornwall, overlooking the River Fowey and close to the ancient town of Lostwithiel. A friendly and relaxed atmosphere, coupled with great facilities, make this a very popular destination. Restaurant, bar, gymnasium, indoor, heated swimming pool, tennis courts, beautiful 18-hole golf course.
Offers:	Cheaper rates if you arrive on a Sunday (or bank holiday Monday) and stay for three or more nights.
Facilities:	

CORNWALL

CORNWALL

MARAZION

Trevarthian Holiday Homes ★★★ Self Catering
Trevarthian House, West End, TR17 0EG

T:	+44 (0) 1208 873550
W:	trevarthian.co.uk
Units:	13 • Sleeps from 1-5 • Low season £166-£391; high season £395-£795 • Credit/debit cards; cash/cheques accepted
Open:	Year round
Description:	Converted from a Victorian hotel in Mount's Bay location, 50 yards from beach. Superb views of St Michael's Mount, Mousehole, Newlyn, Penzance. A selection of the finest self-catering accommodation available. One- to five-minute walk to safe sandy beach. Playground, pubs, restaurants, galleries, shops, bus routes for Land's End, St Ives and Penzance.
Offers:	£100 for two nights per unit in off-peak time.
Facilities:	

NEWQUAY

Degembris Cottage ★★★★ Self Catering
Booking address: St Newlyn East, Newquay, TR8 5HY

T:	+44 (0) 1872 510555
E:	kathy@degembris.co.uk
W:	degembris.co.uk
Units:	2 • Sleeps – call for details • Low season £240; high season £240-£610 • Credit/debit cards; cash/cheques accepted
Open:	Year round
Description:	Self-catering cottages situated in the heart of Cornwall, providing an ideal base from which to explore the whole of the county. Individual design and extensive use of natural wood and carefully chosen furnishings create a warm, homely atmosphere. Views from the french windows stretch for miles.
Offers:	Three-night short breaks November-March.
Facilities:	

POLPERRO

Crumplehorn Cottages ★★★★ Self Catering
Booking address: C/o the Anchorage, Portuan Road, PL13 2DN

T:	+44 (0) 1872 510555
W:	crumplehorncottages.co.uk
Units:	7 • Sleeps from 1-5 • Low season £185-£245; high season £355-£630 • Cash/cheques accepted
Open:	Year round
Description:	Individual Cornish cottages with lots of charm, situated in the beautiful coastal resorts of Polperro and Looe. Just minutes from the harbour, safe beaches and spectacular coastal paths.
Offers:	Three-day breaks November-March: £135 for two people (excluding Christmas and New Year).
Facilities:	

CORNWALL

PORT GAVERNE

Green Door Cottages ★★★★Self Catering
Green Door Cottages, Port Isaac, PL29 3SQ

T:	+44 (0) 1872 510555
W:	greendoorcottages.co.uk
Units:	10 • Sleeps from 2-8 • Low season £323-£515; high season £546-£1124 • Credit/debit cards; cash/cheques accepted
Open:	Year round
Description:	A delightful collection of restored 18thC Cornish buildings built around a sunny enclosed courtyard and two lovely apartments with stunning sea views. Picturesque, tranquil cove ideal for children. Half a mile from Port Isaac, on the South West Coast Path. Polzeath beach and Camel Trail nearby. Traditional pub opposite. Dogs welcome.
Offers:	Three-night weekend or four-night mid-week short breaks available January-May, September-December.
Facilities:	

PORTREATH

Higher Laity Farm ★★★★★Self Catering
Higher Laity Farm, Portreath Road, Redruth, TR16 4HY

T:	+44 (0) 1872 510555
W:	higherlaityfarm.co.uk
Units:	3 • Sleeps from 1-6 • Low season £220-£300; high season £300-£700 • Cash/cheques accepted
Open:	Year round
Description:	Come and relax in our tastefully converted luxury barns. En suite bedrooms, central heating, linen provided, gas cooker, fridge/freezer, microwave, dishwasher, washer/dryer, hi-fi, video, DVD. Close to beaches and the breathtaking North Cornish coast. Ideal for walking, relaxing and exploring Cornwall. A friendly welcome is guaranteed. One cottage wheelchair accessible.
Offers:	Short breaks available October-March, also discounted rates for couples, out of season.
Facilities:	

PORTREATH

Trengove Farm Cottages ★★★★Self Catering
Trengove Farm, Cot Road, Illogan, Redruth, TR16 4PU

T:	+44 (0) 1872 510555
Units:	7 • Sleeps from 2-6 • Low season £200-£300; high season £300-£720 • Credit/debit cards; cash/cheques, euros accepted
Open:	Year round
Description:	Traditional, well-equipped cottages and farmhouse on a 140-acre arable farm. Close to beautiful beaches, cliffs and countryside park, yet within easy reach of the main towns. Centrally heated, some with wood-burners – ideal for winter breaks. A superb location for walking, swimming, touring or just switching off.
Offers:	Short breaks available from £100 during low season.
Facilities:	

CORNWALL

RELUBBUS

River Valley Country Par ★★★★★ Holiday Park
Relubbus, Penzance, Cornwall, TR20 9ER

T:	+44 (0) 1736 763398
E:	rivervalley@surfbay.dircon.co.uk
W:	surfbayholidays.co.uk
Pitches:	Touring caravans: 70; motor caravans: 10; tents: 19; caravan holiday homes: 45 • Per night (caravan) £8.50-£13.50; (motor caravan) £8.50-£12.50; (tent) £7-£12; (caravan holiday home) £115-£505 • Credit/debit cards; cash/cheques accepted
Open:	March to December
Description:	Eighteen-acre, partly wooded park on the banks of a clear, shallow stream. Spacious, well-kept, individual pitches for touring caravans, motor homes and tents. Luxury lodges, some with hot tubs, and caravan holiday homes also available to hire or to buy as a second home. David Bellamy Silver Award.
Offers:	10% discount on 14+ nights between 1 April and 21 July.
Facilities:	

REZARE

Rezare Farmhouse ♦♦♦♦ Guest Accommodation
Rezare, Launceston, PL15 9NX

T:	+44 (0) 1579 371214
E:	info@rezarefarmhouse.co.uk
W:	rezarefarmhouse.co.uk
Rooms:	4 • B&B per room per night (single) £26-£37; (double) £52-£54 • Credit/debit cards; cash/cheques accepted
Open:	Year round
Description:	17thC farmhouse in a peaceful hamlet, offering comfortable, characterful accommodation with an emphasis on good food. Located within the Tamar Valley Area of Outstanding Natural Beauty, midway between Bodmin Moor and Dartmoor, perfectly placed for exploring the region. Freshly prepared, seasonally influenced meals available nightly. Licensed.
Offers:	Mid-week breaks available October-March. Choose minimum two nights Sunday-Thursday, stay an extra night free.
Facilities:	

ROSUDGEON

Kenneggy Cove ★★★★ Holiday, Touring & Camping Park
Higher Kenneggy, Rosudgeon, Penzance, TR20 9AU

T:	+44 (0) 1736 763453
E:	enquiries@kenneggycove.co.uk
W:	kenneggycove.co.uk
Pitches:	Touring: 50; caravan holiday homes: 9 • Per night (caravan, motor caravan, tent) £10-£16; (caravan holiday home) £155-£455 • Cash/cheques accepted
Open:	March to November.
Description:	Flat, lawned pitches in a garden setting with panoramic sea views. Close to South West Coast Path and secluded, sandy beach. Home-made meals available May to September.
Offers:	10% discount for senior citizens March-May/September-October (static hire only). No single-sex groups or large parties.
Facilities:	

RUAN HIGH LANES

Trenona Farm Holidays ♦♦♦ Guest Accommodation
Ruan High Lanes, Truro, Cornwall, TR2 5JS

T:	+44 (0) 1872 501339
E:	info@trenonafarmholidays.co.uk
W:	trenonafarmholidays.co.uk
Rooms:	4 • B&B per room per night (single) £26-£38; (double) £52-£56 • Credit/debit cards; cash/cheques accepted
Open:	March to November
Description:	Enjoy a warm welcome in a Victorian farmhouse on a working farm on the beautiful Roseland Peninsula. Guest bedrooms have en suite or private bathrooms, and children and pets are welcome. Public footpaths lead to Veryan and the south coast (three miles).
Offers:	Discounts for stays of four or more nights for children and for family rooms.
Facilities:	

SENNEN

Surfers ★★★ Self Catering
Surfers, 311 Longford Road, Cannock, WS11 1NF

T:	+44 (0) 1872 501339
Units:	1 • Sleeps from 2-5 • Low season £195-£270; high season £290-£435 • Cash/cheques accepted
Open:	Year round
Description:	A modern, granite, two-bedroom bungalow in a group of converted farm buildings. Bedroom one has three single beds, bedroom two has a double bed, shower and basin. Bathroom with shower over bath, well-equipped kitchen. Quiet location near Sennen Cove's surfing beach and cliff walks and Land's End.
Offers:	Short breaks available October-April. Discount for two people. 10% discount for early booking before 31 January.
Facilities:	

SENNEN

Trevear Farm ★★★★ Self Catering
Trevear Farm, Sennen, Penzance, TR19 7BH

T:	+44 (0) 1736 871205
E:	trevear.farm@farming.co.uk
W:	trevearfarm.co.uk
Units:	1 • Sleeps from 2-10 • From £310 • Cash/cheques accepted
Open:	Year round
Description:	Large farmhouse, completely refurbished; very clean and well equipped; central heating and woodburner. Five minutes' drive to beautiful Sennen Cove. Ample parking, enclosed garden. Great for walking, beaches, cycling and culture. Activity or relaxation – the choice is yours! Also, stunning house for six at Lamorna.
Offers:	Weekend breaks and discount for unit occupancy (excluding school and bank holidays).
Facilities:	

CORNWALL

CORNWALL

ST AGNES

The Owl House ★★★★★ Self Catering
Booking address: Chy Ser Rosow, Barkla Shop, St Agnes, TR5 0XN

T:	+44 (0) 1736 871205
W:	the-owl-house.co.uk
Units:	1 • Sleeps from 1-5 • Low season £295-£395; high season £450-£825 • Credit/debit cards; cash/cheques accepted
Open:	Year round
Description:	Spacious detached cottage enjoying the seclusion of woodland with meandering stream. Superbly equipped and with its own private patio, The Owl House is a luxurious base from which to explore Cornwall, with many walks from the doorstep. The lovely village of St Agnes is less than one mile away. Brochure available.
Offers:	Short breaks available in low season £195.
Facilities:	

ST AUSTELL

Bosinver Farm Cottages ★★★★ Self Catering
Bosinver Farm Cottages, Trelowth, St Austell, PL26 7DT

T:	+44 (0) 1726 72128
E:	reception@bosinver.co.uk
W:	bosinver.co.uk
Units:	19 • Sleeps from 3-12 • Low season £275-£900; high season £600-£2,000 • Credit/debit cards; cash/cheques, euros accepted
Open:	Year round
Description:	Best Self-Catering Establishment 2005 – Cornwall Tourism Awards. Guests often don't want to leave. You can relax in real comfort, enjoy your own private garden, splash in the pool, feed the chickens, watch the wildlife, love the village feel and explore the Cornish coast and countryside.
Offers:	Short breaks September-May, £50 per night for two persons (minimum three nights).
Facilities:	

ST AUSTELL

River Valley ★★★★★ Holiday, Touring & Camping Park
Pentewan Road, London Apprentice, St Austell, Cornwall, PL26 7AP

T:	+44 (0) 1726 73533
W:	cornwall-holidays.co.uk
Pitches:	Touring: 45; caravan holiday homes: 40 • Per night (caravan, motor caravan) £10-£25; (tent) £10-£20; (caravan holiday home) £200-£600 • Credit/debit cards; cash/cheques accepted
Open:	April to October
Description:	Stay at River Valley and you will enjoy high standards. Quality caravans to hire, or bring your own and stay in the level, sheltered meadow. Surrounded by woodlands and bordered by a river with lots of walks. Indoor swimming pool, cycle trail to the beach, immaculate toilet block.
Offers:	Short-break offers in static vans. Seven nights for the price of five in the touring meadow.
Facilities:	

ST AUSTELL
Tregongeeves Farm Cottages ★★★★ Self Catering
Tregongeeves Farm Holiday Cottages, St Austell, PL26 7DS

T:	+44 (0) 1726 73533
W:	cornwall-holidays.co.uk
Units:	7 • Sleeps from 2-6 • Low season £350 • Credit/debit cards; cash/cheques, euros accepted
Open:	Year round
Description:	Tregongeeves combines quality accommodation with excellent leisure facilities. Guests enjoy exclusive, all year round use of the indoor heated swimming pool, spa bath, gym, recreation room and a professional tennis court. Being located in mid-Cornwall just off the A390 at St Austell, both coastlines are within easy reach.
Offers:	Short breaks available November-March inclusive. Free wireless broadband available in all the cottages.
Facilities:	

ST AUSTELL
Trencreek Farm Country Holiday Park ★★★ Holiday Park
Hewas Water, St Austell, PL26 7JG

T:	+44 (0) 1726 882540
E:	reception@trencreek.co.uk
W:	surfbayholidays.co.uk
Pitches:	Touring: 184; touring caravans: 35; caravan holiday homes: 40 • Per night (caravan, motor caravan) £8.95-£15.50; (tent) £7-£13.50; (caravan holiday home) £115-£510 • Credit/debit cards; cash/cheques accepted
Open:	March to October
Description:	Fifty-six acres of idyllic, open meadows, woodland and lakes in a fun farm setting. Six miles from Eden Project. Facilities include tennis court, outdoor pool, fishing lakes, farm animals, entertainment, bar, restaurant and takeaway. Hot tubs available.
Offers:	8 April-21 July, seven nights or more: £52pw (electric pitch) or £45pw (non-electric pitch) – for up to six people and a pet!
Facilities:	

ST IVES
9 Ayr Lane ★★★ Self Catering
Booking address: 115 Earlsfield Road, London, SW18 3DD

T:	+44 (0) 1736 797216
E:	sue.kibby@btinternet.com
W:	btinternet.com/~stives.cottage
Units:	1 • Sleeps from 1-4 • Low season £200-£325; high season £330-£550 • Cash/cheques accepted
Open:	Year round
Description:	Cosy, modernised, ancient, granite, three-storey cottage overlooking town and harbour. Central location. Self-guided walking pack available. Also local history books and maps. Easily accessible by car, train or coach. Perfect all year round. Linen and electricity included.
Offers:	Low season discounts for short breaks of four days or less.
Facilities:	

CORNWALL

CORNWALL

ST IVES

Trevalgan Holiday Farm ★★★★ Self Catering
Trevalgan Holiday Farm, Trevalgan, St Ives, TR26 3BJ

T:	+44 (0) 1736 796433
W:	trevalgan.co.uk
Units:	4 • Sleeps from 2-6 • Low season £195-£370; high season £230-£600 • Cash/cheques accepted
Open:	Year round
Description:	Set in an idyllic location, this working farm combines first-class accommodation and breathtaking scenery with a friendly atmosphere. Attention to detail means the cottages are decorated, furnished and equipped to a very high standard. The farm trail joins the South West Coast Path, and the A30 is close, making it easy to explore.
Offers:	Short breaks available October-April. Special packages for families with pre-school children.
Facilities:	

TRURO

Chy-Vista ★★★★ B&B
Higher Penair, St Clement, Truro, TR1 1TD

T:	+44 (0) 1872 270592
Rooms:	2 • B&B per room per night (single) £35-£38; (double) £50-£55 • Cash/cheques accepted
Open:	March to October
Description:	Chy-Vista is just outside Truro. The house is a converted barn in a tranquil, rural setting with large, well-stocked garden and extensive countryside views. Ideally located only 20 minutes' drive to north or south coast. Within easy reach of all main attractions and many beautiful gardens. Spacious, well-equipped double bedrooms.
Offers:	Reduction for four or more nights.
Facilities:	

WADEBRIDGE

Tregolls Farm Cottages ★★★★ Self Catering
Tregolls Farm Cottages, St Wenn, Bodmin, PL30 5PG

T:	+44 (0) 1208 812154
W:	tregollsfarm.co.uk
Units:	4 • Sleeps from 2-8 • Low season £225-£435; high season £435-£850 • Credit/debit cards; cash/cheques accepted
Open:	Year round
Description:	Well-equipped holiday cottages, tastefully converted from redundant stone barns. Charming, mellow oak beams, slate window sills, fire hearths, and wonderful views of the open countryside with fields of cows and sheep grazing and a stream meandering through the valley. Pets' corner, games room, farm trail and barbecues.
Offers:	Three- and four-night breaks October-April.
Facilities:	

AMBLESIDE

Queens Hotel ★★Hotel
Market Place, Ambleside, Cumbria, LA22 9BU

T:	+44 (0) 15394 32206
E:	enquiries@queenshotelambleside.com
W:	queenshotelambleside.com
Rooms:	26 • B&B per room per night (single) £30-£47; (double) £60-£94 • Credit/debit cards; cash/cheques accepted
Open:	Year round
Description:	Family-owned, 18thC hotel in the centre of village, renowned for warm and friendly atmosphere. Four-poster and Jacuzzi bedrooms. Excellent-value menu served all day in the bar and non-smoking restaurant. Pizzeria cellar bar with satellite TV. Real ales featuring local breweries. Ideally situated for walking and touring the Lakes.
Offers:	Christmas and New Year breaks. Special late-booking deals available. Special offers featured on website.
Facilities:	

AMBLESIDE

Rothay Manor ★★★Hotel
SILVER AWARD
Rothay Bridge, Ambleside, Cumbria, LA22 0EH

T:	+44 (0) 15394 33605
E:	hotel@rothaymanor.co.uk
W:	rothaymanor.co.uk
Rooms:	19 • B&B per room per night (single) £80-£120; (double) £135-£170 • Credit/debit cards; cash/cheques accepted
Open:	Year round except Christmas and New Year
Description:	This Regency country-house hotel stands in its own grounds a short walk from the centre of Ambleside and the head of Lake Windermere. The hotel is renowned for the relaxed, comfortable, friendly atmosphere and excellent food and wine. Free use of nearby leisure centre. Closed 3-26 January.
Offers:	Special short-break rates available. Special-interest holidays October-May: antiques, music, painting, gardening, walking, bridge and Lake District heritage.
Facilities:	

AMBLESIDE

Wateredge Inn ♦♦♦♦Guest Accommodation
Waterhead Bay, Ambleside, Cumbria, LA22 0EP

T:	+44 (0) 15394 32332
E:	stay@wateredgeinn.co.uk
W:	wateredgeinn.co.uk
Rooms:	22 • B&B per room per night (single) £40-£50; (double) £80-£200 • Credit/debit cards; cash/cheques accepted
Open:	Year round
Description:	Delightfully situated family-run inn on the shores of Windermere at Waterhead Bay. Enjoy country-inn-style dining, freshly prepared gourmet bar food, real ales and fine wines, all served overlooking the lake. Pretty bedrooms, many with lake views, offer the best of Lakeland comfort.
Offers:	Three-night mid-week breaks from £105 per person.
Facilities:	

CUMBRIA

CUMBRIA

BORROWDALE

Hazel Bank ♦♦♦♦♦ Guest Accommodation
Rosthwaite, Borrowdale, Keswick, Cumbria, CA12 5XB — GOLD AWARD

T:	+44 (0) 17687 77248
E:	enquiries@hazelbankhotel.co.uk
W:	hazelbankhotel.co.uk
Rooms:	8 • B&B per room per night (single) £33.50-£62.50; (double) £67-£125 • Credit/debit cards; cash/cheques accepted
Open:	Year round except Christmas
Description:	Award-winning, Victorian country house set in four-acre grounds. Peaceful location, superb views of central Lakeland fells. Bedrooms all en suite. Rosette-standard cuisine using local produce. Ideal base for walking. No smokers. No pets. Self-catering cottage for two. Best in Cumbria 2001, 2002 and 2004. Finalist, Best in England 2003.
Offers:	Discounts available when bookings are made more than three months in advance of arrival.
Facilities:	

CALDBECK

Swaledale Watch ★★★★ Guesthouse
Whelpo, Caldbeck, CA7 8HQ

T:	+44 (0) 1697 478409
E:	nan.savage@talk21.com
W:	swaledale-watch.co.uk
Rooms:	5 • B&B per room per night (single) £25-£28; (double) £44-£50 • Cash/cheques accepted
Open:	Year round except Christmas
Description:	A working farm outside picturesque Caldbeck. Enjoy great comfort, excellent food and a warm welcome amidst peaceful, unspoilt countryside. Central for touring, walking or discovering the rolling northern fells. A memorable walk into Caldbeck is through 'The Howk', a limestone gorge. Relax 'at home' with open fires – your happiness is our priority.
Offers:	Honeymoon extras. Special nature walks. Badger-watching evenings.
Facilities:	

CARTMEL

Aynsome Manor Hotel ★★ Country House Hotel
Aynsome Lane, Cartmel, Grange-over-Sands, Cumbria, LA11 6HH SILVER AWARD

T:	+44 (0) 15395 36653
E:	info@aynsomemanorhotel.co.uk
W:	aynsomemanorhotel.co.uk
Rooms:	12 • B&B per room per night (single) £55-£70; (double) £80-£100 • Credit/debit cards; cash/cheques accepted
Open:	Year round except 2-26 January
Description:	Lovely old manor-house nestling in the historic vale of Cartmel. Personally managed for 24 years by the Varley family. An award-winning Georgian dining room, open log fires and elegant lounges create the perfect atmosphere for relaxation. Ideal base for Lakeland and its peninsulas.
Offers:	Special breaks available throughout the year. Two, three and four days from £59 per person per night DB&B.
Facilities:	

CUMBRIA

CASTLE CARROCK

The Weary ★★★★ Restaurant with Room
Castle Carrock, Brampton, CA8 9LU — SILVER AWARD

T:	+44 (0) 1228 670230
W:	theweary.com
Rooms:	5 • Per night (caravan) £65-£85; (motor caravan) £95-£145 Credit/debit cards; cash/cheques accepted
Open:	Year round
Description:	Set in the sleepy village of Castle Carrock, nine miles east of Carlisle. Ideal location for walking, cycling or simply chilling out. The Weary has quickly become a destination for drinkers and diners who wish to enjoy great food in contemporary surroundings in a beautiful part of North Cumbria.
Offers:	For luxury accommodation throughout the year. Check website or ring for details.
Facilities:	

COCKERMOUTH

Rose Cottage ★★★★ Guesthouse
Lorton Road, Cockermouth, Cumbria, CA13 9DX

T:	+44 (0) 1900 822189
E:	bookings@rosecottageguest.co.uk
W:	rosecottageguest.co.uk
Rooms:	8 • B&B per room per night (single) £45-£70; (double) £60-£85 • Credit/debit cards; cash/cheques accepted
Open:	Year round except Christmas and New Year
Description:	In a pleasant position and only a 10-minute walk from the town, this family-run guesthouse is within easy reach of the Lakes and coast. Home cooking. Large, private car park. An ideal base for walking or touring.
Offers:	Mid-week or weekend breaks available all year (minimum two nights). Family group packages also available all year (minimum 12 people).
Facilities:	

COCKERMOUTH

The Stables ★★★ Self Catering
Booking address: Sunnyside, Gib Lane, Hoghton, PR5 0RS

T:	+44 (0) 1900 822189
Units:	1 • Sleeps 6 • Low season £320-£390; high season £450-£680 • Cash/cheques, euros accepted
Open:	Year round
Description:	Delightful 18thC, comfortable, well-equipped cottage with inglenooks, exposed beams and log fires – an excellent base. Dean is a peaceful village, ideally situated for exploring the northern Lakes, West Cumbria, Carlisle and the Scottish Borders. Secluded garden – perfect for a peaceful, relaxing holiday. Walking, cycling, golf, fishing. Ospreys nearby.
Offers:	Three-night breaks available October-March. A 20% discount for two people, dependent on season.
Facilities:	

CUMBRIA

CROSTHWAITE

Damson Dene Hotel ★★★Hotel
Crosthwaite, Nr Bowness on Windermere, Kendal, Cumbria, LA8 8JE

T:	+44 (0) 15395 68676
E:	info@damsondene.co.uk
W:	bestlakesbreaks.co.uk
Rooms:	37 • B&B per room per night (single) £59-£79; (double) £78-£118 • Credit/debit cards; cash/cheques accepted
Open:	Year round
Description:	This lovely hotel is tucked away in one of the prettiest and most tranquil settings in the Lake District, yet is only a short drive from Lake Windermere. Days may be spent touring the area or relaxing in the comfortable lounge and extensive gardens. Superb leisure facilities.
Offers:	Bargain breaks: Three nights from £129 per person DB&B.
Facilities:	

DENT

Middleton's/Fountain Cottages ★★★Self Catering
Booking address: The Old Rectory, Polegate, BN26 5RB

T:	+44 (0) 15395 68676
W:	dentcottages.co.uk
Units:	2 • Sleeps 4 • Low season £190-£245; high season £255-£310 • Cash/cheques accepted
Open:	Year round
Description:	Modernised mid-17thC cottages in centre of small, quaint village, comfortably furnished and decorated to high standards. Dentdale offers a good base for walking, touring and exploring the Yorkshire Dales or the Lake District, with Kendal and Hawes nearby. Brochure available.
Offers:	Short breaks from October-March, weekend or mid-week. Any combination, subject to availability.
Facilities:	

ESKDALE

Bower House Inn ★★Hotel
Irton, Eskdale, Holmrook, Cumbria, CA19 1TD

T:	+44 (0) 19467 23244
E:	info@bowerhouseinn.freeserve.co.uk
W:	bowerhouseinn.co.uk
Rooms:	30 • B&B per room per night (single) £47.50-£60; (double) £60-£80 • Credit/debit cards; cash/cheques, euros accepted
Open:	Year round
Description:	A typical 17thC Lakeland inn set in its own secluded gardens. There is a lovely oak-beamed bar, candlelit restaurant, relaxing lounge and comfortable, en suite accommodation. Noted for good food, and an ideal centre for walking.
Offers:	Christmas: DB&B, Christmas Day lunch, candlelit church service, presents, quiz night, Eskdale tour. New Year: B&B, gala dinner/buffet, dancing.
Facilities:	

GRANGE-OVER-SANDS

Clare House ★Hotel
Park Road, Grange-over-Sands, Cumbria, LA11 7HQ — SILVER AWARD

T:	+44 (0) 15395 34253
E:	info@clarehousehotel.co.uk
W:	clarehousehotel.co.uk
Rooms:	18 • Contact for price details • Credit/debit cards; cash/cheques accepted
Open:	March to November
Description:	Charming hotel in its own grounds, with well-appointed bedrooms, pleasant lounges and super bay views, offering peaceful holidays to those who wish to relax and be looked after. Delightful meals, prepared with care and pride from fresh, local produce, will contribute greatly to the enjoyment of your stay.
Offers:	Early-season terms in April, mid-summer and autumn. Special four-day breaks available all season.
Facilities:	

GRANGE-OVER-SANDS

Netherwood Hotel ★★★Hotel
Lindale Road, Grange-over-Sands, Cumbria, LA11 6ET — SILVER AWARD

T:	+44 (0) 15395 32552
E:	enquiries@netherwood-hotel.co.uk
W:	netherwood-hotel.co.uk
Rooms:	32 • B&B per room per night (single) £80-£115; (double) £150-£190 • Credit/debit cards; cash/cheques accepted
Open:	Year round
Description:	Built in 1893, a building of high architectural and historical interest, set in 14 acres of gardens and woodland overlooking Morecambe Bay estuary. Original oak-panelling, unique log fires in the public rooms. All bedrooms are furnished to extremely high, modern standards. The elevated restaurant maximizes the dramatic views of the estuary.
Offers:	Special mid-week breaks available. Specialised holidays include bridge and gardening. Visit website for late availability rates.
Facilities:	

GRASMERE

Broadrayne Farm Cottages ★★★★Self Catering
Broadrayne Farm, Grasmere, Ambleside, LA22 9RU

T:	+44 (0) 15395 32552
W:	grasmere-accommodation.co.uk
Units:	3 • Sleeps from 2-5 • Low season £265-£300; high season £435-£600 • Cash/cheques accepted
Open:	Year round
Description:	With dramatic mountains, rolling fells, glorious lakes and peaceful valleys, Broadrayne Farm is at the heart of the Lake District, superbly located for wonderful views. The traditional farm properties have been lovingly renovated with today's creature comforts, including open coal fires, central heating and off-street parking. Pets welcome by arrangement.
Offers:	A week booked in the year allows 10% off a second week booked in March (excluding Easter holidays).
Facilities:	

CUMBRIA

CUMBRIA

GRASMERE

The Grasmere Hotel ★★Hotel
Broadgate, Grasmere, Ambleside, Cumbria, LA22 9TA SILVER AWARD

T:	+44 (0) 15394 35277
E:	enquiries@grasmerehotel.co.uk
W:	grasmerehotel.co.uk
Rooms:	13 • Contact for prices • Credit/debit cards; cash/cheques accepted
Open:	Year round
Description:	Our delightful Victorian hotel offers standards synonymous with larger hotels, providing modern levels of comfort and convenience. Sympathetically refurbished for 2006, the hotel boasts an elegant, award-winning restaurant which overlooks our gardens, the River Rothay and fells beyond. The friendly atmosphere encourages many guests to return.
Offers:	Special three- and five-night mid-week breaks available throughout the year. Weekends from £120 per person, DB&B.
Facilities:	

GRASMERE

The Travellers Rest Inn ★★★Inn
Grasmere, Ambleside, Cumbria, LA22 9RR

T:	+44 (0) 500 600725
E:	stay@lakedistrictinns.co.uk
W:	lakedistrictinns.co.uk
Rooms:	8 • Contact for prices • B&B per room per night (double) £50-£100 • Credit/debit cards; cash/cheques accepted
Open:	Year round
Description:	An original 16thC coaching inn, full of old-world charm and character, with oak beams and inglenooks, roaring log fires in winter and beer garden with panoramic views in summer. We offer comfortable bedrooms with picturesque views, real ales and award-winning food.
Offers:	Special mid-week winter breaks from £20 per person per night B&B. Christmas and New Year packages also available.
Facilities:	

GRIZEDALE

High Dale Park Barn ★★★Self Catering
High Dale Park Farm, High Dale Park, Satterthwaite, Ulverston, LA12 8LJ

T:	+44 (0) 500 600725
W:	lakesweddingmusic.com/accomm/
Units:	2 • Sleeps from 2-6 • Low season £195-£445; high season £284-£650 • Cash/cheques accepted
Open:	Year round
Description:	Come and enjoy the peace and tranquillity of Grizedale Forest. Delightfully situated, south-facing, 17thC converted barn attached to owner's farmhouse. Wonderful views down quiet, secluded valley, surrounded by beautiful, broadleaf woodland, rich in wildlife. Oak beams, log fire, central heating, patio. Hawkshead and Beatrix Potter's house nearby.
Offers:	Short breaks available, minimum two nights.
Facilities:	

HUTTON ROOF

Carrock Cottages ★★★★★Self Catering
Carrock Cottages, Carrock House, How Hill, Hutton Roof, CA11 0XY

T:	+44 (0) 1768 484111
E:	info@carrockcottages.co.uk
W:	carrockcottages.co.uk
Units:	4 • Sleeps from 2-20 • Low season £395-£395; high season £2200-£2200 • Credit/debit cards; cash/cheques accepted
Open:	Year round except Christmas and New Year
Description:	Luxury in a quiet, rural location near the lovely villages of Hesket Newmarket, Caldbeck and Greystoke. Explore the northern Lake District or head north to historic Carlisle and on to Hadrian's Wall. Restaurants, fell-walking and other activities. A warm welcome guaranteed.
Offers:	15% discount on second week of stay.
Facilities:	

KENDAL

Riverside Hotel ★★★Hotel
Stramongate Bridge, Beezon Road, Kendal, Cumbria, LA9 6EL

T:	+44 (0) 1539 734861
E:	info@riversidekendal.co.uk
W:	bestlakesbreaks.co.uk
Rooms:	47 • B&B per room per night (single) £65-£85; (double) £80-£120 • Credit/debit cards; cash/cheques accepted
Open:	Year round
Description:	The Riverside Hotel is on the banks of the River Kent. Dating back to 1626, the building was home to renowned makers of leather for 250 years. Today, the modernised hotel offers comfort and convenience. Situated in the heart of the market town of Kendal, it is an ideal base to explore the Lake District.
Offers:	Special three-night DB&B packages available.
Facilities:	

KENDAL

Shaw End Mansion ★★★★Self Catering
Booking address: Haveriggs Farm, Kendal, LA8 9EF

T:	+44 (0) 1539 734861
W:	fieldendholidays.co.uk
Units:	4 • Sleeps from 2-18 • Low season £200-£240; high season £255-£420 • Credit/debit cards; cash/cheques accepted
Open:	Year round
Description:	Shaw End Mansion is set on a 200-acre farm in a beautiful location. Shaw End – a restored Georgian house – contains spacious and elegant apartments with fantastic views and walks from the doorstep. Why not rent the whole house, which is ideal for weddings and parties?
Offers:	Short breaks from two nights available most of the year, prices from £100.
Facilities:	

CUMBRIA

CUMBRIA

KESWICK

Avondale Guesthouse ♦♦♦♦ Guest Accommodation
20 Southey Street, Keswick, Cumbria, CA12 4EF

T:	+44 (0) 17687 72735
E:	enquiries@avondaleguesthouse.com
W:	avondaleguesthouse.com
Rooms:	6 • B&B per room per night (single) £28-£32; (double) £56-£64 • Credit/debit cards; cash/cheques accepted
Open:	Year round
Description:	Comfortable Victorian guesthouse with well-appointed, en suite rooms. Close to town centre, theatre, lake and parks. Excellent English and vegetarian breakfasts. In our lounge you can just relax and chat to fellow guests or read from the choice of books and magazines. Non-smokers only please.
Offers:	Weekly B&B rate £186-£192.
Facilities:	

KESWICK

Belle Vue ★★★★ Self Catering
Booking address: Belle Vue, c/o Hillside, Portinscale, Keswick, CA12 5RS

T:	+44 (0) 17687 72735
E:	lexieryder@hotmail.co.uk
Units:	3 • Sleeps from 1-4 • Low season £140-£210; high season £250-£395 • Cash/cheques accepted
Open:	Year round
Description:	Close to the heart of Keswick, this lovely Lakeland-stone residence has been superbly converted, providing very spacious, comfortable, well-appointed suites. Tariff includes central heating. Personal welcome. Fell-top views of Catbells/Newlands Valley from lounges. Short walk to lake/parks/theatre. Double/separate twin bedrooms.
Offers:	Short breaks, minimum three nights. Reductions for less than four people.
Facilities:	

KESWICK

Croft House Holidays ★★★★ Self Catering
Croft House Holidays, Croft House, Applethwaite, CA12 4PN

T:	+44 (0) 17687 72735
W:	crofthouselakes.co.uk
Units:	5 • Sleeps from 2-8 • Low season £275-£505; high season £430-£940 • Cash/cheques accepted
Open:	Year round
Description:	Escape to stunning, panoramic views of Derwentwater and Borrowdale. Peaceful, rural locations in Applethwaite village, one mile from Keswick. Cottage for four and ground-floor apartment for two in a Victorian country house. Two further cottages for four and six and spacious detached barn conversion for eight with snooker room.
Offers:	Short breaks (minimum two nights) November-March and at other times at short notice. Special two- and four-person rates.
Facilities:	

KESWICK

Croftlands Cottages ★★★★★Self Catering
Croftlands Cottages, Thornthwaite, Keswick, CA12 5SA

T:	+44 (0) 17687 72735
W:	croftlands-cottages.co.uk
Units:	2 • Sleeps from 1-4 • Low season £265-£330; high season £450-£535 • Credit/debit cards; cash/cheques accepted
Open:	Year round
Description:	Stunning cottages surrounded by fells and forest. Luxuriously appointed with log stoves, old beams and antiques. Fox Howe has king-size and twin en suite bedrooms with bath or shower for two. Squirrel has king-size four-poster bed and very special bathroom. Walks from the doorstep. Seven minutes' drive to Keswick.
Offers:	Short breaks available November-March, minimum three nights (excluding Christmas and New Year).
Facilities:	

CUMBRIA

KESWICK

Crow Park Hotel ★★Hotel
The Heads, Keswick, CA12 5ER

T:	+44 (0) 1768 772208
E:	enquiries@crowpark.co.uk
W:	crowpark.co.uk
Rooms:	28 • B&B per room per night (single) £37.50-£42; (double) £75-£95 • Credit/debit cards; cash/cheques accepted
Open:	Year round except Christmas
Description:	Centrally located, but quiet hotel overlooking Crow Park, Derwent Water and Catbells. Hope Park, with its golf course, is 30m away and the Theatre on the Lake 500m. Private parking for 23 cars. Has some of the best views in Keswick.
Offers:	Three or five nights' DB&B breaks available all year.
Facilities:	

KESWICK

Derwent House and Brandelhowe ★★★Self Catering
Booking address: Derwent House Holidays, c/o Stone Heath, Hilderstone, ST15 8SH

T:	+44 (0) 1768 772208
W:	dhholidays-lakes.com
Units:	4 • Sleeps from 1-6 • Low season £115-£220; high season £265-£390 • Cash/cheques accepted
Open:	Year round
Description:	Traditional stone and slate Lakeland building of character in village on north shore of Derwentwater one mile from Keswick. Comfortable, well-equipped holiday suites, one retaining old cottage grate and range and another open beams. Various views over lake and to Skiddaw. Ideal centre for walking and resting.
Offers:	Short breaks available November-March (minimum two nights).
Facilities:	

33

CUMBRIA

KESWICK

Derwentwater Hotel ★★★Hotel
Portinscale, Keswick, Cumbria, CA12 5RE

T:	+44 (0) 17687 72538
E:	info@derwentwater-hotel.co.uk
W:	derwentwater-hotel.co.uk

Rooms:	46 • B&B per room per night (single) £75-£95; (double) £150-£210 • Credit/debit cards; cash/cheques accepted
Open:	Year round
Description:	The epitome of a Lakeland country-house hotel, set in 16 acres of conservation grounds on the shores of Derwent Water. Refurbished to provide high standards of accommodation-sublimely comfortable without being pretentious. Award-winning hospitality, pets welcome, and entry to local leisure club make it the perfect Lakeland retreat.
Offers:	Mid-week saver, four nights for price of three; seven for price of five. Festive package also available.
Facilities:	

KESWICK

Ellergill Guesthouse ♦♦♦♦Guest Accommodation
22 Stanger Street, Keswick, CA12 5JU

T:	+44 (0) 17687 73347
E:	stay@ellergill.co.uk
W:	ellergill.co.uk

Rooms:	4 • B&B per room per night (double) £48-£56 • Cash/cheques accepted
Open:	Year round
Description:	An informal and relaxed atmosphere is assured at this recently refurbished, Lakeland-stone, Victorian guesthouse where period features meet modern design. Ellergill is in the heart of Keswick, yet in a quiet cul-de-sac, with well-appointed, spacious rooms and high standards of comfort and cleanliness.
Offers:	Reduced rates for stays of four or more nights.
Facilities:	

KESWICK

Sweeney's Bar, Restaurant & Rooms ★★★★Inn
18-20 Lake Road, Keswick, Cumbria, CA12 5BX

T:	+44 (0) 500 600725
E:	stay@lakedistrictinns.co.uk
W:	lakedistrictinns.co.uk

Rooms:	4 • B&B per room per night (double) £50-£80 • Credit/debit cards; cash/cheques accepted
Open:	Year round
Description:	Centrally located in the popular market town of Keswick, Sweeney's offers an ideal base from which to explore the beautiful Northern Lakes. We present good food, fine wines and stylish bedrooms, combining traditional Lakeland character with contemporary style.
Offers:	Special mid-week winter breaks from £20 per person per night B&B. Christmas and New Year packages also available.
Facilities:	

KESWICK

The Coach House & Derwent Cottage Mews
★★★★★ Self Catering

Booking address: Derwent Cottage, Portinscale, Keswick, CA12 5RF

T:	+44 (0) 500 600725
W:	derwentcottage.co.uk
Units:	2 • Sleeps from 1-2 • Low season £320-£420; high season £420-£460 • Credit/debit cards; cash/cheques accepted
Open:	Year round
Description:	Both are one-bedroom apartments, decorated to a high standard and fully equipped. Both have access to the garden, the Coach House having double doors opening out from the living room onto an awning-covered patio. Derwent Cottage is set back from the road in its own grounds.
Offers:	Any three consecutive days at £75 per night reducing to £50 per night during winter months, subject to availability.
Facilities:	

KESWICK

The Cottage
★★★ Self Catering

The Cottage, Birkrigg, Newlands Valley, Keswick, CA12 5TS

T:	+44 (0) 500 600725
Units:	1 • Sleeps from 1-4 • Low season £200 • Cash/cheques accepted
Open:	Year round
Description:	Cosy, comfortable, oak-beamed cottage, converted from a stable, nestled between the farm guesthouse and adjoining barn. Very pleasantly situated five miles from Keswick in a peaceful valley with excellent view of the surrounding range of mountains. Ideal for fell-walking. Lounge, kitchen, one double room, one twin room, shower/toilet.
Offers:	Short breaks welcome, out of season only, from November-April.
Facilities:	

KESWICK

The Kings Head Hotel
★★★ Small Hotel

Thirlmere, Nr Keswick, Cumbria, CA12 4TN

T:	+44 (0) 500 600725
E:	stay@lakedistrictinns.co.uk
W:	lakedistrictinns.co.uk
Rooms:	17 • B&B per room per night (single) £25-£50; (double) £50-£100 • Credit/debit cards; cash/cheques accepted
Open:	Year round
Description:	A former 17thC coaching inn offering award-winning food, fine wines and real ales served in two individual restaurants, a traditional bar lounge, local produce store and individually furnished bedrooms, all with spectacular views of the surrounding fells.
Offers:	Special mid-week winter breaks from £20 per person per night B&B. Christmas and New Year packages also available.
Facilities:	

CUMBRIA

CUMBRIA

KING'S MEABURN

Lyvennet Cottages ★★★★ Self Catering
Lyvennet Cottages, Keld Farm, King's Meaburn, Penrith, CA10 3BS

T:	+44 (0) 500 600725
W:	lyvennetcottages.co.uk
Units:	4 • Sleeps from 3-6 • Low season £190-£280; high season £290-£470 • Cash/cheques accepted
Open:	Year round
Description:	Attractive, well-furnished cottages in quiet village, overlooking the beautiful Lyvennet Valley and Lakeland hills. Some log fires in winter. Fishing, fuel and linen inclusive. Children and pets welcome. Good pub. Own woodland walks and bird-watching. Bring your own horse-excellent livery or grass. Ideal centre for Lakes, Dales, Hadrian's Wall and Scottish Borders.
Offers:	Short breaks available October-Mar (excluding Christmas and New Year). Minimum two nights.
Facilities:	

KIRKBY LONSDALE

Sellet Hall Cottages ★★★★ Self Catering
Sellet Hall Cottages, Sellet Hall, Carnforth, LA6 2QF

T:	+44 (0) 500 600725
W:	sellethall.com
Units:	3 • Sleeps – call for details • Low season £260-£360; high season £400-£460 • Cash/cheques accepted
Open:	Year round
Description:	Unique cottages converted from 17thC barn set in the grounds of Sellet Hall, surrounded by open countryside and complemented by far-distance views over the Lune Valley, Trough of Bowland and Yorkshire Dales. All have log fires, fitted kitchens, dishwasher, microwave etc. Own gardens, patio and parking.
Offers:	Short breaks, subject to availability, (excluding Christmas and New Year). Pets welcome
Facilities:	

KIRKBY LONSDALE

Ullathorns Farm ♦♦♦♦ Guest Accommodation
Middleton, Kirkby Lonsdale, Carnforth, Lancashire, LA6 2LZ

T:	+44 (0) 15242 76214
E:	pauline@tossbeck.f9.co.uk
W:	tossbeck.co.uk
Rooms:	2 • B&B per room per night (single) £28-£35; (double) £46-£52 • Cash/cheques accepted
Open:	Year round except Christmas and New Year
Description:	A working farm situated in the unspoilt Lune Valley midway between Sedbergh and Kirkby Lonsdale. An ideal touring base for lakes and dales. Good overnight stopping-off point, situated between junctions of the M6. Refreshments served upon arrival. Individual breakfast tables.
Offers:	Stay three nights or more and receive a 10% discount (excluding bank holidays).
Facilities:	

LAKESIDE

Boathouse Hotel ★★★Inn
Lakeside, Newby Bridge, Cumbria, LA12 8AS

T:	+44 (0) 1539 531381
E:	enquiries@boathousehotel.co.uk
W:	boathousehotel.co.uk
Rooms:	10 • B&B per room per night (single) £45-£59; (double) £70-£120 • Credit/debit cards; cash/cheques accepted
Open:	Year round except Christmas
Description:	The Boathouse Hotel offers a unique combination of excellent accommodation and a sense of homeliness. We are a family-run business, and our main aim is to provide all of our guests with exceptional service from their initial enquiry. Live music. Conference facilities.
Offers:	Three nights for the price of two. Mid-week breaks: £199 per person.
Facilities:	

LANGDALE

Britannia Inn ★★Hotel
Elterwater, Ambleside, Cumbria, LA22 9HP

T:	+44 (0) 15394 37210
E:	info@britinn.co.uk
W:	britinn.co.uk
Rooms:	9 • B&B per room per night (single) £44-£98; (double) £88-£108 • Credit/debit cards; cash/cheques accepted
Open:	Year round
Description:	Traditional, 500-year-old inn nestled in picturesque Elterwater. Relax in front of our cosy log fires or on the sheltered patio with glorious views. Our broad menu comprises home-cooked dishes, many using local produce, complemented by real ales and fine wines. Refurbished, en suite accommodation. Non-smoking.
Offers:	Pets most welcome. Ask for special mid-week-break prices, and mid-week winter offers.
Facilities:	

LANGDALE

Meadow Bank ★★★★Self Catering
Booking address: Langdale Cottages, 17 Shay Lane, Hale Barns, WA15 8NZ

T:	+44 (0) 7854 960716
E:	lockemeadowbank@aol.com
W:	langdalecottages.co.uk
Units:	2 • Sleeps from 2-10 • Low season £240-£870; high season £320-£2200 • Cash/cheques accepted
Open:	Year round
Description:	In the centre of the unspoilt village of Elterwater, Meadow Bank has fine views of the beck and fells. An exceptional property, completely renovated and beautifully furnished. The house has four bedrooms and three bathrooms. There is also the Garden Cottage. Leisure club facilities are included.
Offers:	Four-night winter mid-week breaks for the price of two (Garden Cottage £130, Meadow Bank £300).
Facilities:	

CUMBRIA

CUMBRIA

LINDALE

7 New Cottages ★★★Self Catering
Lindale Property, 37 Egerton Road, Davenport, Stockport, SK3 8TQ

T:	+44 (0) 7854 960716
E:	lindale.cottage@ntlworld.com
W:	lindale-cottage.co.uk
Units:	1 • Sleeps from 4-5 • Low season £200-£300; high season £350-£400 • Cash/cheques, euros accepted
Open:	Year round except Christmas and New Year
Description:	Three-bedroomed semi-detached cottage with wood-burning stove at the edge of a quiet village. Close to shop and pub. Cosy winter, mid-week breaks. One double bed, twin beds, one single plus cot. The Edwardian-style resort of Grange-over-Sands is 1.50 miles away. Closed New Year.
Offers:	Winter mid-week breaks, November-March, three/four nights, £85-£115.
Facilities:	

NEWBY BRIDGE

Newby Bridge Hotel ★★★Hotel
Newby Bridge, Ulverston, Cumbria, LA12 8NA

T:	+44 (0) 15395 31222
E:	info@newbybridgehotel.co.uk
W:	newbybridgehotel.co.uk
Rooms:	38 • B&B per room per night (single) £59-£79; (double) £78-£118 • Credit/debit cards; cash/cheques accepted
Open:	Year round
Description:	This elegant Georgian mansion is in a commanding position overlooking the southern shores of Lake Windermere. Individually styled bedrooms, many with four-poster beds, Jacuzzi bath and lake view. Cosy bar and lounges feature oak panelling and open log fires. Exclusive leisure facilities overlook the mature, Mediterranean-style, five-acre garden.
Offers:	Bargain breaks: Three nights from £129 per person DB&B.
Facilities:	

NEWBY BRIDGE

The Whitewater Hotel ★★★Hotel
Backbarrow, Newby Bridge, Ulverston, Cumbria, LA12 8PX

T:	+44 (0) 15395 31133
E:	enquiries@whitewater-hotel.co.uk
W:	whitewater-hotel.co.uk
Rooms:	35 • B&B per room per night (single) £85-£105; (double) £100-£195 • Credit/debit cards; cash/cheques, euros accepted
Open:	Year round
Description:	Enviable location on banks of the River Leven, 20 minutes from M6. Superb leisure facilities. Our health and fitness club, Cascades, provides every opportunity to unwind in the pool, sauna, steam room and whirlpool or pamper yourself in our exclusive health spa which offers a full range of treatments.
Offers:	Pamper and special mid-week breaks. Family Christmas holiday. Winter jazz festivals. Romantic weekend packages.
Facilities:	

PENRITH

Flusco Wood Caravan Park

★★★★★ Holiday & Touring Park

Flusco, Penrith, Cumbria, CA11 0JB

T:	+44 (0) 17684 80020
E:	admin@fluscowood.co.uk
W:	fluscowood.co.uk
Pitches:	Touring: 52; touring caravans: 45; motor caravans: 7 • Per night (caravan, motor caravan) £15-£18 • Cash/cheques accepted
Open:	Year round except Christmas and New Year
Description:	A very high-standard and quiet woodland touring caravan park with fully serviced pitches and centrally heated amenity building. Short drive to many attractions and places of interest in the Lake District. Open April to October.
Offers:	Luxury pine holiday lodges for sale. Reduction on prices for pre-booked stays of one week or more.
Facilities:	

PENRITH

Hornby Hall Country Guesthouse

★★★★ Guest Accommodation

Brougham, Penrith, Cumbria, CA10 2AR

T:	+44 (0) 1768 891114
E:	enquire@hornbyhall.co.uk
W:	hornbyhall.co.uk
Rooms:	7 • B&B per room per night (single) £32-£57; (double) £52-£84 • Credit/debit cards; cash/cheques accepted
Open:	Year round except Christmas and New Year
Description:	You will receive a warm welcome to this 16thC farmhouse. It is situated in open farmland yet only four miles from the M6. Fresh flowers, log fires in winter and full of antiques. Home-cooked local produce, generous breakfast. Easy reach of Lakes and Yorkshire. Private fishing on River Eamont.
Offers:	Three nights for the price of two October-March.
Facilities:	

PENRITH

Westmorland Hotel

★★★ Hotel

Nr Orton, Penrith, Cumbria, CA10 3SB

T:	+44 (0) 15396 24351
E:	reservations@westmorlandhotel.com
W:	westmorlandhotel.com
Rooms:	51 • B&B per room per night (single) £65-£80; (double) £83-£105 • Credit/debit cards; cash/cheques accepted
Open:	Year round
Description:	The hotel is in the heart of the Cumbrian mountains, with breathtaking views over the Moors. Indulge yourself and let the friendly staff take care of you in the award-winning Bretherdale Restaurant. An ideal location to relax or explore the Lake District, Yorkshire Dales or Scottish Borders.
Offers:	Two-night leisure breaks from £100 per night DB&B, based on two adults sharing a twin/double room.
Facilities:	

CUMBRIA

CUMBRIA

SAWREY

Sawrey Hotel ★★Hotel
Far Sawrey, Ambleside, Cumbria, LA22 0LQ

T:	+44 (0) 15394 43425
E:	sawreyhotel@btopenworld.com
Rooms:	19 • B&B per room per night from £70 • Credit/debit cards; cash/cheques accepted
Open:	Year round except Christmas
Description:	Country inn on the quieter side of Lake Windermere. One mile from the car ferry on the Hawkshead road B5285. It has been run by the Brayshaw family for more than 35 years and a warm welcome awaits guests all year with special rates between November and March.
Offers:	Any three nights' DB&B April-October £143 per person. Any four nights' DB&B October-March (Sunday-Friday) £165 per person. Any two nights £90 per person.
Facilities:	

SILLOTH

Solway Holiday Village ★★Holiday & Touring Park
Skinburness Drive, Silloth, Wigton, Cumbria, CA7 4QQ

T:	+44 (0) 16973 31236
E:	solway@hagansleisure.co.uk
W:	hagansleisure.co.uk
Pitches:	Touring: 150; caravan holiday homes: 50 • Per night (caravan, motor caravan, tent) £4.50-£18; (caravan holiday home) £95-£625 • Credit/debit cards; cash/cheques accepted
Open:	Year round except Christmas
Description:	This 120-acre family park has something for everyone and offers an ideal touring centre for the Scottish Borders and Lake District. Indoor pool, kids' club, indoor and outdoor play areas, small animal farm, themed bars with live entertainment, tennis courts, golf and gymnasium.
Offers:	Touring pitches from £4.50. Bring a friend and get 50% off. Loyalty discounts for repeat bookings.
Facilities:	

ULLSWATER

Land Ends Country Lodge ♦♦♦Guest Accommodation
Watermillock, Penrith, Cumbria, CA11 0NB

T:	+44 (0) 17684 86438
E:	infolandends@btinternet.com
W:	landends.co.uk
Rooms:	9 • B&B per room per night (single) £39.50-£42; (double) £68-£80 • Cash/cheques, euros accepted
Open:	Year round except Christmas and New Year
Description:	A haven of peace and quiet, set in 25 acres with two pretty lakes, ducks, red squirrels and wonderful birdlife, the traditional farmhouse has been tastefully restored providing en suite bedrooms, one with four-poster. Sandwiches available evenings. Cosy lounge and bar. Close to lake, Ullswater and high fells.
Offers:	Reduced rates for three or more nights.
Facilities:	

ULLSWATER

Waterfoot Caravan Park ★★★★★ Holiday & Touring Park
Pooley Bridge, Penrith, Ullswater, Cumbria, CA11 0JF

T:	+44 (0) 17684 86302
E:	enquiries@waterfootpark.co.uk
W:	waterfootpark.co.uk
Pitches:	Touring caravans: 38 • Per night (caravan, motor caravan) £15-£21.50 • Cash/cheques accepted
Open:	March to November
Description:	Situated in the grounds of a Georgian mansion overlooking Ullswater. The park has an excellent touring area with a mix of hardstanding and lawned areas. The reception and shop are open daily. Licensed bar and games room with pool table. Children's play area. David Bellamy Gold Award.
Offers:	Private boat-launching area available.
Facilities:	

CUMBRIA

WHITEHAVEN

Moresby Hall ♦♦♦♦ Guest Accommodation
SILVER AWARD
Moresby, Whitehaven, CA28 6PJ

T:	+44 (0) 1946 696317
E:	etc@moresbyhall.co.uk
W:	moresbyhall.co.uk
Rooms:	4 • B&B per room per night (single) £70-£90; (double) £100-£140 • Credit/debit cards; cash/cheques, euros accepted
Open:	Year round
Description:	A Grade I Listed building (circa 1620) – one of the oldest residences in Cumbria. Delightful four-poster rooms with hydromassage power shower, sauna or Jacuzzi bath and TileVision (waterproof/condensation-proof) colour TV. Delicious breakfasts and imaginative dinners. Semi-rural location, walled gardens, good parking.
Offers:	September-March – book dinner for two or more on consecutive nights to receive a free house wine each night.
Facilities:	

WHITEHAVEN

Rosmerta & Brighida Cottages ★★★★ Self Catering
Booking address: Moresby Hall, Moresby, Whitehaven, CA28 6PJ

T:	+44 (0) 1946 696317
E:	ctb@moresbyhall.co.uk
W:	moresbyhall.co.uk
Units:	2 • Sleeps from 4-6 • Low season £240-£360; high season £290-£480 • Credit/debit cards; cash/cheques, euros accepted
Open:	Year round
Description:	Cottages adjacent to and managed by the owners of Moresby Hall, a historical, Grade I Listed building (circa 1620). Superbly equipped, delightful decor, quality furnishings and deceptively spacious. Its reputation brings many recommendations and repeat visits from satisfied guests each year. Many extras, including a welcome grocery pack.
Offers:	Short breaks (three nights for the price of two) available November-March (excluding Christmas and New Year).
Facilities:	

CUMBRIA

WINDERMERE

Fairfield Garden ♦♦♦♦ Guest Accommodation
Brantfell Road, Bowness Bay, LA23 3AE

T:	+44 (0) 15394 46565
E:	relax@the-fairfield.co.uk
W:	the-fairfield.co.uk
Rooms:	11 • B&B per room per night (single) £29-£37; (double) £58-£94 • Credit/debit cards; cash/cheques, euros accepted
Open:	Year round except Christmas
Description:	Secluded Georgian house set in own grounds with beautiful garden and private car park. Informally run B&B with exceptional breakfasts. King-size four-poster bedrooms available. All rooms en suite, some with state-of-the-art, deluxe bathrooms. Guest lounge with Internet access. Close to Lake Windermere, restaurants, shops and pubs.
Offers:	Reduced prices for three nights during weekdays, or extended weekends in low season.
Facilities:	

WINDERMERE

Holly-Wood Guesthouse ★★★★ Guest Accommodation
Holly Road, Windermere, Cumbria, LA23 2AF

T:	+44 (0) 15394 42219
E:	info@hollywoodguesthouse.co.uk
W:	hollywoodguesthouse.co.uk
Rooms:	6 • B&B per room per night (single) £45-£65; (double) £50-£66 • Credit/debit cards; cash/cheques accepted
Open:	Year round
Description:	Minutes from Windermere village centre and a short stroll from Lake Windermere, Holly-Wood is a family-run guesthouse where you are assured of a warm welcome. Our comfortable bedrooms are equipped with thoughtful extras. Private parking available. Excellent, hearty English breakfast. A perfect base to explore the Lake District.
Offers:	Three- and seven-night breaks (excluding bank holidays). See website for details of all special offers.
Facilities:	

WINDERMERE

Laurel Cottage ♦♦♦♦ Guest Accommodation
St Martins Square, Bowness-on-Windermere, Windermere, Cumbria, LA23 3EF

T:	+44 (0) 15394 45594
E:	enquiries@laurelcottage-bnb.co.uk
W:	laurelcottage-bnb.co.uk
Rooms:	13 • B&B per room per night (single) £24-£35; (double) £50-£94 • Credit/debit cards; cash/cheques accepted
Open:	Year round
Description:	Charming, early-17thC cottage (1613), originally the village grammar school, located one minute's stroll from the lake at Bowness Bay. Free membership of local leisure club.
Offers:	Low season – any two consecutive nights (excluding weekends) deduct £2. High season – any three consecutive nights (excluding weekends) deduct £2.
Facilities:	

WINDERMERE

Lindeth Fell
★★ Country House Hotel

Lyth Valley Road, Bowness-on-Windermere, Cumbria, LA23 3JP GOLD AWARD

T:	+44 (0) 15394 43286
E:	kennedy@lindethfell.co.uk
W:	lindethfell.co.uk
Rooms:	14 • B&B per room per night (single) £45-£65; (double) £90-£130 • Credit/debit cards; cash/cheques accepted
Open:	Year round except Christmas and New Year
Description:	In magnificent private grounds on the hills above Lake Windermere, Lindeth Fell offers brilliant views, stylish surroundings and superb English cooking at very competitive prices. All bedrooms are en suite and many are on the lake side of the house, offering views of the majestic lakeland scenery. Closed three weeks in January.
Offers:	Special breaks available November-April (excluding bank holidays). Mid-week three-day breaks May-September.
Facilities:	

WINDERMERE

Lindeth Howe Country House Hotel
★★★ Hotel

Lindeth Drive, Longtail Hill, Windermere, Cumbria, LA23 3JF SILVER AWARD

T:	+44 (0) 15394 45759
E:	hotel@lindeth-howe.co.uk
W:	lindeth-howe.co.uk
Rooms:	36 • B&B per room per night (single) £48-£112; (double) £96-£190 • Credit/debit cards; cash/cheques, euros accepted
Open:	Year round
Description:	Traditional Lakeland country house, formerly owned by Beatrix Potter. Comfy rooms, award-winning restaurant and affordable wine list, friendly service, private gardens, superb lake and fell views. Indoor pool and leisure facilities including sauna, solarium and fitness room. The perfect place to relax.
Offers:	Two-, three- and four-night inclusive breaks all year. Special autumn, winter and spring rates including golfing, walking and touring.
Facilities:	

WINDERMERE

Linthwaite House Hotel
★★★ Hotel

Crook Road, Bowness-on-Windermere, Cumbria, LA23 3JA GOLD AWARD

T:	+44 (0) 15394 88600
E:	stay@linthwaite.com
W:	linthwaite.com
Rooms:	27 • B&B per room per night (single) £120-£150; (double) £145-£320 • Credit/debit cards; cash/cheques accepted
Open:	Year round
Description:	Spectacular views over Lake Windermere, friendly, unstuffy staff, award-winning food and eclectic wine list all make Linthwaite a great place to unwind. Attractions include Muncaster and Sizergh Castles, Levens and Holker Halls. Fourteen acres of peace, including private tarn for fishing.
Offers:	Romantic breaks: chilled champagne, handmade chocolates and flowers in your room ready for your arrival. Just add £68.
Facilities:	

CUMBRIA

CUMBRIA

WINDERMERE

St John's Lodge ♦♦♦ Guest Accommodation
Lake Road, Windermere, Cumbria, LA23 2EQ

T:	+44 (0) 15394 43078
E:	mail@st-johns-lodge.co.uk
W:	st-johns-lodge.co.uk
Rooms:	14 • B&B per room per night (single) £20-£40; (double) £40-£70 • Credit/debit cards; cash/cheques, euros accepted
Open:	Year round except Christmas
Description:	Attractive guesthouse between Windermere and lake, exclusively for non-smokers. Comfortable, clean, en suite rooms. Large breakfast menu including traditional English, veggie/vegan, fresh fish and some house-speciality dishes. Free Intenet access including radio connectivity for laptops. Free use of nearby leisure club. Parking.
Offers:	Three-day breaks (price per person): Low season £57, mid-season from £69, high season £78.
Facilities:	

WINDERMERE

Tarn Rigg Guesthouse ♦♦♦♦ Guest Accommodation
Thornbarrow Road, Windermere, Cumbria, LA23 2DG

T:	+44 (0) 15394 88777
E:	info@tarnrigg-guesthouse.co.uk
W:	tarnrigg-guesthouse.co.uk
Rooms:	5 • B&B per room per night (single) £45-£50; (double) £40-£70 • Credit/debit cards; cash/cheques, euros accepted
Open:	Year round
Description:	Built in 1903, Tarn Rigg is situated in an ideal position midway between Windermere and Bowness. Panoramic Langdale Pike views. Quiet, convenient location, ample parking, beautiful 0.75-acre grounds. Spacious, en suite rooms with excellent modern facilities. Rooms with lake views available.
Offers:	Special off-peak offer – three nights for £99. Discount from high-season prices available all year for three-night stays.
Facilities:	

WINDERMERE

The Beaumont ♦♦♦♦♦ Guest Accommodation
Holly Road, Windermere, Cumbria, LA23 2AF

T:	+44 (0) 15394 47075
E:	beaumonthotel@btinternet.com
W:	lakesbeaumont.co.uk
Rooms:	10 • B&B per room per night (single) £40-£60; (double) £70-£130 • Credit/debit cards; cash/cheques, euros accepted
Open:	Year round except Christmas
Description:	The Beaumont is an elegant Victorian villa occupying an enviable position for all amenities of Windermere/Bowness and is an ideal base from which to explore Lakeland. The highest standards prevail and the lovely en suite bedrooms are immaculate. Private car park.
Offers:	Please ring or email for details of current special offers. Free leisure facilities at nearby country club.
Facilities:	

CUMBRIA

WINDERMERE

The Lonsdale Hotel ♦♦♦♦ Guest Accommodation
Lake Road, Bowness-on-Windermere, Cumbria, LA23 2JJ SILVER AWARD

T:	+44 (0) 15394 43348
E:	info@lonsdale-hotel.co.uk
W:	lonsdale-hotel.co.uk
Rooms:	10 • B&B per room per night (single) £57-£90; (double) £76-£110 • Credit/debit cards; cash/cheques accepted
Open:	Year round except Christmas
Description:	UK Accommodation of the Year 2004. Traditional Victorian house with luxury, spacious, en suite bedrooms either with lake view or four-poster. Comfortable lounge with well-stocked bar. Central location near to all bars, restaurants, promenade and attractions. Parking. A warm welcome.
Offers:	10% discount on stays over five nights.
Facilities:	

WINDERMERE

Westbury House ♦♦♦ Guest Accommodation
27 Broad Street, Windermere, LA23 2AB

T:	+44 (0) 15394 46839
E:	stay@windermerebnb.co.uk
W:	windermerebnb.co.uk
Rooms:	5 • B&B per room per night (single) £27-£30; (double) £48-£52 • Credit/debit cards; cash/cheques accepted
Open:	Year round
Description:	A charming Victorian residence offering all en suite rooms with hairdryer, radio-alarm clock, tea/coffee facilities and colour TV. Westbury House is a 10-minute walk from the bus/train station and a 15/20-minute walk from Lake Windermere. There are plenty of pubs and restaurants close by.
Offers:	Three-night special: £135 (based on two sharing and excluding bank holidays, Christmas and New Year period).
Facilities:	

DERBYSHIRE

ALSOP-EN-LE-DALE

Rivendale Caravan and Leisure Park
★★★★ Holiday, Touring & Camping Park
Buxton Road, Alsop En le Dale, Ashbourne, Derbyshire, DE6 1QU

T:	+44 (0) 1335 310311
E:	greg@rivendalecaravanpark.co.uk
W:	rivendalecaravanpark.co.uk
Pitches:	Touring: 111; touring caravans: 81; motor caravans: 81; tents: 30 • Per night (caravan, motor caravan, tent) £9.50-£17.20 • Credit/debit cards; cash/cheques accepted
Open:	Year round except Christmas and New Year
Description:	Surrounded by spectacular Peak District, convenient for Alton Towers, Chatsworth, Dove Dale and Carsington Water. Ideal for cyclists and ramblers. Closed 7 January to 1 February.
Offers:	Receive £15 discount for every seven-night stay (includes multiples of seven-night stays).
Facilities:	

DERBYSHIRE

ASHBOURNE

Paddock House Farm ♦Self Catering
Paddock House Farm Holiday Cottages, Alstonefield, Ashbourne, DE6 2FT

T:	+44 (0) 1335 310311
W:	paddockhousefarm.co.uk
Units:	5 • Sleeps from 2-6 • Low season £234-£430; high season £430-£677 • Cash/cheques accepted
Open:	Year round
Description:	Luxury holiday cottages in the heart of the Peak District National Park. Cottages have either three bedrooms, two bedrooms or one bedroom. Wonderful views of the open countryside in a very peaceful location. Excellent attractions, including Alton Towers, Chatsworth and Dovedale.
Offers:	20% reduction for two adults booking a three-bedroom cottage only using one bedroom (off-peak only).
Facilities:	

ASHBOURNE

Sandybrook Country Park ★★★★Self Catering
Pinelodge Holidays, Sandybrook Country Park, Buxton Road, Ashbourne, DE6 2AQ

T:	+44 (0) 1335 310311
W:	pinelodgeholidays.co.uk/sandybrook.ihtml
Units:	41 • Sleeps from 2-8 • Low season £270-£530; high season £370-£995 • Credit/debit cards; cash/cheques accepted
Open:	Year round
Description:	Set in the former grounds of Sandybrook Hall, an elegant, 19thC manor-house with woodland walks and wonderful views. Luxurious, fully equipped pine lodges furnished to the highest standards. Heated indoor swimming pool, indoor and outdoor play areas, restaurant and bar.
Offers:	Mid-week and weekend breaks available all year round (excluding Christmas and New Year).
Facilities:	

ASHBOURNE

The Grooms Quarters ★★★★★Self Catering
The Old Coach House, Hall Lane, Wootton, Ellastone, Ashbourne, DE6 2GW

T:	+44 (0) 1335 324549
W:	groomsquarters.co.uk
Units:	1 • Sleeps from 6-8 • Low season £410-£595; high season £595-£795 • Cash/cheques accepted
Open:	Year round
Description:	Part of 18thC coach house, many original features, converted into a spacious and cosy retreat. Elevated and tranquil with superb views. Good walking from the door, cycling on the trails. Bordering Dovedale and Peak Park. Alton Towers three miles. Wood-burning stove, super-king beds, farmhouse-style kitchen, enclosed, lawned garden and pool table.
Offers:	Short breaks available. 'Just for Two' discounts.
Facilities:	

DERBYSHIRE

BAKEWELL

Housley Cottage ♦♦♦♦ Guest Accommodation
Housley, Nr Foolow, Hope Valley, Derbyshire, S32 5QB

T:	+44 (0) 1433 631505
E:	kevin@housleycottages.co.uk
W:	housleycottages.co.uk
Rooms:	4 • B&B per room per night (single) £32-£36; (double) £48-£53 • Credit/debit cards; cash/cheques, euros accepted
Open:	Year round except Christmas and New Year
Description:	A 16thC farm cottage set in open countryside but within 10 minutes' walk of the Bulls Head pub in Foolow village. Public footpaths pass our garden gate to Millers Dale, Chatsworth House, Eyam and Castleton. All rooms en suite with views over open countryside. Full English breakfast or vegetarian.
Offers:	Family room (sleeps four): children half price. 10% reduction when booking three or more nights. See website for latest.
Facilities:	

BAMFORD

Yorkshire Bridge Inn ★★ Hotel
Ashopton Road, Bamford, Hope Valley, Derbyshire, S33 0AZ SILVER AWARD

T:	+44 (0) 1433 651361
E:	enquiries@ybridge.force9.co.uk
W:	yorkshire-bridge.co.uk
Rooms:	14 • B&B per room per night (single) £50-£0; (double) £68-£94 • Credit/debit cards; cash/cheques accepted
Open:	Year round
Description:	This famous inn enjoys an idyllic setting by the beautiful reservoirs of Ladybower, Derwent and Howden in the Peak District, and was voted one of the top six freehouses of the year for all-year-round excellence. Superb, en suite rooms, lovely bar and dining areas offering excellent cuisine with a friendly welcome all year. Brochure available.
Offers:	Special breaks available for three nights or more; bank holiday special breaks; Christmas and New Year breaks.
Facilities:	

BIGGIN-BY-HARTINGTON

Biggin Hall Hotel ★★ Hotel
Biggin-by-Hartington, Buxton, Derbyshire, SK17 0DH

T:	+44 (0) 1298 84451
E:	enquiries@bigginhall.co.uk
W:	bigginhall.co.uk
Rooms:	20 • B&B per room per night (single) £65-£95; (double) £75-£130 • Credit/debit cards; cash/cheques accepted
Open:	Year round
Description:	Set at 1,000ft in the White Peak District, 17thC, Grade II Listed Biggin Hall has been sympathetically restored, keeping its fine old character while giving room to contemporary comforts. Excellent, uncomplicated, fresh home cooking and home-baked bread! Close to Chatsworth, Haddon Hall etc.
Offers:	Icebreaker specials November-March for stays of two or more nights including breakfast, packed lunch and mulled wine before dinner.
Facilities:	

DERBYSHIRE

BUXTON

Fernydale Farm ♦♦♦♦ Guest Accommodation
Earl Sterndale, Nr Buxton, SK17 0BS
SILVER AWARD

T:	+44 (0) 1298 83236
E:	wjnadin@btconnect.com
Rooms:	3 • B&B per room per night (single) £39-£45; (double) £58-£70 • Cash/cheques accepted
Open:	Year round
Description:	A friendly, warm welcome awaits you at Fernydale. A working farm nestling in the Peaks with a stunning views. Attractive bedrooms with modern bathrooms. Spacious conservatory and garden to relax in. Excellent breakfast to set you up for the day. Buxton, Bakewell, Ashbourne and numerous attractions/walks within easy access.
Offers:	Discounts on stays of four or more nights (excluding bank holidays).
Facilities:	

BUXTON

Kingscroft Guesthouse ♦♦♦♦ Guest Accommodation
10 Green Lane, Buxton, Derbyshire, SK17 9DP
SILVER AWARD

T:	+44 (0) 1298 22757
Rooms:	8 • B&B per room per night (single) £35-£40; (double) £60-£80 • Cash/cheques accepted
Open:	Year round except Christmas
Description:	Late-Victorian luxury guesthouse, in a central yet quiet position in the heart of the Peak District. Comfortable surroundings with period decor. Enjoy our hearty, delicious, home-cooked full English or continental breakfasts.
Offers:	10% discount on stays of four nights or more.
Facilities:	

CHAPEL-EN-LE-FRITH

High Croft ♦♦♦♦♦ Guest Accommodation
Manchester Road, Chapel-en-le-Frith, High Peak, SK23 9UH

T:	+44 (0) 1298 814843
E:	elaine@highcroft-guesthouse.co.uk
W:	highcroft-guesthouse.co.uk
Rooms:	4 • B&B per room per night (single) £45-£55; (double) £60-£80 • Cash/cheques accepted
Open:	Year round
Description:	A luxurious Edwardian country house set in 1.5 acres of peaceful, mature gardens adjoining Chapel-en-le-Frith golf course and Combs Reservoir. Magnificent views and superb walks from the door. Beautifully furnished, en suite bedrooms, spacious, comfortable sitting room, log fires, elegant dining room, and an extensive breakfast menu.
Offers:	Discounts on stays of four or more days (excluding Saturdays).
Facilities:	

DERBYSHIRE

CHESTERFIELD

Pear Tree Farm Barn ★★★★Self Catering
Pear Tree Farm House, Rowthorne Village, Glapwell, Chesterfield, S44 5QQ

T:	+44 (0) 1298 814843
W:	peartreefarmbarn.co.uk
Units:	1 • Sleeps from 2-4 • Low season £175-£250; high season £250-£450 • Cash/cheques accepted
Open:	Year round
Description:	Grade II Listed barn conversion in quiet conservation village. Double bedroom with en suite (extra beds available), lounge/diner and kitchen. Full central heating with wood-burning stove. Ten minutes' walk to Hardwick Hall (National Trust). Ideally situated for visiting Peak District (Chatsworth 40 minutes). Pub and shop within walking distance.
Offers:	Special offers November-February (excluding Christmas and New Year). Short breaks all year.
Facilities:	

HARTINGTON

Cruck & Wolfscote Grange Cottages
★★★★Self Catering

Wolfscote Grange Farm, Hartington, Buxton, SK17 0AX

E:	+44 (0) 1298 814843
W:	wolfscotegrangecottages.co.uk
Units:	4 • Sleeps from 2-7 • Low season £180-£320; high season £480-£650 • Cash/cheques accepted
Open:	Year round
Description:	Unique setting overlooking Dove Valley/Dale, with miles of rolling countryside and picture views, sells Wolfcote Cottages as the perfect place to stay. Cruck Cottage – an oak-beamed hideaway. 'No neighbours, only sheep'. Swallows Cottage – en suites, spa bathroom. Both offer comfort and character. Farm trail with freedom to roam. Central to Peak District.
Offers:	Private farm trail weekend and short breaks available.
Facilities:	

HORSLEY

Horsley Lodge ♦♦♦♦Guest Accommodation
Smalley Mill Road, Horsley, Derby, Derbyshire, DE21 5BL

T:	+44 (0) 1332 780838
E:	enquiries@horsleylodge.co.uk
W:	horsleylodge.co.uk
Rooms:	10 • B&B per room per night (single) £65-£75; (double) £90-£100 • Credit/debit cards; cash/cheques, euros accepted
Open:	Year round
Description:	Magnificent stone country-house hotel. This hidden gem specialises in exclusive golf breaks for couples (maximum 10). Great restaurant, lovely views, championship golf course. All rooms individually themed.
Offers:	'Learn to golf' breaks. Discounts available Sunday nights.
Facilities:	

DERBYSHIRE

MATLOCK

Mooredge Barns ★★★★★ Self Catering
Mooredge Farm, Knabb Hall Lane, Tansley, Matlock, DE4 5FS

T:	+44 (0) 1332 780838
W:	mooredgefarmcottages.co.uk
Units:	3 • Sleeps from 4-18 • Low season £270-£630; high season £385-£880 • Cash/cheques accepted
Open:	Year round
Description:	These barns are set in a very rural location down a quiet country lane, having splendid panoramic views from the grounds of the whole surrounding area with Riber Castle sitting on the horizon overlooking Matlock. Choice of cottages. Heated indoor pool.
Offers:	Enjoy swimming in our heated indoor pool all year round, free to cottage guests.
Facilities:	

YOULGREAVE

Sunnyside ★★★ Self Catering
Booking address: Falkland House, 10 New Road, Bakewell, DE45 1WP

T:	+44 (0) 1332 780838
Units:	1 • Sleeps 2 • Price from £190 • Cash/cheques accepted
Open:	Year round
Description:	Sunnyside is a homely, self-contained, very private apartment. From its patio, which is well-stocked with hanging baskets, various old farm implements and stone troughs, there are lovely views to the hills. Close to local amenities (including good pubs!), long/short walks from the door and tourist attractions (Chatsworth, Bakewell etc). Off-street parking.
Offers:	Three-night breaks available November-April.
Facilities:	

DEVON

BABBACOMBE

Sefton Hotel ★★ Hotel
Babbacombe Downs Road, Torquay, TQ1 3LH

T:	+44 (0) 1803 326591
E:	seftonhotel@yahoo.com
W:	seftonhotel.info
Rooms:	69 • B&B per room per night (single) £26-£32; (double) £52-£64 • Credit/debit cards; cash/cheques accepted
Open:	Year round
Description:	The Sefton is on the seafront and has comfortable bedrooms with private bath/shower and toilet en suite, colour TV, direct-dial telephone and tea/coffee-making facilities. Some have a balcony and magnificent sea views. Sandy beaches, boating, model village, golf and theatre are nearby.
Offers:	Weekend and mid-week breaks (two nights minimum) including Murder Mystery, line dance and country and western. From £60 per person for two nights.
Facilities:	

DEVON

BAMPTON

Three Gates Farm ★★★★Self Catering
Three Gates Farm, Huntsham, Tiverton, EX16 7QH

T:	+44 (0) 1803 326591
W:	threegatesfarm.co.uk
Units:	5 • Sleeps from 2-6 • Low season £150-£285; high season £355-£910 • Cash/cheques accepted
Open:	Year round
Description:	Relax in one of our excellent converted barns, in the beautiful countryside. Spend hours in our superb indoor heated pool, sauna or fitness room. Play in the grounds, with play tower and games rooms. The perfect place to unwind and explore the beaches, river valleys and attractions of Devon.
Offers:	Short breaks October-May (excluding school holidays).
Facilities:	

BAMPTON

Wonham Barton ★★★Self Catering
Wonham Barton, Bampton, Tiverton, EX16 9JZ

T:	+44 (0) 1803 326591
W:	wonham-country-holidays.co.uk
Units:	1 • Sleeps 6 • Low season £200-£360; high season £360-£400 • Credit/debit cards; cash/cheques accepted
Open:	Year round
Description:	From friendly accommodation overlooking Exe Valley, conveniently explore secretive, historic Devon, rolling moorlands and dramatic coastlines; enjoy country pursuits and leisurely cream teas. Savour 300 tranquil acres, glimpsing Exmoor red deer, soaring buzzards and traditional shepherding; share romantic scenes from TV drama and 'Landgirls', filmed here. Tell us when you're coming!
Offers:	Short breaks available October-March minimum two nights. Prices on request. Dogs accepted by arrangement.
Facilities:	

BARNSTAPLE

Broomhill Farm ★★★★Farmhouse
Muddiford, Barnstaple, North Devon, Devon, EX31 4EX

T:	+44 (0) 1271 850676
E:	rwmmills@hotmail.co.uk
Rooms:	3 • B&B per room per night (single) £25-£30; (double) £50-£60 • Cash/cheques, euros accepted
Open:	Year round
Description:	Farmhouse in pretty rural setting, yet only two miles from town centre; adjacent to the renowned Broomhill Sculpture Gardens. Attractive bedrooms, ample parking, local produce and a warm welcome. Ideal base for exploring Exmoor and the beautiful beaches of Woolacombe and Croyde.
Offers:	Discounts on stays of four or more nights.
Facilities:	

DEVON

BIGBURY-ON-SEA

Apartment 5, Burgh Island Causeway
★★★★★ Self Catering & Serviced Apartments
Booking address: Mill Street, Chagford, Newton Abbott, TQ13 8AW

T:	+44 (0) 1271 850676
E:	help@helpfulholidays.com
Units:	1 • Sleeps from 1-4 • Low season £429-£958; high season £1,068-£1,497 • Credit/debit cards; cash/cheques accepted
Open:	Year round
Description:	Luxury, modern, ground-floor apartment set into cliff with panoramic views from large patio. Facilities include pool, gym, sauna, cafe/bar, grassy cliff-top grounds and direct access to beautiful large sandy beach and coastal path. Popular for surfing and near golf course and village shop/post office.
Offers:	Bargain weekend and short-stay breaks available in autumn and winter months.
Facilities:	

BOVEY TRACEY

Brookfield House ♦♦♦♦♦ Guest Accommodation
Challabrook Lane, Bovey Tracey, Devon, TQ13 9DF   GOLD AWARD

T:	+44 (0) 1626 836181
E:	brookfieldh@tinyworld.co.uk
W:	brookfield-house.com
Rooms:	3 • B&B per room per night (single) £45-£52; (double) £60-£74 • Credit/debit cards; cash/cheques accepted
Open:	February to November
Description:	Spacious, early-Edwardian residence on the edge of Bovey Tracey and Dartmoor and set in two acres with panoramic moor views. Secluded tranquillity yet within easy walk of town. Individually decorated bedrooms, all with comfortable seating areas. Gourmet breakfasts, including home-made breads and preserves.
Offers:	Special rates on application for stays of four or more nights, and also weekly terms.
Facilities:	

BRIXHAM

Devoncourt Holiday Flats ★★ Self Catering
Devoncourt Holiday Flats, Berry Head Road, Brixham, TQ5 9AB

T:	+44 (0) 1626 836181
E:	bookings@devoncourt.net
W:	devoncourt.info
Units:	6 • Sleeps from 1-5 • Low season £299-£300; high season £299-£499 • Credit/debit cards; cash/cheques, euros accepted
Open:	Year round
Description:	Panoramic sea views from your balcony and lounge over Torbay, Brixham harbour and marina. The beach is opposite, only 50m. Each flat is fully self-contained and carpeted, with colour TV and full cooker. Private gardens. Car park. Children, pets and credit cards welcome. For colour brochure telephone (01803) 853748 or 07050 853748.
Offers:	10% discount for Senior Citizens.
Facilities:	

DEVON

BRIXHAM

The Berry Head Hotel ★★★Hotel
Berry Head, Brixham, Devon, TQ5 9AJ

T:	+44 (0) 1803 853225
E:	stay@berryheadhotel.com
W:	berryheadhotel.com
Rooms:	32 • B&B per room per night (single) £48-£66; (double) £96-£168 • Credit/debit cards; cash/cheques, euros accepted
Open:	Year round
Description:	Steeped in history, nestling on the water's edge. Traditional hospitality, excellent, friendly and personal service with attention to detail. Imaginative menus, varied dining options, feature quality local produce and fresh fish. Lounge, bars and terrace, equally popular with locals and residents.
Offers:	Special-event packages. Extensive range of conference and business facilities. Weddings and special occasions. Christmas and New Year celebrations.
Facilities:	

BURRINGTON

Northcote Manor ♦Country House Hotel
Burrington, Umberleigh, Devon, EX37 9LZ

T:	+44 (0) 1769 560501
E:	rest@northcotemanor.co.uk
W:	northcotemanor.co.uk
Rooms:	11 • B&B per room per night (single) £100-£170; (double) £150-£250 • Credit/debit cards; cash/cheques accepted
Open:	Year round
Description:	Northcote Manor is a cherished country-house hotel set in stunning grounds at the foothills of the Exmoor National Park. Enjoy open fires, cream teas on our sun terrace and award-winning cuisine in our beautiful restaurant. Licensed for civil ceremonies (up to 100 guests).
Offers:	Special rates on stays of two or more nights.
Facilities:	

CHARDSTOCK

Barn Owls Cottage ★★★★Self Catering
Barn Owls Cottage, Chardstock, Axminster, EX13 7BY

T:	+44 (0) 1769 560501
W:	cottageguide.co.uk/barnowlscottage
Units:	1 • Sleeps – call for details • Low season £200-£275; high season £250-£345 • Cash/cheques accepted
Open:	Year round
Description:	Peaceful and relaxing cottage with emphasis on quality and comfort. King-size posture-sprung bed. Beautiful views over River Axe valley. Bird-watching, large garden, conservatory. Near Lyme Regis, Beer, Branscombe, Forde Abbey (National Trust). Located within Blackdown Hills, an area designated as an Area of Outstanding Natural Beauty. Local walks. Faces south/south-west. Owner's personal attention.
Offers:	Three-night short breaks March or October.
Facilities:	

DEVON

CHURSTON FERRERS

Alston Farm Cottages ★★★★★Self Catering
Alston Lane, Churston Ferrers, Brixham, TQ5 0HT

T:	+44 (0) 1769 560501
W:	alstonfarm.co.uk
Units:	2 • Sleeps from 4-7 • Low season £290-£390; high season £730-£960 • Cash/cheques accepted
Open:	Year round
Description:	Delightfully furnished accommodation in converted, Grade II Listed barns. Baytree comprises two en suite bedrooms and cloakroom; Laurel comprises three bedrooms and two bathrooms. Designed for year-round comfort. Welcome tray, fresh flowers.
Offers:	Short breaks available off season: Two nights from £205, three nights from £215.
Facilities:	

COLYTON

Smallicombe Farm ★★★★Guest Accommodation
Northleigh, Colyton, Devon, EX24 6BU   SILVER AWARD

T:	+44 (0) 1404 831310
E:	maggie_todd@yahoo.com
W:	smallicombe.com
Rooms:	3 • B&B per room per night (single) £35-£45; (double) £56-£65 • Credit/debit cards; cash/cheques accepted
Open:	Year round
Description:	Relax in a really special place, an idyllic rural setting abounding with wildlife, yet close to the coast. Enjoy scrumptious farmhouse breakfasts including prize-winning Smallicombe sausages from our rare-breed pigs. All rooms en suite, overlooking an unspoilt valley landscape. The Garden Suite of sitting room, bedroom and bathroom is wheelchair accessible.
Offers:	Short breaks or 'piggy' weekends and 'introduction to pig-keeping' courses.
Facilities:	

COMBE MARTIN

Stowford Farm Meadows ★★★★Touring & Camping Park
Combe Martin, Ilfracombe, Devon, EX34 0PW

T:	+44 (0) 1271 882476
E:	enquiries@stowford.co.uk
W:	stowford.co.uk
Pitches:	Touring: 710; touring caravans: 610; motor caravans: 50; tents: 50 • Per night (caravan) £7-£20; (motor caravan) £8-£20; (tent) £7-£23 • Credit/debit cards; cash/cheques accepted
Open:	Year round
Description:	Recent winner of numerous awards and situated on the fringe of the Exmoor National Park, this park has a reputation for superb facilities and unrivalled value.
Offers:	Low season: one week, only £39.90 (incl electric hook-up). Mid season: one week, only £59.90 (incl electric hook-up).
Facilities:	

DEVON

DAWLISH

Cofton Country Holiday Park ★★★★ Self Catering
Cofton Country Cottage Holidays, Cofton, Starcross, Exeter, EX6 8RP

T:	+44 (0) 1271 882476
W:	coftonholidays.co.uk
Units:	5 • Sleeps from 4-6 • Low season £285-£325; high season £675-£735 • Credit/debit cards; cash/cheques accepted
Open:	Year round
Description:	On the edge of privately owned Cofton Country Holiday Park, converted 100-year-old farm buildings overlooked by ancient Cofton church. Coarse-fishing lakes. Woodland walks. Within a short drive of the Exe Estuary and Dawlish Warren. All amenities of the park available during season, including swimming pool and pub.
Offers:	Short breaks early and late season. Three- or four-night breaks at most times. Free coarse fishing November-March.
Facilities:	

DAWLISH

Cofton Country Holidays
★★★★ Holiday, Touring & Camping Park

Cofton, Starcross, Exeter, EX6 8RP

T:	+44 (0) 1626 890111
E:	info@coftonholidays.co.uk
W:	coftonholidays.co.uk
Pitches:	Touring: 450; touring caravans: 450; motor caravans: 450; tents: 450; caravan holiday homes: 66 • Per night (caravan, motor caravan) £12.50-£21; (tent) £9-£21; (caravan holiday home) £170-£645 • Credit/debit cards; cash/cheques accepted
Open:	April to October
Description:	Family-run holiday park in 30 acres of delightful parkland. Heated outdoor pools. Fun-packed visitor attractions. David Bellamy Gold Conservation Award.
Offers:	£2 off standard pitch per night, low and mid season. Senior citizens save an extra £1 each per night.
Facilities:	

EAST BUDLEIGH

Brook Cottage ★★★★ Self Catering
Booking address: Foxcote, Noverton Lane, Prestbury, Cheltenham, GL52 5BB

T:	+44 (0) 1626 890111
W:	brookcottagebudleigh.co.uk
Units:	1 • Sleeps from 6-8 • Low season £275-£495; high season £545-£750 • Cash/cheques accepted
Open:	Year round
Description:	Spacious thatched cottage. Two showers and bathroom. Beaches, walking, golf, karting, bird-watching, riding nearby but the cottage is so comfortable it's a pleasure to be indoors. Two living rooms with TVs, one for the adults, and a snug, with sofa bed, for the children! Visit website for photos.
Offers:	Reduced-rate winter breaks for three-night stays with or without linen (excluding Christmas and New Year).
Facilities:	

55

DEVON

EXETER

Bussells Farm Cottages ★★★★ Self Catering
Bussells Farm, Huxham, Nr Stoke Canon, Exeter, EX5 4EN

T:	+44 (0) 1626 890111
E:	bussellsfarm@aol.com
W:	bussellsfarm.co.uk
Units:	7 • Sleeps from 6-7 • Low season £340-£480; high season £465-£835 • Credit/debit cards; cash/cheques accepted
Open:	Year round
Description:	Lovely barn-conversion cottages, heated outdoor swimming pool, from May to September, adventure playground, well-equipped games room and excellent coarse fishing in the private lakes. We offer a wonderful base from which to explore the beautiful Exe Valley, Dartmoor, the South Devon beaches and the ancient city of Exeter.
Offers:	Three-night stays available. Low season discounts for one or two people. Pets welcome.
Facilities:	

EXETER

St Andrews Hotel ♦♦♦♦ Guest Accommodation
28 Alphington Road, Exeter, EX2 8HN

T:	+44 (0) 1392 276784
E:	standrewsexeter@aol.com
W:	standrewsexeter.co.uk
Rooms:	17 • B&B per room per night (single) £45-£65; (double) £65-£85 • Credit/debit cards; cash/cheques accepted
Open:	Year round except Christmas
Description:	St Andrews is a long-established, family-run hotel offering a high standard of comfort and service in a friendly, relaxing atmosphere. Excellent home cooking. Large car park at rear. Weekend breaks. Brochure on request.
Offers:	Weekend breaks all year, must include Saturday night. Ideally situated for Christmas shopping or summer touring breaks.
Facilities:	

HEMYOCK

Pounds Farm ♦ Farmhouse
Hemyock, Devon, EX15 3QS

T:	+44 (0) 1823 680802
E:	shillingscottage@yahoo.co.uk
W:	poundsfarm.co.uk
Rooms:	1 • B&B per room per night (double) £30 • Cash/cheques accepted
Open:	Year round except Christmas and New Year
Description:	Stone farmhouse set in large gardens. Relax beside the outdoor heated pool or next to a log fire. Gorgeous bedroom, en suite with walk-in shower. Extensive views over the Culm Valley Area of Outstanding Natural Beauty. Delicious farmhouse breakfasts. Half a mile to village pub.
Offers:	Discounts on stays of two or more days. Telephone or see website for details.
Facilities:	

ILFRACOMBE

Beachside Holiday Park ★★★★★ Holiday Park
33 Beach Road, Hele, Ilfracombe, Devon, EX34 9QZ

T:	+44 (0) 1271 863006
E:	enquiries@beachsidepark.co.uk
W:	beachsidepark.co.uk
Units:	Caravan holiday homes: 27 • From £165-£650 • Credit/debit cards; cash/cheques accepted
Open:	Mid-March to end of October
Description:	At Beachside, the sea views and the beach are right outside your door; you don't have to get in the car and drive. Peaceful, relaxing, tranquil, unspoilt, quiet, great for all ages and families alike-these are words often used to describe a holiday at Beachside.
Offers:	Short breaks out of high season. For specials see our website.
Facilities:	

DEVON

ILFRACOMBE

The Admirals House ★★★★ Self Catering
Admirals House, Quayfield Road, Ilfracombe, EX34 9EN

T:	+44 (0) 1271 863006
W:	theadmiralshouse.co.uk
Units:	5 • Sleeps from 2-4 • Low season £225-£425; high season £350-£710 • Cash/cheques accepted
Open:	Year round
Description:	Georgian manor-house converted into stunning apartments and cottage, situated right on Ilfracombe's famous heritage harbourside. Superb views, great location near restaurants, pubs, theatre, coastal paths and the sea. Watch the fishing boats land lobsters and crabs and buy one for your supper!
Offers:	Short breaks off-season. Special discounts for couples.
Facilities:	

KENTISBEARE

Forest Glade ★★★★ Holiday & Touring Park
Kentisbeare, Cullompton, Devon, EX15 2DT

T:	+44 (0) 1404 841381
E:	nwellard@forest-glade.co.uk
W:	forest-glade.co.uk
Pitches:	Touring: 80; caravan holiday homes: 26 • Per night (caravan, motor caravan) £12-£16.50; (tent) £9.50-£13.50; (caravan holiday home) £185-£450 • Credit/debit cards; cash/cheques accepted
Open:	Mid-March to end of October.
Description:	Free indoor heated pool on small, family-managed park surrounded by forest with deer. Large, flat, sheltered pitches.
Offers:	Club members £1 per night discount on pitch fees. Short breaks available in holiday homes during most of season. Pet-free and non-smoking holiday homes available.
Facilities:	

DEVON

LEE

Lower Campscott Farm ★★★★Self Catering
Lower Campscott Farm, Lee, Ilfracombe, EX34 8LS

T:	+44 (0) 1404 841381
W:	lowercampscott.co.uk
Units:	8 • Sleeps from 2-8 • Low season £195-£475; high season £415-£980 • Credit/debit cards; cash/cheques accepted
Open:	Year round
Description:	Charming, tastefully furnished character cottages converted from our farm buildings. Everything supplied to make your stay special. Also holiday homes and lodges. Peaceful farm setting with views across the Bristol Channel. Lee and Woolacombe beaches are easily accessible.
Offers:	Short breaks available out of school holidays. Residential craft and hobby courses second and third weeks of the month.
Facilities:	

LYNTON

Cloud Farm ★★★★Self Catering
Booking address: Oare, Lynton, EX35 6NU

T:	+44 (0) 1404 841381
W:	doonevalleyholidays.co.uk
Units:	3 • Sleeps from 2-8 • Low season £210-£440; high season £470-£895 • Credit/debit cards; cash/cheques accepted
Open:	Year round
Description:	Cloud Farm is a lovely riverside farmhouse in the heart of Exmoor's beautiful Doone Valley. The cottages, with tea room, shop, off-licence and gardens, provide an idyllic base for families, walkers and tourers seeking an 'away-from-it-all' break at any time of year. Riding for all ages and abilities.
Offers:	Short breaks and weekend breaks available during off-peak seasons. Special rates for advanced and late bookings.
Facilities:	

LYNTON

Royal Castle Lodge ★★★★Self Catering
Booking address: Primespot Character Cottages,
c/o Stag Cottage, Holdstone Down, Combe Martin, EX34 0PF

T:	+44 (0) 1404 841381
Units:	1 • Sleeps from 1-2 • Low season from £245 • Cash/cheques, euros accepted
Open:	Year round
Description:	Something special! High-quality, 16thC, detached, thatched stone cottage with rustic balcony, stable door, real fire, garden. Idyllic coastal setting in England's 'Little Switzerland'. Exmoor National Park, wooded outlook with harbour, pubs, restaurants, shops within walking distance. Spectacular walks. Spotless, warm and cosy. Off-season short breaks. Perfect honeymoon/anniversaries.
Offers:	De-stressing breaks November-March.
Facilities:	

DEVON

LYNTON

The Denes ♦♦♦♦ Guest Accommodation
15 Longmead, Lynton, Devon, EX35 6DQ

T:	+44 (0) 1598 753573
E:	j.e.mcgowan@btinternet.com
W:	thedenes.com
Rooms:	5 • B&B per room per night (double) £42-£55 • Credit/debit cards; cash/cheques accepted
Open:	Year round except Christmas
Description:	Peacefully located close to Valley of Rocks, but a short walk to the heart of the village, The Denes is an ideal base to explore Exmoor, whether walking, cycling or driving. Bedrooms are spacious, all with en suite or private facilities. Freshly cooked breakfasts and evening meals appeal to discerning appetites.
Offers:	Beaujolais Nouveau weekend. New Year specials. Gift vouchers. Three-night DB&B.
Facilities:	

MAIDENCOMBE

Bowden Close House ★★★ Self Catering
Bowden Close House, Teignmouth Road, Maidencombe, Torquay, TQ1 4TJ

T:	+44 (0) 1598 753573
W:	bowdenclose.co.uk
Units:	6 • Sleeps from 2-4 • Low season £200-£360; high season £290-£560 • Cash/cheques, euros accepted
Open:	Year round
Description:	Relax in very comfortable apartments or two-storey, self-contained wings of large Victorian house overlooking Lyme Bay, four miles from Torquay. Acre of gardens with stunning views. Minutes from sheltered Maidencombe Cove and the South West Coast Path. Easy access to Dartmoor and the lovely South Devon countryside.
Offers:	Short breaks available. Low season: 20% discount for couples (except for 'Poppy' unit).
Facilities:	

MARLDON

Lower Tor Cot ★★★★ Self Catering
Booking address: Thorn Cottage, Burn Lane, Brentor, Tavistock, PL19 0ND

T:	+44 (0) 1598 753573
W:	sallysholidaycottages.co.uk
Units:	1 • Sleeps 5 • Low season £250-£320; high season £285-£600 • Cash/cheques accepted
Open:	Year round
Description:	On a steep lane, this comfortable, well-equipped cottage offers panoramic views towards Dartmoor. Three bedrooms (double, twin and single). Multi-fuel stove and night-storage heaters for winter warmth. Patio/garden. Maximum of two dogs very welcome. Network of footpaths from door. Torbay, beaches, Dartmouth and Totnes very accessible.
Offers:	Short breaks available November-March inclusive, minimum two nights (excluding main school holiday dates).
Facilities:	

DEVON

MOTHECOMBE

The Flete Estate ★★★★★ Self Catering
The Flete Estate Holiday Cottages, Pamflete, Plymouth, PL8 1JR

T:	+44 (0) 1598 753573
W:	flete.co.uk
Units:	7 • Sleeps from 5-12 • Low season £530-£965; high season £1,290-£1,975 • Cash/cheques accepted
Open:	Year round
Description:	Undoubtedly the Jewel in the Crown of the beautiful South Hams. This private, 5,000-acre estate is designated an Area of Outstanding Natural Beauty, encompassing large, broadleaf woodlands, rolling pastures, cliff paths and sandy beaches, secluded cottages, little hamlets and a tantalising lacework of private drives and pathways.
Offers:	Winter breaks November-March (excluding Christmas and New Year) from £150 per night, minimum three nights.
Facilities:	

NEWTON ABBOT

Dornafield ★★★★★ Touring & Camping Park
Two Mile Oak, Newton Abbot, Devon, TQ12 6DD

T:	+44 (0) 1803 812732
E:	enquiries@dornafield.com
W:	dornafield.com
Pitches:	Touring caravans: 135 • Per night (caravan, motor caravan) £12.50-£19.80; (tent) £13.50-£20.80 • Credit/debit cards; cash/cheques accepted
Open:	Year round except Christmas and New Year
Description:	Beautiful 14thC farmhouse located in 30 acres of glorious countryside. Quiet and peaceful, yet convenient for Torbay and Dartmoor. Superb facilities to suit the discerning caravanner, including many hardstanding, all-service pitches. Shop, games room, adventure play area, tennis and golf.
Offers:	Early- and late-season bookings. Book for seven days and only pay for five. Details on request.
Facilities:	

NORTH BOVEY

Ring of Bells Inn ♦♦♦♦ Guest Accommodation
The Village, North Bovey, Devon, TQ13 8RB

T:	+44 (0) 1647 440375
E:	info@ringofbellsinn.com
W:	ringofbellsinn.com
Rooms:	8 • B&B per room per night (single) £45-£55; (double) £80-£100 • Credit/debit cards; cash/cheques accepted
Open:	Year round
Description:	A 13thC thatched inn in North Bovey, the quintessential Dartmoor village. It offers extremely comfortable, en suite accommodation, four-posters, great atmosphere, real ales, excellent wines and locally farmed produce prepared to order by our top chefs. We offer a choice of bar meals and fine-dining menus. Ideally situated for exploring the Moors.
Offers:	Out-of-season, mid-week and weekend breaks often offered.
Facilities:	

DEVON

OKEHAMPTON

Beer Farm ★★★★Self Catering
Beer Farm, Okehampton, EX20 1SG

E:	+44 (0) 1647 440375
W:	beerfarm.co.uk
Units:	4 • Sleeps from 4-6 • Low season £190-£360; high season £370-£650 • Cash/cheques accepted
Open:	Year round
Description:	Enjoy a peaceful holiday on our small farm situated on the northern edge of Dartmoor in mid-Devon. Comfortable and well-equipped two- and three-bedroomed cottages with DVDs and CD players. One offers accessibility for the less mobile. Games room, some covered parking. Dogs/horses by arrangement. Good walking, cycling and touring base.
Offers:	5% discount on second (lower price) cottage if booked together. Short breaks often available (minimum three nights).
Facilities:	

OKEHAMPTON

Week Farm Country Holidays ★★★★Farmhouse
Bridestowe, Okehampton, Devon, EX20 4HZ

T:	+44 (0) 1837 861221
E:	accom@weekfarmonline.com
W:	weekfarmonline.com
Rooms:	5 • B&B per room per night (single) £30-£32; (double) £27-£28 • Credit/debit cards; cash/cheques accepted
Open:	Year round except Christmas
Description:	200-acre sheep farm. A warm welcome awaits at this homely 17thC farmhouse six miles from Okehampton. Three coarse-fishing lakes. Good home cooking assured and every comfort. Ideal touring base Dartmoor and coasts, walking, cycling, pony-trekking, fishing. Outdoor heated swimming pool. Cream tea on arrival. Come and spoil yourselves.
Offers:	Fishing weekend breaks. Three well-stocked coarse-fishing lakes, something for the whole family.
Facilities:	

OTTERY ST MARY

Salston Manor Hotel ★★★Hotel
Fluxton Road, Ottery St Mary, EX11 1RQ

T:	+44 (0) 1404 815581
E:	enquiries@salstonhotel.co.uk
W:	salstonhotel.co.uk
Rooms:	27 • Contact for prices • Credit/debit cards; cash/cheques, euros accepted
Open:	Year round
Description:	Early-Victorian country-house hotel is excellent touring base with indoor heated pool and sauna. Ideal for business or pleasure, superb cuisine at affordable prices. Special-interest breaks include golf, walking, antiques, houses and gardens. Exeter, Dartmoor, Sidmouth are all within easy reach.
Offers:	Ask for getaway breaks for two days or more. Discounts of up to 20% on normal rates.
Facilities:	

61

DEVON

PAIGNTON

Beecroft Lodge ♦♦♦ Guest Accommodation
10 St Andrews Road, Paignton, TQ4 6HA

T:	+44 (0) 1803 558702
E:	info@beecrofthotel.co.uk
W:	beecrofthotel.co.uk
Rooms:	9 • B&B per room per night (single) £23-£27; (double) £46-£54 • Credit/debit cards; cash/cheques accepted
Open:	Year round
Description:	Situated in an elevated position near the beach, harbour and town. Ideal for exploring Torbay, walking the coastal path or relaxing on the beach. Enjoy a home-cooked evening meal, relax with a drink, and be free to come and go. Best of all, just unwind in the friendly atmosphere.
Offers:	Discounts and special offers – see website for details.
Facilities:	

PAIGNTON

Newbarn Farm Cottages and Angling Centre
★★★★ Self Catering

Totnes Road, Collaton St Mary, Paignton, TQ4 7PT

T:	+44 (0) 1803 558702
W:	newbarnfarm.com
Units:	7 • Sleeps from 2-12 • Low season £190-£280; high season £315-£1,590 • Credit/debit cards; cash/cheques accepted
Open:	Year round
Description:	A selection of well-equipped, self-catering cottages set in 40 acres of pasture and woodland. Magnificent hill-top views of Dartmoor and the South Hams. Peaceful and tranquil, with on-site fishing lakes. Close to Paignton, Totnes and Torquay. Many places of interest within easy reach. Beach 2.5 miles.
Offers:	Short breaks available October-April three-, four-, and five-night stays.
Facilities:	

PLYMOUTH

Kitley House Hotel and Restaurant ★★★ Hotel
Kitley Estate, Yealmpton, Plymouth, Devon, PL8 2NW

T:	+44 (0) 1752 881555
E:	sales@kitleyhousehotel.com
W:	kitleyhousehotel.com
Rooms:	19 • B&B per room per night (single) £75-£125; (double) £85-£145 • Credit/debit cards; cash/cheques, euros accepted
Open:	Year round
Description:	Unique Grade I Listed building, set in valley overlooking a trout lake. Luxury suites and standard bedrooms feature contemporary facilities with magnificent views. Restaurant is popular with locals and is open for lunch and dinner.
Offers:	Christmas and New Year events. Mid-week and weekend short breaks available all year. Murder Mystery events autumn-spring. Honeymoon destination.
Facilities:	

DEVON

SALCOMBE

Bolberry Farm Cottages ★★★★★Self Catering
Bolberry Farm Cottages, Bolberry, Kingsbridge, TQ7 3DY

T:	+44 (0) 1752 881555
W:	bolberryfarmcottages.co.uk
Units:	3 • Sleeps from 4-6 • Low season £310-£440; high season £690-£820 • Credit/debit cards; cash/cheques accepted
Open:	Year round
Description:	Luxury two- and three-bedroom, tasteful barn-conversion cottages. Each individually designed, retaining true character whilst creating modern, high-quality living accommodation. Hand-crafted furniture, TV, video, washer/dryer, microwave, dishwasher. Full central heating and coal-effect gas open fire. Enclosed garden, car park and pet/boot wash area.
Offers:	Short breaks out of season; discount off evening meals taken at our nearby Port Light hotel.
Facilities:	

SEATON

West Ridge Bungalow ★★★Self Catering
West Ridge Bungalow, Harepath Hill, Seaton, EX12 2TA

T:	+44 (0) 1752 881555
W:	cottageguide.co.uk/westridge
Units:	1 • Sleeps from 1-4 • Low season £195-£295; high season £315-£525 • Cash/cheques accepted
Open:	March to October
Description:	Comfortably furnished bungalow on elevated ground in 1.5 acres of gardens. Beautiful, panoramic views of Axe Estuary and sea. Close by are Beer and Branscombe. Lyme Regis seven miles, Sidmouth 10 miles. Excellent centre for touring, walking, sailing, fishing, golf. Full gas central heating, double glazing throughout.
Offers:	10% reduction for two persons only, throughout booking period.
Facilities:	

SIDMOUTH

Boswell Farm Cottages ★★★★Self Catering
Boswell Farm, Harcombe, Sidmouth, EX10 0PP

T:	+44 (0) 1752 881555
W:	boswell-farm.co.uk
Units:	7 • Sleeps from 4-6 • Low season £264-£364; high season £754-£1,038 • Credit/debit cards; cash/cheques accepted
Open:	Year round
Description:	Two miles from the World Heritage Coastline and beaches, cradled in 45 acres of peaceful valley. Listed, 17thC farmhouse with period cottages, lovingly converted from original farm buildings, each with own enclosed flower-filled cottage garden. Idyllic walks, ideal touring base. Tennis court, trout pond. 14thC inn and amenities within walking distance.
Offers:	25% reduction – two people (or two people and baby) November-March (full week only, excluding bank holidays).
Facilities:	

DEVON

SIDMOUTH

Hotel Riviera ★★★★ Hotel
The Esplanade, Sidmouth, EX10 8AY GOLD AWARD

T:	+44 (0) 1395 515201
E:	enquiries@hotelriviera.co.uk
W:	hotelriviera.co.uk

Rooms:	26 • B&B per room per night (single) £90-£142; (double) £180-£262 • Credit/debit cards; cash/cheques accepted
Open:	Year round
Description:	The hotel has a long tradition of hospitality and is perfect for unforgettable holidays, long weekends, unwinding breaks and all the spirit of the glorious festive season… you will be treated to the kind of friendly, personal attention that can only be found in a private hotel of this quality.
Offers:	Luxury three-day breaks and carefree weekend breaks at certain times of year. Christmas and New Year programme also available.
Facilities:	

SIDMOUTH

Southern Cross ★★★ Guesthouse
High Street, Newton Poppleford, Sidmouth, EX10 0DU

T:	+44 (0) 1395 568439
E:	southerncrossguesthouse@tesco.net
W:	southerncrossguesthouse.co.uk

Rooms:	7 • B&B per room per night (single) £28-£38; (double) £50-£56 • Cash/cheques, euros accepted
Open:	March to December (excluding Christmas).
Description:	14thC, thatched, Grade II Listed cottage and tea room with walled rear gardens. Hearty breakfasts, lunches, famous cream teas. Sidmouth and Bicton Park three miles, Exeter 10 miles, Westpoint Showground and airport six miles. Jurassic Coast and excellent eating places nearby. Walking, golf and fishing on our doorstep.
Offers:	Discount for three or more nights. Phone for details.
Facilities:	

SIDMOUTH

The Salty Monk ★★★★★ Restaurant with Rooms
Church Street, Sidford, Sidmouth, EX10 9QP GOLD AWARD

T:	+44 (0) 1395 513174
E:	saltymonk@btconnect.com
W:	saltymonk.co.uk

Rooms:	5 • B&B per room per night (single) £65-£85; (double) £95-£175 • Credit/debit cards; cash/cheques accepted
Open:	Year round
Description:	A haven of luxury, this 16thC restaurant ideally located for exploring Dartmoor and the Heritage Coast. Individual, superbly appointed bedrooms, spa baths and two stunning suites. Award-winning, elegant restaurant overlooking beautiful gardens. Imaginative food using finest ingredients, all made on the premises by resident chef proprietors.
Offers:	Three nights for two low season.
Facilities:	

SOURTON

Collaven Manor Hotel ★★Country House Hotel
Sourton, Okehampton, EX20 4HH SILVER AWARD

T:	+44 (0) 1837 861522
E:	collavenmanor@supanet.com
W:	collavenmanor.co.uk
Rooms:	9 • B&B per room per night (single) £62-£62; (double) £98-£140 • Credit/debit cards; cash/cheques, euros accepted
Open:	Year round except Christmas and New Year
Description:	Historic 15thC manor on edge of Dartmoor. Characterful bedrooms, log fires, four-posters, glorious views. Delicious home-cooked, home-grown food including vegetarian specialities. Ideal touring centre, three minutes from A30 yet peacefully located in four-acre grounds and surrounded by open countryside. Riding, fishing and golf nearby.
Offers:	Off-season breaks – 25%-35% discount for two nights' or more DB&B.
Facilities:	

TAVISTOCK

Edgemoor Cottage ★★★★Self Catering
Edgemoor, Middlemoor, Tavistock, PL19 9DY

T:	+44 (0) 1837 861522
W:	edgemoorcottage.co.uk
Units:	1 • Sleeps from 1-4 • Low season £200-£300; high season £300-£400 • Cash/cheques, euros accepted
Open:	Year round
Description:	Attractive country cottage in peaceful hamlet. Two en suite bedrooms (one twin, one double, both with TV), kitchen/dining room, upstairs living room leading into a sun lounge/diner with patio overlooking fields. Perfect base to explore Dartmoor, Devon and Cornwall. North and south coasts are within an hour's drive.
Offers:	£25 discount to holidaymakers booking a second week. Same discount to guests booking a subsequent holiday.
Facilities:	

TAVISTOCK

Harford Bridge ★★★★Holiday, Touring & Camping Park
Peter Tavy, Tavistock, Devon, PL19 9LS

T:	+44 (0) 1822 810349
E:	enquiry@harfordbridge.co.uk
W:	harfordbridge.co.uk
Pitches:	Touring: 120; touring caravans: 40; motor caravans: 40; tents: 40; caravan holiday homes: 12 • Per night (caravan, motor caravan) £9.50-£18; (tent) £9.50-£13.50; (caravan holiday home) £195-£440 • Credit/debit cards; cash/cheques accepted
Open:	Year round
Description:	Beautiful, level, sheltered park set in Dartmoor with delightful views of Cox Tor. The River Tavy forms a boundary, offering riverside and other spacious, level camping pitches. Luxury, self-catering caravan holiday homes.
Offers:	Camping: 10% discount for week paid in full on arrival. Holiday let: £15 off two-week booking. £10 senior citizen discount.
Facilities:	

DEVON

DEVON

TAVISTOCK

Langstone Manor ★★★★ Holiday, Touring & Camping Park
Moortown, Tavistock, Devon, PL19 9JZ

T:	+44 (0) 1822 613371
E:	jane@langstone-manor.co.uk
W:	langstone-manor.co.uk
Pitches:	Touring: 40; touring caravans: 40; motor caravans: 40; tents: 40; caravan holiday homes: 7 • Per night (caravan, motor caravan, tent) £9-£11; (caravan holiday home) £160-£400 • Credit/debit cards; cash/cheques accepted
Open:	Year round except Christmas and New Year
Description:	Fantastic location with direct access onto moor. Peace and quiet, with secluded pitches. Bar and restaurant. Discover Dartmoor's secret!
Offers:	£15 discount for two-week booking in holiday homes. £30 discount for two people sharing, on weekly bookings, booked on certain weeks.
Facilities:	

TEIGNMOUTH

Britannia House B&B ♦♦♦♦♦ Guest Accommodation
26 Teign Street, Teignmouth, Devon, TQ14 8EG   SILVER AWARD

T:	+44 (0) 1626 770051
E:	gillettbritannia@aol.com
W:	britanniahouse.org
Rooms:	3 • B&B per room per night (single) £40-£60; (double) £60-£80 • Credit/debit cards; cash/cheques, euros accepted
Open:	Year round except January
Description:	This 17thC listed house is situated in a conservation area of old Teignmouth. Recently refurbished to a high standard, bedrooms are luxuriously equipped, en suite and have high-pressure, thermostatically controlled showers. A sumptuous breakfast can be taken in the beautiful dining room or peaceful, walled garden.
Offers:	Prices reduce by £5 per night up to three nights for a double room.
Facilities:	

TORQUAY

Corbyn Head Hotel ★★★ Hotel
Torbay Road, Torquay, TQ2 6RH   SILVER AWARD

T:	+44 (0) 1803 213611
E:	info@corbynhead.com
W:	corbynhead.com
Rooms:	45 • B&B per room per night (single) £45-£150; (double) £70-£0 • Credit/debit cards; cash/cheques, euros accepted
Open:	Year round
Description:	The Corbyn Head Hotel is one of Torquay's finest three-star hotels with its seafront location. Many of the bedrooms boast sea views and have private balconies. With two award-winning restaurants to choose from, and with its outstanding service, you can expect an enjoyable stay.
Offers:	Please enquire about special promotions. Stay seven nights for the price of six.
Facilities:	

DEVON

TORQUAY

South Sands Apartments ★★★Self Catering
Torbay Road, Livermead, Torquay, TQ2 6RG

T:	+44 (0) 1803 213611
W:	southsands.co.uk
Units:	18 • Sleeps from 1-5 • Low season £130-£220; high season £260-£490 • Credit/debit cards; cash/cheques, euros accepted
Open:	Year round
Description:	Specifically designed holiday apartments offering a high degree of comfort and cleanliness. Spacious and tastefully decorated with fitted kitchens. Apartments with bath or shower. No meters. Towels available upon request. Ground and first floor only. Seafront location. Beach 100 yards. Main bus route. Families and couples only. Parking on site.
Offers:	Short breaks and mid-week bookings in low season. Discount available for two consecutive weeks or more.
Facilities:	

TOTNES

The Old Forge at Totnes ★★★★Guesthouse
Seymour Place, Totnes, TQ9 5AY

T:	+44 (0) 1803 862174
E:	enq@oldforgetotnes.com
W:	oldforgetotnes.com
Rooms:	10 • B&B per room per night (single) £52-£72; (double) £62-£85 • Credit/debit cards; cash/cheques accepted
Open:	Year round
Description:	A warm welcome assured at this 600-year-old stone building with walled garden and car parking. Whirlpool spa. Extensive breakfast menu. Quiet, yet close to town and river. Coast and Dartmoor nearby, Eden Project 1.5 hours. Two-bedroomed cottage suite and family room with roof terrace available.
Offers:	Three-day breaks (November-March) – £4 off price of room per night.
Facilities:	

TWO BRIDGES

Prince Hall Hotel ★★Hotel
Two Bridges, Princetown, Yelverton, Devon, PL20 6SA — SILVER AWARD

T:	+44 (0) 1822 890403
E:	info@princehall.co.uk
W:	princehall.co.uk
Rooms:	9 • B&B per room per night (single) £60-£165; (double) £130-£180 • Credit/debit cards; cash/cheques accepted
Open:	Year round
Description:	With its vibrant cuisine, using local and seasonal produce, and genuine hospitality to human and canine visitors alike, this stunningly situated Georgian country house embodies the essence and tranquillity of Dartmoor. Rooms are spacious and stylish, most with magnificent moorland views. Walking, fishing, riding and golf are easily accessible.
Offers:	Fishing breaks; art courses; private house parties.
Facilities:	

DEVON

WEST DOWN

The Long House ♦♦♦♦ Guest Accommodation
The Square, West Down, Ilfracombe, Devon, EX34 8NF

T:	+44 (0) 1271 863242
W:	long-house.com
Rooms:	4 • B&B per room per night (double) from £27 • Cash/cheques accepted
Open:	Year round
Description:	Picturesque, 18thC cottage guesthouse in a quiet village, yet within 10 minutes of Blue Flag beaches and Exmoor. Our cosy, yet spacious, centrally heated bedrooms are all en suite and our delicious breakfasts, using local produce, are served in what was originally the village smithy.
Offers:	Two-night winter weekend breaks. Three-course dinner with bottle of house wine per couple included. Prices and availability on request.
Facilities:	

WILLAND

Bradfield Cottages ★★★★ Self Catering
Bradfield, Willand, Cullompton, EX15 2RA

T:	+44 (0) 1271 863242
E:	reservations@bradfieldcottages.co.uk
W:	bradfieldcottages.co.uk
Units:	2 • Sleeps 4 • Low season £340-£475; high season £475-£720 • Cash/cheques accepted
Open:	Year round
Description:	Stylish and comfortable single-storey cottages, set in 18 acres of beautiful Devon countryside, with private gardens, woodland and a fishing lake. Each cottage has direct access to its own patio and walled garden. Easy access to all of Devon's activities and attractions. The perfect place for relaxing.
Offers:	Short breaks available October-March and at short notice March-October.
Facilities:	

YELVERTON

The Rosemont ♦♦♦♦ Guest Accommodation
Greenbank Terrace, Yelverton, Devon, PL20 6DR

T:	+44 (0) 1822 852175
E:	office@therosemont.co.uk
W:	therosemont.co.uk
Rooms:	7 • B&B per room per night (single) £27-£45; (double) £52-£60 • Credit/debit cards; cash/cheques, euros accepted
Open:	Year round except Christmas and New Year
Description:	Overlooking the village green, The Rosemont has all en suite rooms with modern facilities offering remote-control colour TV (with Freeview), tea and coffee facilities, hairdryer, complimentary biscuits and bottled water etc. Breakfast is free range using local produce.
Offers:	Book two nights and get a third at half price (excluding bank holidays).
Facilities:	

DORSET

ALTON PANCRAS

Whiteways Farmhouse Accommodation ★★★★B&B
Bookham, Dorchester, DT2 7RP SILVER AWARD

T:	+44 (0) 1300 345511
E:	andy.foot1@btinternet.com
W:	bookhamcourt.co.uk
Rooms:	1 • B&B per room per night (single) £35-£40; (double) £54-£70 • Cash/cheques accepted
Open:	Year round except Christmas
Description:	A warm welcome awaits you at this hamstone and flint farmhouse, situated at the head of the Blackmore Vale. The double/family character rooms enjoy panoramic views over unspoilt countryside. Ideal for walks along the Wessex Way and Hardy Trail, with own fishing lake, farm trail and hide.
Offers:	Wildlife breaks – see birds and badgers from our wildlife hide. Fishing lake also available to guests.
Facilities:	

ATHELHAMPTON

White Cottage ★★★★B&B
Dorchester, Dorset, DT2 7LG SILVER AWARD

T:	+44 (0) 1305 848622
W:	white_cottage_bandb.co.uk
Rooms:	2 • B&B per room per night (single) £40-£45; (double) £60-£70 • Cash/cheques accepted
Open:	Year round except Christmas
Description:	A beautiful 300-year-old cottage, newly refurbished. Room one, with en suite, looks over river and hills. Room two, with private bathroom, looks over field and woodland. Each room has dressing gowns, fresh fruit and flowers and a mini-fridge with complimentary water, fresh milk etc. Athelhampton House 200 yards.
Offers:	Three nights or more – single £35-£40, double £50-£60. Children under three – free; under 12 – £15 sharing room.
Facilities:	

BLANDFORD FORUM

Lower Bryanston Farm B&B ★★★★B&B
Lower Bryanston, Blandford Forum, DT11 0LS

T:	+44 (0) 1258 452009
E:	aj.jones@onetel.net
W:	brylow.co.uk
Rooms:	5 • B&B per room per night (single and double) from £55 • Cash/cheques accepted
Open:	Year round except Christmas and New Year
Description:	Attractive Georgian farmhouse with spacious rooms and beautiful rural views. All rooms equipped with hospitality tray and TV/DVD. Fantastic full English breakfast. Safe off-road parking. Superb location to explore the interesting county of Dorset. Within walking distance of Blandford. Blandford Camp and Bryanston school nearby.
Offers:	B&B for your horse is available.
Facilities:	

69

DORSET

BOURNEMOUTH

Alexander Lodge Hotel ★★★★ Guesthouse
21 Southern Road, Bournemouth, BH6 3SR

T:	+44 (0) 1202 421662
E:	alexanderlodge@yahoo.com
W:	alexanderlodgehotel.co.uk
Rooms:	6 • B&B per room per night (single) £25-£50; (double) £44-£64 • Credit/debit cards; cash/cheques accepted
Open:	Year round except Christmas and New Year
Description:	Delightful, small, no-smoking hotel in quiet Bournemouth suburb, 200 yards from Blue Flag sandy beach, cliff top and lift. Excellent home-cooked meals, comfortable en suite rooms, licensed bar, parking. Ideal for holidays, short breaks and stopovers. Perfect for Christchurch, New Forest, Bournemouth and Dorset. Finalist – Landlady of the Year.
Offers:	Three-night specials available from September-June. Prices from £62 per person B&B, £90 per person DB&B.
Facilities:	

BOURNEMOUTH

Best Western Connaught Hotel ★★★ Hotel
West Hill Road, West Cliff, Bournemouth, BH2 5PH

T:	+44 (0) 1202 298020
E:	sales@theconnaught.co.uk
W:	theconnaught.co.uk
Rooms:	56 • B&B per room per night (single) £45-£70; (double) £90-£160 • Credit/debit cards; cash/cheques accepted
Open:	Year round
Description:	Superbly presented hotel, centrally located to town centre, Bournemouth International Centre, pier and sandy beaches. Outdoor pool and patio area. Magnificent indoor leisure centre with large pool, spa, saunas, steam rooms and gym. Attractive, en suite bedrooms, some with balconies. Good food and wine. Traditional good service and modern facilities.
Offers:	Minimum lengths of stay may apply. Christmas, New Year, Easter and bank holiday programmes.
Facilities:	

BOURNEMOUTH

The Chine Hotel ★★★ Hotel
Boscombe Spa Road, Bournemouth, BH5 1AX

T:	+44 (0) 1202 396234
E:	reservations@chinehotel.co.uk
W:	fjbhotels.co.uk
Rooms:	87 • B&B per room per night (single) £70-£90; (double) £140-£190 • Credit/debit cards; cash/cheques, euros accepted
Open:	Year round
Description:	A delightful, quality hotel with a rosette awarded for fine food. Excellent leisure facilities including indoor/outdoor pools, outdoor hot tub, sauna, Jacuzzi, gym and children's indoor/outdoor play areas. The hotel is set in three acres of beautifully manicured gardens which lead down to the beach.
Offers:	Wine tasting and gourmet weekends, Christmas and New Year packages, Easter and special short breaks available.
Facilities:	

DORSET

BOURNEMOUTH

Ullswater Hotel ★★Hotel
Westcliff Gardens, Bournemouth, BH2 5HW

T:	+44 (0) 1202 555181
E:	enquiries@ullswater.uk.com
W:	ullswater.uk.com
Rooms:	42 • B&B per room per night (single) £33-£39; (double) £66-£78 • Credit/debit cards; cash/cheques accepted
Open:	Year round
Description:	The Ullswater is within sight of the sea in the most favoured position on the West Cliff and within a few minutes' walk of the beach, town centre and Bournemouth International Centre. The Ullswater offers a high degree of comfort in tasteful surroundings, with good food and personal service.
Offers:	Regular Murder Mystery weekends, Turkey and Tinsel breaks and party weekends. Speciality breaks for gardening, heritage and ramblers.
Facilities:	

BRIDPORT

Britmead House ♦♦♦♦Guest Accommodation
West Bay Road, Bridport, Dorset, DT6 4EG

T:	+44 (0) 1308 422941
E:	britmead@talk21.com
W:	britmeadhouse.co.uk
Rooms:	8 • B&B per room per night (single) £40-£50; (double) £54-£70 • Credit/debit cards; cash/cheques accepted
Open:	Year round
Description:	An elegant Edwardian house situated just off the A35 between the historic market town of Bridport and the harbour at West Bay, the ideal location for exploring the beautiful Dorset countryside. Family-run, en suite accommodation with many thoughtful extras. Ten minutes' walk to harbour, beaches, golf course and the coastal path.
Offers:	Discounts available on stays of three or more nights.
Facilities:	

BRIDPORT

Freshwater Beach Holiday Park
★★★★Holiday, Touring & Camping Park

Burton Bradstock, Bridport, Dorset, DT6 4PT

T:	+44 (0) 1308 897317
E:	office@freshwaterbeach.co.uk
W:	freshwaterbeach.co.uk
Pitches:	Touring: 500; touring caravans: 350; motor caravans: 50; tents: 100; caravan holiday homes: 60 • Per night (caravan, motor caravan) £9-£30; (tent) £4-£30; (caravan holiday home) £150-£715 • Credit/debit cards; cash/cheques accepted
Open:	Mid-March to mid-November.
Description:	Family park with a large touring and camping field. Own private beach on spectacular World Heritage Coastline.
Offers:	Pitch prices include up to six people and club membership.
Facilities:	

DORSET

CHARMOUTH

Monkton Wyld Farm Caravan & Camping Park
★★★★ Touring & Camping Park

Monkton Wyld, Bridport, Dorset, DT6 6DB

T:	+44 (0) 1297 34525
E:	simonkewley@mac.com
W:	monktonwyld.co.uk
Pitches:	Touring: 60 • Per night (caravan, motor caravan, tent) £8.50-£18 • Credit/debit cards; cash/cheques, euros accepted
Open:	Easter to 31 October.
Description:	Beautifully landscaped, level park. Only three miles from sandy beaches and surrounded by lovely countryside. Excellent access, yet away from noisy main roads. All the amenities you would expect to find in a quality park.
Offers:	Weekly special-offer rates: £65 low season, £75 mid-season.
Facilities:	

CHARMOUTH

The Poplars
★★★ Self Catering

Booking address: Wood Farm Caravan Park, Axminster Road, Bridport, DT6 6BT

T:	+44 (0) 1297 34525
W:	woodfarm.co.uk
Units:	1 • Sleeps 4 • Low season £210-£0 • Credit/debit cards; cash/cheques accepted
Open:	Easter to end of October.
Description:	With breathtaking views and superb facilities, The Poplars offers spacious, comfortable accommodation specifically designed for disabled guests. See our Heritage Coast and spectacular rural scenery.
Offers:	10% discount for two-week stays. Early Bird offer for bookings received before 1 March.
Facilities:	

CHARMOUTH

Wood Farm Caravan and Camping Park
★★★★★ Holiday, Touring & Camping Park

Charmouth, Bridport, Dorset, DT6 6BT

T:	+44 (0) 1297 560697
E:	holidays@woodfarm.co.uk
W:	woodfarm.co.uk
Pitches:	Touring: 206; touring caravans: 186; tents: 20; caravan holiday homes: 3 • Per night (caravan, motor caravan) £12.50-£26; (tent) £10.50-£22; (caravan holiday home) £210-£550 • Credit/debit cards; cash/cheques accepted
Open:	Easter to October.
Description:	Breathtaking views and superb facilities are both on offer at Wood Farm. Heritage Coast and spectacular rural scenery are just waiting to amaze you.
Offers:	Low- and mid-season offers for one- and two-week stays.
Facilities:	

DORSET

EVERSHOT

The Acorn Inn ♦♦♦♦ Guest Accommodation
28 Fore Street, Evershot, Dorchester, Dorset, DT2 0JW

T:	+44 (0) 1935 83228
E:	stay@acorn-inn.co.uk
W:	acorn-inn.co.uk
Rooms:	10 • B&B per room per night (single) £75-£140; (double) £100-£235 • Credit/debit cards; cash/cheques accepted
Open:	Year round
Description:	A delightful 16thC coaching inn in an Area of Outstanding Natural Beauty. Charming bedrooms, individually decorated. Award-winning restaurant specialising in local produce and fresh fish. Oak-panelled bar with flagstone floor and open fire, serving real ales. Thirty minutes from World Heritage Coastline. Short breaks our speciality.
Offers:	Three-, four- and five-night DB&B breaks from £370 per room, Sunday-Thursday.
Facilities:	

EYPE

Eype's Mouth Country Hotel ★★ Hotel
Eype, Bridport, Dorset, DT6 6AL

T:	+44 (0) 1308 423300
E:	info@eypesmouthhotel.co.uk
W:	eypesmouthhotel.co.uk
Rooms:	18 • B&B per room per night (single) £50-£70; (double) £82-£100 • Credit/debit cards; cash/cheques, euros accepted
Open:	Year round
Description:	Set in the picturesque small village of Eype, the hotel nestles amid the downland and cliff tops that form the Heritage Coastline. Stunning sea views in a peaceful setting are matched by excellent hospitality. Good food and drink, served in the comfortable surroundings of this family-run hotel, make the perfect venue for a relaxing break.
Offers:	Special DB&B three-night breaks available throughout year.
Facilities:	

LULWORTH COVE

Cromwell House Hotel ★★ Hotel
Lulworth Cove, West Lulworth, Wareham, Dorset, BH20 5RJ

T:	+44 (0) 1929 400253
E:	cromwell@lulworthcove.co.uk
W:	lulworthcove.co.uk
Rooms:	18 • B&B per room per night (single) £42.50-£60; (double) £66-£95 • Credit/debit cards; cash/cheques accepted
Open:	Year round except Christmas and New Year
Description:	Lulworth Cove 200 yards, all en suite rooms, spectacular sea views, direct access Jurassic Coast, excellent walking and country pursuits. Good home cooking – local fish, including Lulworth Cove lobsters, a speciality. Bar and extensive wine list, beautiful gardens and sea-facing terrace, home-made cream teas, all-day refreshments, pool (May to October).
Offers:	Art and photography courses – apply for details. Three-day special breaks available.
Facilities:	

DORSET

NORTH WOOTTON

Stoneleigh Barn ♦♦♦♦ Guest Accommodation
North Wootton, Sherborne, Dorset, DT9 5JW — SILVER AWARD

T:	+44 (0) 1935 815964
E:	stoneleighbarn@aol.com
W:	stoneleighbarn.com
Rooms:	4 • B&B per room per night (single) £27.50-£35; (double) £55-£80 • Cash/cheques accepted
Open:	Year round
Description:	Attractive, tastefully refurbished, converted stone barn, modern en suite bathrooms, comfortable four-poster beds, spacious ground-floor en suite room, delicious breakfasts, pretty landscaped gardens, South African rotunda and pond, heated outdoor pool, Jacuzzi room with mini-gym, off-road parking, inn 250 yards. Ideal touring base.
Offers:	Weekend breaks from £140 per couple (minimum two nights). Anniversary and honeymoon stays from £210.
Facilities:	

ORGANFORD

Organford Manor ★★★ Holiday, Touring & Camping Park
The Lodge, Organford, Poole, Dorset, BH16 6ES

T:	+44 (0) 1202 622202
E:	organford@lds.co.uk
W:	organfordmanor.co.uk
Pitches:	Touring: 70; touring caravans: 30; motor caravans: 10; tents: 30; caravan holiday homes: 4 • Per night (caravan, tent) £10.50-£12; (motor caravan) £9.50-£11; (caravan holiday home) £180-£250 • Cash/cheques, euros accepted
Open:	Year round except Christmas and New Year
Description:	A quiet country site in the wooded grounds of the manor-house, level and grassy. Good facilities; surrounded by farmland but centrally placed.
Offers:	10% discount off a four-night stay in May, June and September, low season times only (excluding bank holidays).
Facilities:	

SHERBORNE

The Eastbury Hotel ★★★ Hotel
Long Street, Sherborne, Dorset, DT9 3BY — SILVER AWARD

T:	+44 (0) 1935 813131
E:	enquiries@theeastburyhotel.co.uk
W:	theeastburyhotel.co.uk
Rooms:	21 • B&B per room per night (single) £55-£70; (double) £100-£120 • Credit/debit cards; cash/cheques accepted
Open:	Year round
Description:	Gracious Georgian townhouse just five minutes' walk from the centre of historic Sherborne. Typical of the period, it has graceful, light and spacious rooms offering home-from-home comfort throughout. Comfortable, attractive, en suite rooms. One-acre walled garden, private car park. The rosette-awarded restaurant features modern English cuisine.
Offers:	Stay for free Sunday nights when on a DB&B package.
Facilities:	

STUDLAND

The Manor House Hotel ★★Hotel
Manor Road, Studland, BH19 3AU — SILVER AWARD

T:	+44 (0) 1929 450288
E:	themanorhousehotel@lineone.net
Rooms:	21 • Contact for prices • Credit/debit cards; cash/cheques accepted
Open:	Year round
Description:	Romantic 18thC manor-house in 20 acres of secluded grounds overlooking the sea. Residential and restaurant licence. All rooms en suite with central heating, TV, telephone, radio, hairdryer, tea/coffee-making facilities. Four-poster beds. Menus feature fresh local seafood. Oak-panelled bar and dining room with conservatory. Two hard tennis courts. Riding and golf nearby.
Offers:	Good discounts on stays of three nights or more. Christmas three-day package and New Year two-day package available.
Facilities:	

SWANAGE

11 Wordsworth Court ★★★Self Catering
Booking address: Hidden Cottage, 20 Sidbury Close, Ascot, SL5 0PD

T:	+44 (0) 1929 450288
Units:	1 • Sleeps from 4 • Low season £240-£350; high season £350-£495 • Cash/cheques accepted
Open:	Year round
Description:	South-facing, two-bedroomed apartment in a sunny position adjacent to the Downs. Short stroll to Swanage beach, pier and town centre. Beautiful cliff-top walks to Durleston Country Park and the Jurassic Coast. Sea views from balcony, lounge and kitchen. Central heating. Fully equipped kitchen. Communal gardens. Off-road parking.
Offers:	Short breaks available from £50 per night September-June (minimum two nights).
Facilities:	

SWANAGE

Swanage Cottage Holidays ★★★★Self Catering
60 Bell Street, Swanage, BH19 2SB

T:	+44 (0) 1929 450288
W:	swanagecottageholidays.co.uk
Units:	3 • Sleeps from 5-8 • Low season £200-£500; high season £500-£1,000 • Cash/cheques, euros accepted
Open:	Year round
Description:	Comfortable, well-equipped stone cottages in old seaside resort near World Heritage Coastline and outstanding countryside. The Grade II Listed Plum Tree Cottage has four bedrooms and a large garden. Others have three bedrooms and small, south-west facing gardens. Everything provided to make your holiday successful. Your home away from home.
Offers:	£50 discount if couple and baby. Three/four-night stays October-April (excluding school/bank holidays).
Facilities:	

DORSET

75

DORSET

SWANAGE

Swanage Haven ★★★Guesthouse
3 Victoria Road, Swanage, BH19 1LY

T:	0870 285 1745
E:	info@swanagehaven.com
W:	swanagehaven.com
Rooms:	9 • B&B per room per night (single) £30-£35; (double) £60-£70 • Credit/debit cards; cash/cheques accepted
Open:	Year round
Description:	The Swanage Haven is a family-run B&B, where a warm welcome awaits you. Fluffy towels, crisp linen and friendly service make your stay a relaxed, comfortable treat. Child-friendly and will go extra mile to accommodate your needs.
Offers:	Weekly bookings: Seven nights for the price of six.
Facilities:	

TOLLER PORCORUM

Old School Cottage ★★★Self Catering
2 School Lane, Toller Porcorum, Dorchester, DT2 0DF

T:	0870 285 1745
W:	oldschooltoller.co.uk
Units:	3 • Sleeps 4 • Low season £170-£380; high season £390-£480 • Credit/debit cards; cash/cheques, euros accepted
Open:	Year round
Description:	Set in a tranquil village, The Old School offers relaxing, well-equipped accommodation with fantastic views, ideal for walkers and nature lovers. Within easy reach of West Bay, Burton Bradstock and Abbotsbury on the stunning Jurassic Coast. All properties have one double and one twin room, one with both bedrooms en suite.
Offers:	Three-night stays available November-April (excluding Christmas, Easter and bank holidays).
Facilities:	

WAREHAM

Beryl's B&B ★★B&B
2 Heath Cottages, Sandford, Wareham, BH20 7DF

T:	+44 (0) 1929 550138
E:	beryl@dakevar.demon.co.uk
Rooms:	3 • B&B per room per night (single) £30-£50; (double) £40-£70 • Cash/cheques accepted
Open:	Year round except Christmas and New Year
Description:	An attractive Victorian house set in wooded area with Sandford Heath at rear. Close to Wareham, the Isle of Purbeck, the Jurassic Coast, Swanage Railway, Corfe Castle, Lulworth Cove, Monkey World and Tank Museum. Ideal for walking and bird-watching. Cyclists welcome (overnight storage for cycles).
Offers:	Off-peak, mid-week breaks (minimum three nights, two sharing) £55 per person. Discounts for cyclists year round.
Facilities:	

DORSET

WIMBORNE MINSTER

Ashton Lodge ♦♦♦♦ Guest Accommodation
10 Oakley Hill, Wimborne Minster, Dorset, BH21 1QH   SILVER AWARD

T:	+44 (0) 1202 883423
E:	ashtonlodge@ukgateway.net
W:	ashtonlodge.ukgateway.net
Rooms:	5 • B&B per room per night (single) from £35; (double) £60-£65 • Cash/cheques accepted
Open:	Year round
Description:	Spacious, detached family house with ample off-street parking. Relaxed, friendly atmosphere with all the comforts of home on offer, including full English breakfast served in the dining room overlooking the attractively laid garden. All bedrooms are centrally heated, tastefully decorated and furnished to a high standard.
Offers:	Spring/autumn/winter savers: 10% discount for couples staying three nights or more October-March.
Facilities:	

DURHAM

BARNARD CASTLE

Staindrop House Mews & The Arches
★★★★ Self Catering

Booking address: 14 Front Street, Darlington, DL2 3NH

T:	+44 (0) 1202 883423
E:	harry-1937@hotmail.com
Units:	2 • Sleeps from 2-5 • Low season £190-£225; high season £270-£425 • Cash/cheques accepted
Open:	Year round
Description:	Converted stable units comprising one/two reception rooms, bathroom, shower room, fitted kitchen and small balcony. The unit with two reception rooms also has a beamed ceiling. Pretty countryside village. Use of large, landscaped garden with children's play area. All linen provided. No pets in Arches unit.
Offers:	Coal fire (first bucket of coal free). Bottle of wine in fridge.
Facilities:	

CONSETT

Bee Cottage Guesthouse ★★★★ Guesthouse
Castleside, Consett, County Durham, DH8 9HW

T:	+44 (0) 1207 508224
E:	welcome@beecottagefarmhouse.freeserve.co.uk
W:	smoothhound.co.uk/hotels/beecottage.html
Rooms:	8 • B&B per room per night (single) £41-£46; (double) £33-£36 • Credit/debit cards; cash/cheques accepted
Open:	Year round except Christmas and New Year
Description:	Situated on the edge of the Durham Dales with stunning views. A wonderful place to relax. Peaceful walking and cycling (next to C2C). Ideal base for Beamish, Durham, Newcastle, Hadrian's Wall, Hexham and Corbridge. Some ground-floor rooms, all en suite. Dinner available. Licensed. Non-smoking. You will be most welcome.
Offers:	Short breaks available – contact for details.
Facilities:	

DURHAM

Kingslodge Hotel & Restaurant ★★★Hotel
Flass Vale, Durham, DH1 4BG

T:	+44 (0) 1913 709977
E:	reservations@kingslodge.fsnet.co.uk
W:	kingslodge.info
Rooms:	20 • B&B per room per night (single) £65-£80; (double) £85-£100 • Credit/debit cards; cash/cheques accepted
Open:	Year round
Description:	One of Durham's top independent hotels, nestled among the beautiful woodland of Flass Vale, just a short walk from the centre of the historic city and the railway station. With ample on-site, complimentary parking, Kingslodge provides a countryside setting within the heart of Durham City.
Offers:	Weekend DB&B rates are available for both one- and two-night stays. Please contact the hotel direct to benefit from discounted rates.
Facilities:	

DURHAM

Whitworth Hall Country Park Hotel ★★★Hotel
Nr Spennymoor, Durham, County Durham, DL16 7QX   SILVER AWARD

T:	+44 (0) 1388 811772
E:	etc@whitworthhall.co.uk
W:	whitworthhall.co.uk
Rooms:	29 • B&B per room per night (single) £125-£145; (double) £145-£165 • Credit/debit cards; cash/cheques accepted
Open:	Year round
Description:	This Grade II Listed building, the former home of Bonnie Bobby Shafto, stands in extensive parkland with gardens, deer park and lake. Well-appointed, en suite bedrooms, three diverse restaurants, catering for all tastes, and comfortable lounges combine to deliver short breaks to remember in the heart of a 73-acre deer park.
Offers:	Weekend breaks: DB&B £150 per couple per night. Special rates for weddings, functions and groups on request.
Facilities:	

BILLERICAY

Pump House Apartment ★★★★★Self Catering
Pump House, Church Street, Billericay, CM11 2TR

T:	+44 (0) 1388 811772
W:	thepumphouseapartment.co.uk
Units:	1 • Sleeps from 1-6 • Low season £475-£950; high season £600-£1,050 • Credit/debit cards; cash/cheques, euros accepted
Open:	Year round
Description:	The apartment is on two floors and luxuriously furnished, with air-conditioning. The accommodation comprises two living rooms, fully fitted kitchen/diner and the option of one, two or three bedrooms with one, two or three bath/shower rooms. Guests have use of heated outdoor pool (May to September), hot tub, gazebo and gardens. Personal supervision.
Offers:	5% discount for stays of four weeks; 10% discount for stays of eight weeks against two- or three-bedroom options.
Facilities:	

ESSEX

CLACTON-ON-SEA

The Chudleigh ★★★★ Guest Accommodation
13 Agate Road, Marine Parade West, Clacton-on-Sea, Essex, CO15 1RA

T:	+44 (0) 1255 425407
E:	reception@chudleighhotel.com
W:	essex-sunshine-coast.org.uk
Units:	Rooms: 10 • B&B per room per night (single) from £41; (double) £60-£65 • Credit/debit cards; cash/cheques, euros accepted
Open:	Year round
Description:	An oasis in a town centre location, 200m from seafront gardens, near pier and main shops. Ideal for the business visitor, the tourist and for overnight stays. Free parking. The Chudleigh, owned by the same family since 1963, welcomes you and assures you of every comfort, with friendly atmosphere and attention to detail.
Offers:	Reduced terms by negotiation October-March (excluding Christmas and bank holidays).
Facilities:	

HARWICH

Continental ★★ Hotel
28-29 Marine Parade, Dovercourt, CO12 3RG

T:	+44 (0) 1255 551298
E:	hotconti@btconnect.com
W:	thehotelcontinental.com
Rooms:	14 • B&B per room per night (single) £40-£75; (double) £70-£95 • Credit/debit cards; cash/cheques, euros accepted
Open:	Year round
Description:	Boutique hotel overlooking Blue Flag beach and ever-changing seascape which is busy with shipping activity. Only minutes from Harwich International port. All rooms en suite, all unique. Quality food, cooked to order, with organically grown ingredients used extensively. Well-stocked bar and restaurant open to public all day.
Offers:	Perfect for ship-spotters: special three-day breaks – fishing trips at sea combined with accommodation and dinner.
Facilities:	

LITTLE BENTLEY

Spring Hall Cottage ★★★★ Self Catering
Spring Hall, Little Bentley, CO7 8SR

T:	+44 (0) 1206 251619
Units:	1 • Sleeps 4 • Low season £200-£295; high season £300-£400 • Cash/cheques, euros accepted
Open:	Year round
Description:	Grade II Listed, 17thC thatched cottage with a wealth of character and original features including exposed beams and inglenook fireplace. Two double bedrooms, double cart lodge, 0.33-acre enclosed garden, patio area and barbecue. Ideal location for Constable Country, Manningtree, historical Harwich/Colchester and Essex coast. Excellent selection of pubs/restaurants nearby.
Offers:	Short breaks available (minimum three nights). Welcome pack and complimentary bottle of wine per couple.
Facilities:	

ESSEX

SAFFRON WALDEN

The Cricketers ◆◆◆◆ Guest Accommodation
Wicken Road, Clavering, Saffron Walden, Essex, CB11 4QT SILVER AWARD

T:	+44 (0) 1799 550442
E:	cricketers@lineone.net
W:	thecricketers.co.uk
Rooms:	14 • B&B per room per night (single) £75; (double) £110 • Credit/debit cards; cash/cheques accepted
Open:	Year round except Christmas
Description:	16thC freehouse near Stansted Airport with beamed interior. Well-established restaurant and bar-meal trade with adjacent accommodation. Jamie Oliver grew up here and cooked here from the age of eight. Although he no longer cooks here, it is still owned and run by his parents, Trevor and Sally Oliver. Wireless Internet access.
Offers:	20% reduction for B&B on any Sunday or Friday. Please quote 'English Tourism Council'.
Facilities:	

GLOUCESTERSHIRE

BIBURY

The Swan Hotel ★★★ Small Hotel
Bibury, Cirencester, Gloucestershire, GL7 5NW

T:	+44 (0) 1285 740695
E:	info@swanhotel.co.uk
W:	cotswold-inns-hotels.co.uk/swan
Rooms:	18 • B&B per room per night (double) £140-£260 • Credit/debit cards; cash/cheques accepted
Open:	Year round
Description:	Standing alongside the River Coln, featuring beautifully decorated bedrooms and cosy lounges with real log fires. The delightful gardens are the perfect place to relax in the summer. The elegant Gallery Restaurant and Cafe Swan are renowned for their excellent cuisine. Relax in the recently developed Swan Sanctuary beauty rooms.
Offers:	Romantic mid-week breaks. Stay two nights (DB&B) in a luxury superior room – £95 per person per night.
Facilities:	

BOURTON-ON-THE-WATER

The Dial House Hotel ★★ Hotel
The Chestnuts, Bourton-on-the-Water, Cheltenham, GL54 2AN GOLD AWARD

T:	+44 (0) 1451 822244
E:	info@dialhousehotel.com
W:	dialhousehotel.com
Rooms:	13 • B&B per room per night (single) £60-£210; (double) £110-£210 • Credit/debit cards; cash/cheques accepted
Open:	Year round
Description:	The Dial House has been completely refurbished to combine a wonderful mix of old and new. Some rooms have four-posters with views over the village, others have sumptuously large beds. The food here is of a very high standard. Large 1.5-acre garden. Private parking.
Offers:	Bargain breaks available all year, mid-week. November-February, stay two nights mid-week and get third night free.
Facilities:	

GLOUCESTERSHIRE

BUCKLAND

Buckland Manor – Relais & Chateaux ★★★ Hotel
Buckland, Broadway, WR12 7LY — GOLD AWARD

T:	+44 (0) 1386 852626
E:	info@bucklandmanor.com
W:	bucklandmanor.com
Rooms:	13 • B&B per room per night (single) £215-£410; (double) £225-£420 • Credit/debit cards; cash/cheques accepted
Open:	Year round
Description:	13thC country-house hotel set in 10 acres, immaculate gardens, stream and waterfalls. Guests can relax before warming log fires and enjoy antiques reflecting the tastes of several centuries. Some bedrooms with four-poster beds and working fireplaces. The superb cuisine has been awarded many accolades. Ideal for Stratford-on-Avon and Cotswolds.
Offers:	Special, minimum two-night stay from £295 per room per night, DB&B.
Facilities:	

CHELTENHAM

Butlers ★★★★ Guest Accommodation
Western Road, Stretton Lodge, Cheltenham, GL50 3RN — SILVER AWARD

T:	+44 (0) 1242 570771
E:	info@butlers-hotel.co.uk
W:	butlers-hotel.co.uk
Rooms:	6 • B&B per room per night (single) £50-£65; (double) £70-£120 • Credit/debit cards; cash/cheques accepted
Open:	Year round
Description:	Welcome to Butlers. This unique Regency home is situated in a central, yet quiet, area, and just a short stroll to the promenade and the quaint Montpellier district. The rooms are named after well-known butlers from literature and history. Facilities include free WI-FI Internet, guest lounge, garden and parking.
Offers:	Self-catering studios within hotel also available for vacation and professional lets.
Facilities:	

CHELTENHAM

Charlton Kings Hotel ★★★ Small Hotel
London Road, Charlton Kings, Cheltenham, Gloucestershire, GL52 6UU

T:	+44 (0) 1242 231061
E:	enquiries@charltonkingshotel.co.uk
W:	charltonkingshotel.co.uk
Units:	Rooms: 13 • B&B per room per night (single) £65-£85; (double) £98-£125 • Credit/debit cards; cash/cheques accepted
Open:	Year round
Description:	Surrounded by Cotswold Hills, on outskirts of Cheltenham. Quality, comfort and friendliness are hallmarks of this privately owned hotel. All rooms are beautifully refurbished and have satellite TV. Very comfortable standard rooms. Excellent restaurant open seven days a week. Ample parking.
Offers:	Two-night weekend break special DB&B from £60 per person per night sharing. Three- and five-night breaks also available.
Facilities:	

GLOUCESTERSHIRE

CHELTENHAM

Priory Cottage ★★★Self Catering
Booking address: Church Gate, Southam Lane, Cheltenham, GL52 3NY

T:	+44 (0) 1242 231061
W:	countrycottagesonline.net
Units:	1 • Sleeps from 1-4 • Low season £250-£280; high season £280-£350 • Cash/cheques accepted
Open:	Year round except Christmas
Description:	Old Cotswold-stone cottage in own garden overlooking apple orchard. Cosy and warm in winter with wood-burning stove. Two bedrooms, one double, one twin; sitting room, dining room, modern fitted kitchen. Ideal base for Cotswolds, Cheltenham and Area of Outstanding Natural Beauty. Good walking country including Cotswold Way.
Offers:	Short breaks available all year from £150.
Facilities:	

CHIPPING CAMPDEN

The Eight Bells ♦♦♦♦Guest Accommodation
Church Street, Chipping Campden, GL55 6JG

T:	+44 (0) 1386 840371
E:	neilhargreaves@bellinn.fsnet.co.uk
W:	eightbellsinn.co.uk
Rooms:	7 • B&B per room per night (single) £50-£85; (double) £80-£115 • Credit/debit cards; cash/cheques accepted
Open:	Year round
Description:	This unspoilt 14thC Cotswold inn features open fires in winter and candle-lit tables all year round. There is a sun-drenched courtyard and terraced beer garden which overlooks the church. All accommodation has recently been refurbished to a high standard, and all bedrooms are en suite. Food is of the very highest standard, and a friendly welcome awaits you.
Offers:	Mid-January to mid-March '2 for 1' specials Monday-Thursday.
Facilities:	

CHIPPING CAMPDEN

Three Ways House ★★★Hotel
SILVER AWARD
Chapel Lane, Mickleton, Chipping Campden, GL55 6SB

T:	+44 (0) 1386 438429
E:	threeways@puddingclub.com
W:	puddingclub.com
Rooms:	48 • B&B per room per night (single) £75-£93; (double) £128-£185 • Credit/debit cards; cash/cheques accepted
Open:	Year round
Description:	Close to Chipping Campden, Broadway and Stratford-upon-Avon. Comfortable bedrooms, some with pudding themes, cosy bar, good food and attentive service. Regularly on TV as 'Home of The Pudding Club' where meetings of pudding lovers occur regularly. Stylish, air-conditioned restaurant.
Offers:	Pudding Club, walking weekends, chocoholic and gardens of Gloucestershire breaks available throughout the year.
Facilities:	

GLOUCESTERSHIRE

CIRENCESTER

Riverside House ♦♦♦♦ Guest Accommodation
Watermoor Road, Cirencester, Gloucestershire, GL7 1LF

T:	+44 (0) 1285 647642
E:	riversidehouse@mitsubishi-cars.co.uk
W:	riversidehouse.org.uk
Rooms:	24 • B&B per room per night (single) from £45; (double) from £60 • Credit/debit cards; cash/cheques accepted
Open:	Year round
Description:	Located 15 minutes' walk from the centre of the historic market town of Cirencester with easy access to and from M4/M5 and the Cotswolds. Riverside House is fully licensed and provides superb B&B for private and corporate guests. Built in the grounds of Mitsubishi UK headquarters.
Offers:	Special group discounts are available at weekends. Ideal for clubs and societies.
Facilities:	

DAGLINGWORTH

Corner Cottage ★★★★ Self Catering
Booking address: Brook Cottage, 23 Farm Court, Daglingworth, Cirencester, GL7 7AF

T:	+44 (0) 1285 647642
Units:	1 • Sleeps 2 • £235 – confirm with owner • Cash/cheques, euros accepted
Open:	Year round
Description:	Well-equipped, cosy cottage in small village. Excellent centre for exploring the Cotswolds Area of Outstanding Natural Beauty and glorious Gloucestershire. All-inclusive tariff. No hidden extras. All you need provide is food and transport. Allergy-friendly accommodation free from fur, feathers and tobacco smoke.
Offers:	No high-season charges. Single, flat-rate tariff throughout the year.
Facilities:	

GLOUCESTER

Middletown Farm Cottages ★★★★ Self Catering
Middletown Farm, Middletown Lane, Upleadon, Newent, GL18 1EQ

T:	+44 (0) 1285 647642
W:	middletownfarm.co.uk
Units:	2 • Sleeps 2 • Low season £200-£265; high season £265-£345 • Cash/cheques accepted
Open:	Year round
Description:	Delightful cottages surrounded by tranquil countryside. Refurbished to a high standard and very well equipped with everything you could need for a relaxing break in the country. Easy access to Gloucester, the Malvern Hills, the enchanting Royal Forest of Dean, the scenic Cotswolds and much more.
Offers:	Three-/four-night stays available November-March.
Facilities:	

GLOUCESTERSHIRE

MISERDEN

Sudgrove Cottages ★★★Self Catering
Sudgrove Cottages, Sudgrove, Miserden, Stroud, GL6 7JD

T:	+44 (0) 1285 647642
W:	sudgrovecottages.co.uk
Units:	3 • Sleeps from 2-6 • Low season £240-£350; high season £300-£430 • Cash/cheques accepted
Open:	Year round
Description:	Attractive Cotswold-stone cottages with views across fields, in a peaceful hamlet on a no-through road. Footpaths lead through valleys, woods and pasture to picturesque villages, while Cirencester, Stroud, Cheltenham and Gloucester are easily reached by car. You will find Sudgrove a place to relax and unwind.
Offers:	Short breaks available November-March, minimum two nights. Special offer– three nights for the price of two.
Facilities:	

MORETON-IN-MARSH

Manor House Hotel ♦Hotel
High Street, Moreton-in-Marsh, Gloucestershire, GL56 0LJ

T:	+44 (0) 1608 650501
E:	info@manorhousehotel.info
W:	cotswold-inns-hotels.co.uk/manor
Rooms:	38 • B&B per room per night (single) £115-£155; (double) £135-£210 • Credit/debit cards; cash/cheques accepted
Open:	Year round
Description:	This historic hotel, tastefully furnished throughout in a country-house style, was formerly a 16thC manor. The award-winning Mulberry Restaurant overlooks a sun terrace and garden. Guests can unwind and relax with afternoon tea in the traditional English gardens.
Offers:	Food lovers' Cotswold Break – two nights' DB&B, includes four-poster room/suite, complimentary coffee/tea, half bottle champagne and menu upgrade – £90 per person per night.
Facilities:	

STOW-ON-THE-WOLD

Broad Oak Cottages ★★★★★Self Catering
Counting House, Oddington Road, Stow-on-the-Wold, Cheltenham, GL54 1AL

T:	+44 (0) 1608 650501
E:	mary@broadoakcottages.co.uk
W:	broadoakcottages.co.uk
Units:	4 • Sleeps from 1-4 • Prices from £285 • Cash/cheques, euros accepted
Open:	Year round
Description:	Delightful cottages situated within a few minutes' walk of the centre of Stow. The cottages are furnished and equipped to the highest standard comprising both double and twin bedrooms, full central heating, log fires and fully modernised bathrooms and kitchens. Parking, south-facing patios, gardens and lovely views.
Offers:	Short breaks available (except in high season).
Facilities:	

GLOUCESTERSHIRE

STOW-ON-THE-WOLD

Stow Lodge Hotel
★★★ Hotel
SILVER AWARD

The Square, Stow-on-the-Wold, Cheltenham, GL54 1AB

T:	+44 (0) 1451 830485
E:	chris@stowlodge.com
W:	stowlodge.com
Rooms:	21 • B&B per room per night (single) £60-£130; (double) £80-£160 • Credit/debit cards; cash/cheques accepted
Open:	Year round except Christmas and New Year
Description:	Stow Lodge Hotel is situated in its own picturesque grounds overlooking the market square of the historic town of Stow-on-the-Wold. The hotel has been family owned and run for over 40 years and has built up a fine reputation for its friendly hospitality and excellent service.
Offers:	We offer special half-board rates if staying two or more nights.
Facilities:	

STROUD

Bear of Rodborough Hotel
★★★ Hotel
SILVER AWARD

Rodborough Common, Stroud, Gloucestershire, GL5 5DE

T:	+44 (0) 1453 878522
E:	info@bearofrodborough.info
W:	cotswold-inns-hotels.co.uk/bear
Rooms:	46 • B&B per room per night (double) £120-£215 • Credit/debit cards; cash/cheques accepted
Open:	Year round
Description:	Former 17thC coaching inn offers comfortable accommodation in an area of outstanding beauty. The hotel has many original features and the en suite bedrooms are exquisite, blending traditional architecture with luxurious interiors. The superb bar is renowned for its large selection of traditional beers.
Offers:	Three nights for the price of two DB&B.
Facilities:	

STROUD

Hillenvale
♦♦♦♦ Guest Accommodation

The Plain, Whiteshill, Stroud, GL6 6AB

T:	+44 (0) 1453 753441
E:	bobsue@hillenvale.co.uk
W:	hillenvale.co.uk
Rooms:	3 • B&B per room per night (single) from £30; (double) from £50 • Credit/debit cards; cash/cheques accepted
Open:	Year round
Description:	A warm welcome, comfort and high-quality accommodation are guaranteed in this country house between Bath and Cheltenham on the edge of the Cotswold Way. The conservatory/lounge and gardens have stunning panoramic views. M5 and M4 a short distance away
Offers:	Introductory offer – Friday night to Monday morning on selected weekends only £100 per couple; £70 single for B&B.
Facilities:	

GLOUCESTERSHIRE

STROUD

Pretoria Villa ♦♦♦♦ Guest Accommodation
Wells Road, Eastcombe, Stroud, Gloucestershire, GL6 7EE   SILVER AWARD

T:	+44 (0) 1452 770435
E:	glynis@gsolomon.freeserve.co.uk
W:	bedandbreakfast-cotswold.co.uk
Rooms:	3 • B&B per room per night (single) from £28; (double) from £56 • Cash/cheques accepted
Open:	Year round except Christmas
Description:	Enjoy luxurious B&B in a relaxed, family country house set in peaceful secluded gardens. Spacious bedrooms with many home comforts. Guest lounge with TV. Superb breakfast served at your leisure. Excellent base from which to explore the Cotswolds. Personal service and your comfort guaranteed.
Offers:	Discounted rates for four+ nights.
Facilities:	

HAMPSHIRE

ASHURST

Forest Gate Lodge ♦♦♦♦ Guest Accommodation
161 Lyndhurst Road, Ashurst, Southampton, SO40 7AW

T:	+44 (0) 23 8029 3026
W:	ukworld.net/forestgatelodge
Rooms:	5 • B&B per room per night (single) £25-£35; (double) £50-£60 • Cash/cheques accepted
Open:	Year round except Christmas
Description:	Large Victorian house with direct access to New Forest and its attractions – walks, riding, cycling. Pubs and restaurants nearby, Lyndhurst, 'capital of the New Forest', five minutes' drive. Multi-choice breakfast or vegetarian by prior arrangement. London direct, railway station five minutes' walk, golf course nearby, also local bike hire.
Offers:	Special rates: Three nights for price of two, weekdays only, Seven nights+ 50% off. 1 October- 1 April inclusive.
Facilities:	

BASINGSTOKE

The Hampshire Centrecourt ★★★★ Hotel
Great Binfields Road, Chineham, Basingstoke, RG24 8FY   SILVER AWARD

T:	+44 (0) 1256 319700
E:	hampshirec@marstonhotels.com
W:	marstonhotels.com
Rooms:	90 • B&B per room per night (single) £69.50-£174.50; (double) £90-£226 • Credit/debit cards; cash/cheques, euros accepted
Open:	Year round
Description:	With two indoor pools, nine tennis courts (indoor/outdoor), gym, fitness studio, sauna and spa offering beauty treatments, it offers leisure facilities second to none. Comfort and style runs throughout. Convenient for many attractions.
Offers:	Save 20% on our two-night HB break in July/August and November-February (excluding bank holidays, 23 December-1 January and Valentine's Day.
Facilities:	

HAMPSHIRE

BEAULIEU

Dale Farm House ♦♦♦♦ Guest Accommodation
Manor Road, Applemore Hill, Dibden, Southampton, Hampshire, SO45 5TJ

T:	+44 (0) 23 8084 9632
W:	dalefarmhouse.co.uk
Units:	Rooms: 6 • B&B per room per night (single) from £30; (double) from £48 • Cash/cheques accepted
Open:	Year round
Description:	Beautiful 18thC farmhouse in secluded wooded setting with direct access for walks or cycling. Peaceful garden in which to unwind and a bird-watcher's paradise. Excellent food to satisfy your appetite. Barbecues on request. Near beaches and ferry link to Southampton. Spoil yourself at this BBC *Holiday* programme-featured B&B.
Offers:	10% discount for Christmas breaks on a room-only basis. Three-for-two weekend breaks October-March (excluding bank holidays).
Facilities:	

HOOK

Tylney Hall Hotel ★★★★ Hotel
GOLD AWARD
Tylney Hall, Rotherwick, Hook, Hampshire, RG27 9AZ

T:	+44 (0) 1256 764881
E:	sales@tylneyhall.com
W:	tylneyhall.com
Rooms:	112 • B&B per room per night (single) £140-£335; (double) £170-£365 • Credit/debit cards; cash/cheques accepted
Open:	Year round
Description:	Set in manicured, historic gardens, Tylney Hall is in a perfect location. Elegant lounges, fine leisure facilities, exquisite bedrooms with breathtaking views. The spa makes this perfect for guests to be pampered in relaxing surroundings. A tranquil, romantic country house of distinction.
Offers:	Romantic breaks: champagne, chocolates, flowers in room. Full English breakfast, newspaper, use of hotel's luxury spa, from £240 per room per night.
Facilities:	

LYMINGTON

Stanwell House Hotel ★★★ Hotel
SILVER AWARD
15 High Street, Lymington, Hampshire, SO41 9AA

T:	+44 (0) 1590 677123
E:	sales@stanwellhousehotel.co.uk
W:	stanwellhousehotel.co.uk
Rooms:	29 • B&B per room per night (single) £85-£125; (double) £110-£170 • Credit/debit cards; cash/cheques, euros accepted
Open:	Year round
Description:	Privately owned Georgian townhouse with award-winning accommodation and dining. Four-poster suites, lovely bedrooms, candlelit dining and dramatic decor. Huge, lofty conservatory, charming, flower-filled terrace and walled garden for alfresco dining. Friendly and relaxed.
Offers:	Stay Friday and Saturday or Monday and Tuesday and get Sunday free (excluding bank holidays).
Facilities:	

HAMPSHIRE

LYMINGTON

Wheathill ★★★ Self Catering
Booking address: Three Corners, Centre Lane, Everton, Lymington, SO41 0JP

T:	+44 (0) 1590 677123
W:	halcyonholidays.com
Units:	1 • Sleeps 12 • Low season £420-£800; high season £840-£1,280 • Credit/debit cards; cash/cheques, euros accepted
Open:	Year round
Description:	In a semi-rural location on the outskirts of Lymington, on a leafy road leading to the New Forest, this beautifully refurbished house has mature gardens. An ideal base for exploring Lymington Quay, the New Forest, coastal walks and marshes. See website for further pictures and information/guest comments.
Offers:	Discounted weekend/mid-week bookings available all year round.
Facilities:	

NEW MILTON

Taverners Cottage ♦♦♦♦ Guest Accommodation
Bashley Cross Road, Bashley, New Milton, Hampshire, BH25 5SZ   SILVER AWARD

T:	+44 (0) 1425 615403
E:	jbaines@supanet.com
W:	tavernerscottage.co.uk
Rooms:	2 • B&B per room per night (double) £50-£60 • Cash/cheques, euros accepted
Open:	Year round except Christmas and New Year
Description:	Attractive 300-year-old cob cottage overlooking open farmland. Warm welcome guaranteed. Great breakfasts. Care and attention to detail a priority. Ideal for touring, golf, cycling, walking and riding.
Offers:	Winter discounts (excluding bank holidays). Discount for more than seven days.
Facilities:	

NEW MILTON

Willy's Well ★★★★ B&B
Bashley Common Road, New Milton, Hampshire, BH25 5SF

T:	+44 (0) 1425 616834
E:	moyramac2@hotmail.com
Rooms:	2 • B&B per room per night (single) £40-£50; (double) £60-£70 • Cash/cheques accepted
Open:	Year round
Description:	A warm welcome awaits you at this mid-1700s Listed thatched cottage standing in one acre of mature gardens, also available for your enjoyment. Willy's Well has direct forest access through six acres of pasture and is three miles from the sea. Ideal for walking, cycling, horse-riding.
Offers:	Mid-week reduced breaks – four nights for the price of three.
Facilities:	

HAMPSHIRE

ODIHAM

George Hotel
High Street, Odiham, Hook, Hampshire, RG29 1LP

★★Hotel
SILVER AWARD

T:	+44 (0) 1256 702081
E:	reception@georgehotelodiham.com
W:	georgehotelodiham.com
Rooms:	28 • B&B per room per night (single) £65-£90; (double) £85-£125 • Credit/debit cards; cash/cheques accepted
Open:	Year round except Christmas
Description:	15thC coaching inn with visible beams and wattle and daub walls. Oak-panelled, fine-dining restaurant with flagstone floor and ornate fireplace, specialising in seafood. Also offers contemporary cafe bar and bistro. Rooms beautifully refurbished with every modern comfort for today's travellers. Four-poster rooms feature in the oldest parts of the building.
Offers:	Special weekend and mid-week breaks available throughout the year – phone for special offers.
Facilities:	

WINCHESTER

South Winchester Lodges ★★★★★Self Catering
Booking address: 18 the Green, South Winchester Golf Club, Romsey Road, Winchester, SO22 5QX

T:	+44 (0) 1256 702081
W:	golfholidaywinchester.com
Units:	2 • Sleeps 6 • Low season £385-£520; high season £590-£740 • Cash/cheques accepted
Open:	Year round
Description:	Luxury three-bedroom, two-bathroom log cabins with spacious, open-plan living area and large decked balcony overlooking private putting green. Tranquil setting at the heart of South Winchester Golf Club. Two miles from the centre of historic Winchester and close to tourist attractions of the south coast and New Forest.
Offers:	10% discount for bookings made before 1 April 2007. See website for other current offers.
Facilities:	

HEREFORDSHIRE

HEREFORD

Castle Cliffe East ★★★★Self Catering
Booking address: Castle Cliffe West, 14 Quay Street, Hereford, HR1 2NH

T:	+44 (0) 1256 702081
W:	castlecliffe.net
Units:	1 • Sleeps 6 • Low season £350-£550; high season £600-£850 • Cash/cheques accepted
Open:	Year round
Description:	Originally a medieval watergate, Castle Cliffe provides luxury accommodation which is both tranquil and convenient. Set in parkland, it has period furniture, open fires and a south-facing riverside garden. Shops, restaurants and the cathedral are all within a few minutes' walk.
Offers:	Short breaks available all year. Claim a 10% discount by mentioning VisitBritain.
Facilities:	

HEREFORDSHIRE

LEDBURY

The Woodhouse Farm Cottages ★★★★★ Self Catering
The Woodhouse, Staplow, Ledbury, HR8 1NP

T:	+44 (0) 1256 702081
W:	thewoodhousefarm.co.uk
Units:	2 • Sleeps from 2-6 • Low season £250-£500; high season £450-£1,000 • Credit/debit cards; cash/cheques accepted
Open:	Year round
Description:	Tranquil retreats. Barn Croft and The Wainhouse share 15 acres of grounds with The Woodhouse, a medieval, Grade II Listed, semi-moated hall house. Comfortably furnished to very high standards with antiques and prints. All bedrooms are en suite. Each cottage has a private garden. Choice of dining solutions and food hampers.
Offers:	Romantic breaks. Three- and four-night breaks available.
Facilities:	

LEDBURY

White House Cottages ★★★★ Self Catering
The White House, Aylton, Ledbury, HR8 2RQ

T:	+44 (0) 1256 702081
W:	whitehousecottages.co.uk
Units:	5 • Sleeps from 2-5 • Low season £190-£380; high season £240-£499 • Cash/cheques accepted
Open:	Year round
Description:	Well-equipped, self-catering cottages situated in a hamlet four miles west of Ledbury. Surrounded by Herefordshire's idyllic countryside, these former farm buildings have been carefully adapted to create very comfortable and individual holiday accommodation. Perfect for exploring the Wye Valley, the Malverns and surrounding area. Resident owners.
Offers:	Three-night short breaks available all year, subject to certain booking restrictions. Please ring for details.
Facilities:	

ROSS-ON-WYE

Broome Farm ♦♦♦ Guest Accommodation
Peterstow, Ross-on-Wye, HR9 6QG

T:	+44 (0) 1989 562824
E:	enquiries@broomefarmhouse.co.uk
W:	broomefarmhouse.co.uk
Rooms:	3 • B&B per room per night (single) £20-£35; (double) £35-£60 • Cash/cheques, euros accepted
Open:	Year round
Description:	Working cider farm, providing en suite accommodation. Licensed dining room with a la carte menu featuring local produce. Set in tranquil countryside, looking over rural Herefordshire. Only two miles from the town of Ross-on-Wye. Orchard walks, cream teas and cider tasting available.
Offers:	Pay a maximum of £18.50 for an a la carte dinner, regardless of the menu price, if you are a resident.
Facilities:	

HEREFORDSHIRE

ROSS-ON-WYE

The Game Larders and The Old Bakehouse
★★★Self Catering

Wythall Estate, Bulls Hill, Ross-on-Wye, HR9 5SD

T:	+44 (0) 1989 562824
W:	wythallestate.co.uk
Units:	2 • Sleeps from 2-4 • Low season £195-£230; high season £250-£350 • Cash/cheques accepted
Open:	Year round
Description:	Self-contained cottages in the wing of a 16thC manor-house in a secluded setting with garden, duck pond and wooded grounds. You will enjoy peace and quiet here and see an abundance of wildlife. Well equipped and furnished in period style, the cottages are warm and comfortable.
Offers:	Short breaks available October-March three-night stay.
Facilities:	

HERTFORDSHIRE

HERTFORD

Ponsbourne Park Hotel
★★★★Hotel SILVER AWARD

Newgate Street Village, Hertford, Hertfordshire, SG13 8QT

T:	+44 (0) 1707 876191
E:	enquiries@ponsbournepark.co.uk
W:	ponsbournepark.co.uk
Rooms:	51 • B&B per room per night (single) £119-£182; (double) £119-£182 • Credit/debit cards; cash/cheques, euros accepted
Open:	Year round
Description:	Ponsbourne Park Hotel is a peaceful oasis set in 250 acres of Hertfordshire countryside. The hotel is an ideal venue for weekend breaks, boasting an award-winning restaurant, nine-hole golf course, gymnasium, outdoor heated pool and five all-weather tennis courts. Complemented by a high level of service, Ponsbourne Park has a truly unique environment.
Offers:	Weekend celebration package – DB&B with champagne and chocolates £110 per person.
Facilities:	

ISLE OF WIGHT

FRESHWATER

Farringford Hotel
★★★Self Catering

Farringford Hotel, Bedbury Lane, Freshwater, PO40 9PE

T:	+44 (0) 1707 876191
W:	farringford.co.uk
Units:	29 • Sleeps from 2-7 • Low season £270-£430; high season £440-£900 • euros accepted
Open:	Year round
Description:	Once the home of Alfred Lord Tennyson, now a country-style house with self-catering units of three different styles to suit individual needs. Set within 35 acres of mature pastureland incorporating a 9-hole, par 3 golf course, tennis, outdoor heated pool, Bistro Bar and bowls.
Offers:	Fully inclusive Christmas packages available. Ferry-inclusive deals available. Subsidised child and pet rates available.
Facilities:	

ISLE OF WIGHT

GODSHILL

Koala Cottage Retreat ★★★★★ Guest Accommodation
Church Hollow, Godshill, Ventnor, PO38 3DR   SILVER AWARD

T:	+44 (0) 1983 842031
E:	info@koalacottage.co.uk
W:	koalacottage.co.uk
Rooms:	3 • B&B per room per night (double) £132-£150 • Cash/cheques accepted
Open:	Year round
Description:	Exclusive, unique boutique retreat for couples looking for a very special breakaway. First-class facilities including de luxe suites, spa, sauna and complimentary gift pack. Optional extras including health treatments, champagne, picnics, grand high teas. An exceptional personal service is provided.
Offers:	Complimentary gift pack: personalised wine, luxury chocolates, flowers and gift card. One night free for mid-week Monday-Friday breaks.
Facilities:	

SHANKLIN

Orchardcroft Hotel ★★ Hotel
Victoria Avenue, Shanklin, PO37 6LT

T:	+44 (0) 1983 862133
Rooms:	16 • B&B per room per night (single) £30-£50; (double) £60-£100 • Credit/debit cards; cash/cheques, euros accepted
Open:	Year round
Description:	This elegant, but friendly, hotel has a private leisure complex, secluded gardens, and a reputation for good food and service. One guest couple wrote: "A very family-friendly hotel who do all they can to ensure a pleasant stay. Friendly staff, good food and wonderful pool and games facilities".
Offers:	Excellent-value, ferry-inclusive breaks available October-May. Christmas and New Year packages. Discounts on ferry prices all year.
Facilities:	

SHANKLIN

Priory Manor Hotel ★★ Hotel
Priory Road, Shanklin, PO37 6RJ

T:	+44 (0) 1983 862854
E:	info@priorymanorhotel.co.uk
W:	priorymanorhotel.co.uk
Rooms:	38 • B&B per room per night (single) £35-£45; (double) £70-£90 • Credit/debit cards; cash/cheques accepted
Open:	Year round
Description:	Standing at the top of the famous Shanklin Chine, the hotel offers en suite bedrooms with TV and tea-/coffee-making facilities, and a licensed bar. The restaurant caters for up to 100 people and there is a function room, pool and large car park. Ideal for parties or couples looking for a relaxing break.
Offers:	Special breaks to include a ferry crossing from Southampton or Portsmouth, for two people plus car.
Facilities:	

ISLE OF WIGHT

VENTNOR

Garden House ♦ Self Catering
Booking address: 67 Strode Road, London, SW6 6BL

T:	+44 (0) 1983 862854
W:	holidaylets.net/prop_detail.asp?id=13874
Units:	1 • Sleeps from 2-8 • Low season £500-£750; high season £800-£1000 • Cash/cheques accepted
Open:	Year round
Description:	Comfortable and spacious family house with pretty, secluded garden, children's playhouse, barbecue and outside eating area. Garden House provides a perfect holiday setting for families and walkers. A few minutes' walk from pretty beaches, the stunning South Wight Coastal Path, Bonchurch village and the quiet Victorian resort of Ventnor.
Offers:	Long weekends and short breaks (ideal for families and walkers) available off-peak.
Facilities:	

KENT

ASHFORD

Eastwell Manor Hotel ★★★★Hotel
Eastwell Park, Boughton Lees, Ashford, Kent, TN25 4HR   GOLD AWARD

T:	+44 (0) 1233 213000
E:	enquiries@eastwellmanor.co.uk
W:	eastwellmanor.co.uk
Rooms:	62 • B&B per room per night (single) £110-£190; (double) £140-£220 • Credit/debit cards; cash/cheques accepted
Open:	Year round
Description:	Set in 62 acres of Kent countryside, with award-winning restaurant. Carved oak panelling, comfortable lounges and roaring oak fires in winter. The ultimate luxury spa houses a 20m pool, hydrotherapy pool, sauna, Jacuzzi and 'Dreams' beauty salon. Also 20m outdoor pool, tennis court, croquet, petanque terrains.
Offers:	Weekend breaks – one night DB&B for two people sharing, from £295-£440. Sunday night B&B per person sharing, £70.
Facilities:	

CANTERBURY

Canterbury Cathedral Lodge ★★★Metro Hotel
The Precincts, Canterbury, CT1 2EH

T:	+44 (0) 1227 865350
E:	stay@canterbury-cathedral.org
W:	canterburycisc.org
Rooms:	29 • B&B per room per night (single) £71-£79; (double) £89-£119 • Credit/debit cards; cash/cheques accepted
Open:	Year round except Christmas and New Year
Description:	Stay in welcoming and inspiring surroundings. We are situated within the beautiful walled and secluded grounds of Canterbury Cathedral, part of a UNESCO World Heritage Site. All bedrooms are comfortable and stylish and boast uninterrupted, magnificent cathedral views.
Offers:	Overnight accommodation includes the cost of entrance to the cathedral and grounds. Cathedral tours can be arranged.
Facilities:	

KENT

CANTERBURY

Canterbury Country Houses ★★★★★ Self Catering
Booking address: Woolton Farm, Bekesbourne, Canterbury, CT4 5EA

T:	+44 (0) 1227 865350
W:	canterburycountryhouses.co.uk
Units:	3 • Sleeps from 2-14 • Low season £400-£700; high season £700-£1,200 • Credit/debit cards; cash/cheques, euros accepted
Open:	Year round
Description:	Choice of houses within three miles of Canterbury. The Oast and The Old Tannery are Grade II Listed and are situated in the village of Littlebourne. Ellen's Cottage is a typical Kentish house on a fruit farm with large garden overlooking the fields.
Offers:	Short breaks of three or four nights (excluding June, July and August). The Oast and Tannery can be combined for groups of up to 14.
Facilities:	

CANTERBURY

Clare Ellen Guesthouse ♦♦♦♦ Guest Accommodation
9 Victoria Road, Wincheap, Canterbury, Kent, CT1 3SG

T:	+44 (0) 1227 760205
E:	loraine.williams@clareellenguesthouse.co.uk
W:	clareellenguesthouse.co.uk
Rooms:	6 • B&B per room per night (single) £30-£35; (double) £56-£64 • Credit/debit cards; cash/cheques accepted
Open:	Year round
Description:	A warm welcome and B&B in style. Large, quiet, elegant, en suite rooms all with colour TV, clock radio, mini-fridge, hairdryer and tea-/coffee-making facilities. Full English breakfast. Vegetarian and special diets on request. Six minutes' walk to city centre, five minutes to Canterbury East train station. Car park/garage available.
Offers:	Discounts for two-/three-night stay November-March (excluding Christmas and New Year).
Facilities:	

DOVER

Walletts Court Country House Hotel, Restaurant and Spa
★★★ Hotel SILVER AWARD
Westcliffe, St Margaret's at Cliffe, Dover, Kent, CT15 6EW

T:	+44 (0) 1304 852424
E:	wc@wallettscourt.com
W:	wallettscourt.com
Rooms:	17 • B&B per room per night (single) £110-£150; (double) £130-£170 • Credit/debit cards; cash/cheques, euros accepted
Open:	Year round except Christmas
Description:	Think rolling green hills a stone's throw from the sea, your own sumptuous four-poster bed. Roll-top baths, candles, fluffy towels, luxury bath goodies. A superb spa, pool, Jacuzzi, sauna and hot-stone massage...
Offers:	Two-night/three-day spa break – £239 per person includes two nights' DB&B and 90-minute massage or beauty treatment.
Facilities:	

FOLKESTONE

The Rob Roy Guesthouse ★★★Guesthouse
227 Dover Road, Folkestone, CT19 6NH

T:	+44 (0) 1303 253341
E:	robroy.folkestone@ntlworld.com
W:	therobroyguesthouse.co.uk
Rooms:	7 • B&B per room per night (single) £28-£29; (double) £42-£47 • Credit/debit cards; cash/cheques, euros accepted
Open:	Year round except Christmas
Description:	The Rob Roy – friendly service, comfortable accommodation and tasty breakfasts. Ideally situated 10 minutes from M20 and Channel Tunnel and 20 minutes from Dover ferries and Eurostar Ashford. Only minutes from Folkestone's famous Leas, cliffs, beaches and promenade and the lovely Folkestone Downs and North Downs Way.
Offers:	Weekend and mid-week breaks from £80-£106 per person, minimum two nights. Also free child off-peak offers.
Facilities:	

HIGH HALDEN

The Granary & The Stables ★★★★Self Catering
Booking address: Vintage Years Co Ltd, High Halden, Ashford, TN26 3JQ

T:	+44 (0) 1303 253341
W:	vintage-years.co.uk
Units:	2 • Sleeps from 2-8 • Low season £315-£455; high season £480-£520 • Cash/cheques, euros accepted
Open:	Year round
Description:	The Granary is beautifully converted and heavily beamed, with one double and one twin. The Stables has two en suite bedrooms on one level, one designed for wheelchair access. Both units are comfortably furnished and fully equipped. Set in 10 acres of gardens, they provide tranquillity and an excellent touring base.
Offers:	Swim for free at Tenterden Leisure Centre. Enjoy dinner and cinema evenings. Details on request.
Facilities:	

HOLLINGBOURNE

Well Cottage ★★★★★Self Catering
Booking address: North Downs Country Cottages, The Courtyard, Hollingbourne House, Hollingbourne, Maidstone, ME17 1QJ

T:	+44 (0) 1303 253341
E:	info@wellcottagekent.co.uk
W:	wellcottagekent.co.uk
Units:	1 • Sleeps from 7 • Low season £625-£795; high season £850-£1,195 • Credit/debit cards; cash/cheques accepted
Open:	Year round
Description:	On the North Downs Well Cottage is Grade II Listed and restored to the highest standards. Large farmhouse kitchen/diner, characterful lounge with wood-burning stove, atmospheric dining room, two double bedrooms with en suites, a twin and single bedroom and family bathroom.
Offers:	Short breaks all year (excluding Christmas and New Year).
Facilities:	

KENT

KENT

MAIDSTONE

Ringlestone House ★★★★★ Guest Accommodation
Ringlestone Road, Harrietsham, Maidstone, Kent, ME17 1NX

T:	+44 (0) 1622 859911
E:	bookings@ringlestone.com
W:	ringlestone.com
Rooms:	3 • B&B per room per night (single) £84-£145; (double) £99-£160 • Credit/debit cards; cash/cheques accepted
Open:	Year round except Christmas
Description:	Situated in tranquil, landscaped gardens on the North Downs, this charming former farmhouse has luxury accommodation with spacious en suite bathrooms, and one bedroom has a canopied four-poster bed. Near jct 8 of M20 and Leeds Castle, opposite Ringlestone Inn.
Offers:	Third night free if booking two+ nights to include a Sunday.
Facilities:	

MARGATE

Salmestone Grange ♦ Self Catering
Salmestone Grange, Nash Road, Margate, CT9 4BX

T:	+44 (0) 1622 859911
W:	salmestonegrange.co.uk
Units:	3 • Sleeps from 4-6 • All year £400-£600 • Credit/debit cards; cash/cheques accepted
Open:	Year round
Description:	Unique 14thC monastic grange set in beautiful gardens. The lovingly restored apartments have many original features which capture a 'modern meets medieval' experience. Salmestone Grange is centrally located to the area's five main sandy beaches, with other tourist attractions, festivals, shopping centre and public transport also close by.
Offers:	Mid-week and nightly stay visitors are also welcome (a nightly tariff applies). Please call for further information.
Facilities:	

ROCHESTER

Bridgewood Manor ★★★★ Hotel
Waldersalde Woods, Chatham, Kent, ME5 9AX SILVER AWARD

T:	+44 (0) 1634 201333
E:	bridgewoodmanor@marstonhotels.com
W:	marstonhotels.com
Rooms:	100 • B&B per room per night (single) £92-£172.50; (double) £119-£245 • Credit/debit cards; cash/cheques accepted
Open:	Year round
Description:	Relax around the indoor pool at the luxurious Bridgewood Manor. Convenient for excellent shopping at Bluewater and sightseeing in the historical town of Rochester or fascinating Chatham dockyards, this hotel offers fine dining in an award-winning restaurant. Rooms built around a beautiful courtyard.
Offers:	Save 20% on our two-night HB break in July and August and November-February (excluding bank holidays, 23 December-1 January and Valentine's Day).
Facilities:	

KENT

ROYAL TUNBRIDGE WELLS

Manor Court Farm ♦♦♦♦ Guest Accommodation
Ashurst Road, Ashurst, Tunbridge Wells, Kent, TN3 9TB

T:	+44 (0) 1892 740279
E:	jsoyke@jsoyke.freeserve.co.uk
W:	manorcourtfarm.co.uk
Rooms:	3 • B&B per room per night (single) £28-£40; (double) £56-£66 • Cash/cheques, euros accepted
Open:	Year round
Description:	Georgian farmhouse with friendly atmosphere, spacious rooms and lovely views of Medway Valley. Mixed 350-acre farm, many animals. Good base for walking. Penshurst Place, Hever Castle, Chartwell, Sissinghurst etc all within easy reach by car. Excellent camping facilities. London within easy reach from Ashurst station (two minutes away).
Offers:	Reductions for longer stays; children.
Facilities:	

SITTINGBOURNE

Hempstead House ★★★ Hotel
SILVER AWARD
London Road, Bapchild, Sittingbourne, Kent, ME9 9PP

T:	+44 (0) 1795 428020
E:	info@hempsteadhouse.co.uk
W:	hempsteadhouse.co.uk
Rooms:	27 • B&B per room per night (single) £80-£100; (double) £90-£110 • Credit/debit cards; cash/cheques, euros accepted
Open:	Year round
Description:	Exclusive, privately owned Victorian country-house hotel and restaurant situated in rural location, but on the main A2 between Canterbury and Sittingbourne. Set in four acres of beautifully landscaped gardens, it offers superbly appointed accommodation; fine cuisine, prepared solely from fresh, local produce; elegant reception rooms.
Offers:	Brand new facilities include 13 extra en suite rooms and fully equipped conference suites and function rooms.
Facilities:	

TENTERDEN

Quince Cottage ★★★★ Self Catering
38 Ashford Road, Tenterden, Kent, TN30 6LL

T:	+44 (0) 1795 428020
W:	quincecottage.co.uk
Units:	1 • Sleeps 5 • Low season £250-£365; high season £410-£450 • Cash/cheques, euros accepted
Open:	Year round
Description:	Listed, beamed cottage on residential side of tree-lined high street. Comfortable home from home. One single, two double bedrooms, cot available. Rear secluded courtyard. Close to all amenities, including steam railway and leisure centre. Children welcome. Sorry no pets, no smoking. Good for exploring Kent and East Sussex. Brochure available.
Offers:	10% discount on booking two or more consecutive weeks. Short breaks (minimum three nights) possible October-March.
Facilities:	

KENT

TONBRIDGE

Oast Barn ★★★★Self Catering
Oast Barn, 5 Bourne Lane, Tonbridge, TN9 1LG

T: W:	+44 (0) 1795 428020 kentcottage.co.uk
Units:	1 • Sleeps from 1-4 • Low season £300-£395; high season £450-£500 • Cash/cheques, euros accepted
Open:	Year round
Description:	Character, detached, converted barn in quiet lane within 10 minutes' walk of central Tonbridge. Comfortably furnished, fully equipped, own garden, welcome pack. Every effort made to ensure your stay is as comfortable and relaxing as possible. Ideal location for touring Kent and Sussex, with many places of historical interest nearby.
Offers:	Weekend or short breaks of up to four nights offered at 75% of weekly rate (subject to availability).
Facilities:	

WALMER

Hardicot Guesthouse ♦♦♦♦Guest Accommodation
Kingsdown Road, Walmer, Deal, Kent, CT14 8AW

T: E: W:	+44 (0) 1304 373867 guestboss@btopenworld.com smoothhound.co.uk/hotels/hardicot.html
Rooms:	3 • B&B per room per night (single) £30; (double) £56-£60 • Cash/cheques, euros accepted
Open:	Year round except Christmas
Description:	Large, quiet, detached Victorian house with Channel views and secluded garden, 100 yards from the beach. Guests have unrestricted access to rooms. Close to three championship golf courses, ferries and the Channel Tunnel. Ideal centre for cliff walks and exploring Canterbury and the castles and gardens of East Kent.
Offers:	Seven nights for the price of six.
Facilities:	

LANCASHIRE

BARNOLDSWICK

Hill Top Barn ★★★★★Self Catering
Hill Top Farm, Manchester Road, Barnoldswick, BB18 5QT

T: W:	+44 (0) 1304 373867 hilltopbarn.com
Units:	1 • Sleeps 5 • Low season £275-£305; high season £355-£465 • Cash/cheques, euros accepted
Open:	Year round
Description:	Award-winning, mid-18thC split-level barn comprising one double, one twin and one single bedroom, bathroom, through lounge/dining room with underfloor heating, and dining room/kitchen with gas Aga. Fully centrally heated elsewhere, superb panoramic views of Yorkshire Dales and Ribble Valley. Lots of walks and places to visit.
Offers:	Permanent special offers on last-minute availability.
Facilities:	

LANCASHIRE

BLACKBURN

Northcote Manor Hotel ◆Country House Hotel
Northcote Road, Blackburn, BB6 8BE

T:	+44 (0) 1254 240555
E:	sales@northcotemanor.com
W:	northcotemanor.com
Rooms:	14 • B&B per room per night (single) £120-£155; (double) £155-£190 • Credit/debit cards; cash/cheques, euros accepted
Open:	Year round except Christmas and New Year
Description:	Northcote Manor is an award-winning restaurant with highly individual rooms offering total luxury and comfort. Elegant wood panelling, warm welcoming lounges with sumptuous leather sofas and impressive staircases add to the atmosphere. Breathtaking views of the Ribble Valley.
Offers:	Gourmet Breaks available from £105 per person includes Champagne, five-course gourmet dinner, overnight stay and stunning Lancashire breakfast.
Facilities:	

BLACKPOOL

Berwick Hotel ◆◆◆◆Guest Accommodation
23 King Edward Avenue, Blackpool, FY2 9TA

T:	+44 (0) 1253 351496
E:	theberwickhotel@btconnect.com
W:	theberwickhotel.co.uk
Rooms:	8 • B&B per room per night (single) £25-£35; (double) £44-£60 • Credit/debit cards; cash/cheques accepted
Open:	Year round
Description:	Adjacent to Queens Promenade and close to Gynn Gardens. Conveniently placed for all Blackpool's attractions. Close to local transport. A friendly home-from-home welcome awaits visitors to this attractively decorated, fully non-smoking hotel. All meals are home cooked and served in pleasant dining room.
Offers:	Weekend breaks from £20 per person per night and special rates for over-55s (both excluding bank holidays).
Facilities:	

BLACKPOOL

Big Blue Hotel ◆Hotel
Ocean Boulevard, Pleasure Beach, Blackpool, FY4 1ND

T:	0845 367 3333
E:	reservations@bigbluehotel.com
W:	bigbluehotel.com
Rooms:	156 • B&B per room per night (single) £70-£105; (double) £80-£155 • Credit/debit cards; cash/cheques accepted
Open:	Year round
Description:	The only contemporary boutique hotel in Blackpool. An ideal place to experience the thrills of Britain's top tourist attractions or simply for a relaxing stay in luxury. Family rooms feature a separate children's area.
Offers:	Family-fun breaks available including Pleasure Beach wristbands and show tickets from £125 per night. Special-occasion packages available.
Facilities:	

LANCASHIRE

BLACKPOOL

Number One ♦♦♦♦♦ Guest Accommodation
1 St Lukes Road, Blackpool, FY4 2EL
GOLD AWARD

T:	+44 (0) 1253 343901
E:	info@numberoneblackpool.com
W:	numberoneblackpool.com
Rooms:	3 • B&B per room per night (single) £70-£120; (double) £120-£140 • Credit/debit cards; cash/cheques, euros accepted
Open:	Year round
Description:	Car park, gardens, putting green, elegantly appointed rooms, sumptuous beds with crisp, freshly laundered linen, pristine en suite bathrooms – plus every contemporary and hi-tech convenience. If this is your idea of holiday heaven then visit Number One for the best B&B experience ever.
Offers:	Book thee or more nights and receive a complimentary champagne breakfast hamper on morning of your choice-usually £15 supplement!
Facilities:	

BLACKPOOL

Raffles Hotel ★★★★ Guest Accommodation
73-75 Hornby Road, Blackpool, FY1 4QJ

T:	+44 (0) 1253 294713
E:	enq@raffleshotelblackpool.fsworld.co.uk
W:	raffleshotelblackpool.co.uk
Rooms:	19 • B&B per room per night (single) £26-£35; (double) £52-£66 • Credit/debit cards; cash/cheques accepted
Open:	Year round
Description:	Excellent central location for promenade, shopping centre, Winter Gardens, theatres. All rooms en suite. Licensed bar, English tea rooms, parking and daily housekeeping. Imaginative choice of menus. Listed in the *Good Hotel Guide* and the *Which? Guide to Good Hotels*. Two new family apartments each sleeping up to four people.
Offers:	Three nights for the price of two, Monday-Friday (excluding bank holidays), January-August.
Facilities:	

BLACKPOOL

The Vidella Hotel ♦♦♦ Guest Accommodation
80-82 Dickson Road, North Shore, Blackpool, FY1 2BU

T:	+44 (0) 1253 621201
E:	info@videllahotel.com
W:	videllahotel.com
Rooms:	29 • B&B per room per night (single) £25-£42; (double) £50-£84 • Credit/debit cards; cash/cheques accepted
Open:	Year round
Description:	It is all the little extras that really count to give you the most relaxing and enjoyable stay, from fresh flowers to greet you in reception, to helping with your luggage and shopping when leaving. Close to the North Pier and bus/rail stations.
Offers:	Summer senior specials. Discounts for mid-week, children, three+ nights. Christmas package. New Year package. Flexible times for contractors.
Facilities:	

LANCASHIRE

GARSTANG

Garstang Hotel & Golf Club ★★★Hotel
Bowgreave, Garstang, Preston, Lancashire, PR3 1YE

T:	+44 (0) 1995 600100
E:	reception@garstanghotelandgolf.co.uk
W:	garstanghotelandgolf.co.uk
Rooms:	32 • B&B per room per night (single) £60-£75; (double) £80-£98 • Credit/debit cards; cash/cheques, euros accepted
Open:	Year round
Description:	Conveniently situated for the M6, this smart, purpose-built hotel enjoys a peaceful location alongside its own 18-hole golf course. Modern, spacious bedrooms are well equipped for both business and leisure guests, while public areas include the informal Kingfisher Bar, a comfortable lounge bar and a choice of dining areas.
Offers:	Special weekend and mid-week golf breaks available throughout the year.
Facilities:	

GARSTANG

Guys Thatched Hamlet ♦♦♦♦ Guest Accommodation
Canalside, St Michael's Road, Bilsborrow, Preston, PR3 0RS

T:	+44 (0) 1995 640010
E:	info@guysthatchedhamlet.com
W:	guysthatchedhamlet.com
Rooms:	65 • B&B per room per night (single) £51-£74; (double) £56-£80 • Credit/debit cards; cash/cheques accepted
Open:	Year round except Christmas
Description:	A canalside haven of thatched-roof buildings, just off the A6 at Bilsborrow near Garstang. Here you will find Guy's Lodge, Owd Nell's Tavern, Guy's Restaurant and Pizzeria, craft shops, bowling green and cricket ground. Guy's Lodge offers rooms from only £49.50. All rooms have Sky TV, tea/coffee etc.
Offers:	Rooms with spas available. Champagne weekend, from £160. Sunday saver only £65 for two people, DB&B.
Facilities:	

LYTHAM ST ANNES

Lindum Hotel ★★Hotel
63-67 South Promenade, Lytham St Annes, FY8 1LZ

T:	+44 (0) 1253 722516
E:	info@lindumhotel.co.uk
W:	lindumhotel.co.uk
Rooms:	78 • B&B per room per night (single) £30-£45; (double) £60-£85 • Credit/debit cards; cash/cheques accepted
Open:	Year round
Description:	This family-run, seafront hotel is opposite all amenities including cinemas, casino, pools and mini-golf. The hotel is renowned for its excellent food and comfortable accommodation. Close to championship golf courses.
Offers:	Theatre trips, racing weekends, bridge holidays, Christmas/New Year breaks, weekend and mid-week offers throughout the year. Tailor-made golfing holidays.
Facilities:	

LANCASHIRE

LYTHAM ST ANNES

The Chadwick Hotel ★★★Hotel
South Promenade, Lytham St Annes, FY8 1NP

T:	+44 (0) 1253 720061
E:	sales@thechadwickhotel.com
W:	thechadwickhotel.com

Rooms:	75 • B&B per room per night (single) £56-£62; (double) £68-£88 • Credit/debit cards; cash/cheques, euros accepted
Open:	Year round
Description:	Panoramic views across the Ribble Estuary and Irish Sea. Award-winning family hotel provides excellent cuisine, comforts and facilities unsurpassed for value. Exclusive health and leisure suite. Children's soft-play amenities. Great for relaxing short breaks or longer. Dinner dances and theme-weekend parties. Truly a hotel for all seasons.
Offers:	Special five-day breaks from December: DB&B £199.50-£235 (sharing double room). Weekend breaks from £103.50.
Facilities:	

LEICESTERSHIRE

LOUGHBOROUGH

Forest Rise Hotel ♦♦♦Guest Accommodation
55-57 Forest Road, Loughborough, Leicestershire, LE11 3NW

| T: | +44 (0) 1509 215928 |

Rooms:	23 • B&B per room per night (single) £30-£60; (double) £55-£80 • Credit/debit cards; cash/cheques accepted
Open:	Year round except Christmas and New Year
Description:	Family-run establishment, friendly, personal service, excellent standards throughout. Short walking distance to the town centre, university. Easy access to M1, M42, airport, Donington Park, Prestwold and Beaumanour Halls. Ample, secure car parking, bar, a la carte menu and night porter. En suite bedrooms including executive, bridal, family and four-poster rooms.
Offers:	Stay seven consecutive nights and only pay for six (not including weekend prices).
Facilities:	

MELTON MOWBRAY

Sysonby Knoll Hotel ★★★Hotel
Asfordby Road, Melton Mowbray, LE13 0HP

T:	+44 (0) 1664 563563
E:	reception@sysonby.com
W:	sysonby.com

Rooms:	30 • B&B per room per night (single) £64-£84; (double) £77.50-£110 • Credit/debit cards; cash/cheques accepted
Open:	Year round except Christmas and New Year
Description:	Family-run hotel in five acres on the edge of town with a well-deserved reputation for its warm hospitality, comfortable accommodation and quality of food. The colonial-style restaurant offers outstanding views and a wide choice of menus. Local real ales are served in the cosy bar.
Offers:	Weekend breaks from £56 DB&B based on two people sharing a twin/double room for two nights.
Facilities:	

LINCOLNSHIRE

BOSTON

Elms Farm Cottages ★★★★ Self Catering
Elms Farm Cottages, The Elms, Hubberts Bridge, Boston, PE20 3QP

T:	+44 (0) 1664 563563
E:	carol@elmsfarmcottages.co.uk
W:	elmsfarmcottages.co.uk
Units:	8 • Sleeps from 1-6 • Low season £290-£320; high season £370-£395 • Credit/debit cards; cash/cheques accepted
Open:	Year round
Description:	Award-winning barn conversion of high-quality cottages, some with wood-burning stoves. Private patio with picnic bench. All cottages are accessible, four with disabled shower rooms especially suitable for wheelchair users. Grass field with wild-flower meadow for guests to enjoy. Communal laundry and built-in barbecue.
Offers:	Tastes of Lincolnshire welcome pack on weekly stays.
Facilities:	

GAINSBOROUGH

The Beckett Arms ♦♦♦ Guest Accommodation
25 High Street, Corringham, Gainsborough, DN21 5QP

T:	+44 (0) 1427 838201
Rooms:	12 • B&B per room per night (single) £30-£35; (double) £50-£60 • Credit/debit cards; cash/cheques accepted
Open:	Year round
Description:	A warm welcome awaits you at this family-run country pub. It is ideal for Lincoln, Hemswell, Scunthorpe and Doncaster, all within a 30-minute drive. Golf and fishing on the doorstep.
Offers:	Coaches, lunches, racing parties etc by negotiation.
Facilities:	

HORNCASTLE

Green Court ★★★ Self Catering
Booking address: 401 Brant Road, Waddington, Lincoln, LN5 9AH

T:	+44 (0) 1427 838201
W:	woldscottages.co.uk
Units:	2 • Sleeps from 4-6 • Low season £220-£290; high season £365-£400 • Cash/cheques accepted
Open:	Year round
Description:	Very pleasant converted buildings in the centre of the Lincolnshire Wolds, approximately 25 miles from the coast and Lincoln. The master bedrooms in both cottages have four-poster beds and en suites. Carpenters has its own games room. Seating is available outside with grassed areas for children to play on.
Offers:	Special rates for booking both cottages for Christmas, New Year or any other week of the year.
Facilities:	

LINCOLNSHIRE

LINCOLN

Branston Hall Hotel ★★★Country House Hotel
Lincoln, LN4 1PD
SILVER AWARD

T:	+44 (0) 1522 793305
E:	mail@branstonhall.co.uk
W:	branstonhall.com
Rooms:	50 • B&B per room per night (single) £70-£99; (double) £99-£184 • Credit/debit cards; cash/cheques accepted
Open:	Year round
Description:	An elegant country-house hotel set in 88 acres of wooded parkland, just five minutes' drive from historic Lincoln. Our Parklands Leisure Suite is perfect for relaxation, with its impressive murals, indoor heated pool, sauna and spa. We offer a superb array of conference and banqueting facilities.
Offers:	Mid-week breaks, £105 per room per night.
Facilities:	

LINCOLN

The Stable ★★★★Self Catering
Booking address: Sunnyside, Lincoln Road, Lincoln, LN1 2SQ

T:	+44 (0) 1522 793305
W:	lincolncottages.co.uk
Units:	1 • Sleeps from 2-4 • Low season £190-£250; high season £250-£375 • Cash/cheques, euros accepted
Open:	Year round
Description:	300-year-old cottage of character converted from a former stone and pantile stable. Peace and tranquillity in a conservation village, yet only six miles from the historic cathedral city of Lincoln. Tastefully furnished and decorated. Own enclosed cottage garden and views over open fields.
Offers:	Four nights for the price of three in low season.
Facilities:	

LOUTH

Mill Lodge ★★★Self Catering
Mill Lodge, Benniworth House Farm, Donington on Bain, Louth, LN11 9RD

T:	+44 (0) 1507 343265
Units:	1 • Sleeps from 1-4 • Low season £200-£300; high season £250-£350 • Cash/cheques accepted
Open:	Year round
Description:	Ezra and Pamela Cade welcome you to a comfortable, warm, detached cottage, with conservatory, garden and garage, on lovely farm/nature reserve. Fitted kitchen, open log fire. Free first snack with home-produced honey. Good footpaths join the Viking Way, open access to countryside stewardship area. Children welcome.
Offers:	Special rates for just two visitors. Discounted honey available.
Facilities:	

LINCOLNSHIRE

SKEGNESS

Carmelle Hotel ★★★Guesthouse
16 Castleton Boulevard, Skegness, Lincolnshire, PE25 2TY

T:	+44 (0) 1754 764587
E:	carmelle@ukonline.co.uk
W:	skegness-resort.co.uk/carmelle
Rooms:	10 • B&B per room per night (double) £40-£45 • Credit/debit cards; cash/cheques accepted
Open:	Year round
Description:	Close to bowling greens. Enjoy your breakfast in our Elvis-themed dining room and a drink in the evening in our Egyptian-themed bar. One of our latest guests was Chris Quinten (Brian Tilsley) from Coronation Street who quoted us as being 'the best place in town'.
Offers:	For that special occasion book our four-poster room. Two nights minimum.
Facilities:	

SUTTON-ON-SEA

Country Retreat Equestrian Lodges ♦Self Catering
Huttoft Road, Mablethorpe, Sutton-on-Sea, LN12 2QY

T:	+44 (0) 1754 764587
W:	blackcatequestriancentre.co.uk
Units:	2 • Sleeps from 2-8 • Low season £100-£300; high season £400-£500 • Cash/cheques accepted
Open:	Year round
Description:	Ideally situated near the sandy beaches of Sutton-on-Sea, enjoy a 'get away from it all' holiday in our handmade luxury Scandinavian log cabins. Explore the coast and countryside, or relax in the landscaped grounds of the Black Cat Equestrian Centre. A holiday to remember.
Offers:	Three-night breaks available during non-peak periods.
Facilities:	

THORPE-ON-THE-HILL

Railway Inn Lodges ♦Guest Accommodation
Station Road, Thorpe-on-the-Hill, Lincoln, Lincolnshire, LN6 9BS

T:	+44 (0) 1522 500495
E:	chris.smith20@btconnect.com
Rooms:	4 • B&B per room per night (double) £40-£50 • Credit/debit cards; cash/cheques accepted
Open:	Year round except Christmas and New Year
Description:	The self-contained, en suite lodges are set in a beautiful location within the grounds of a country public house which serves home-cooked, traditional English fayre. There are visitor attractions nearby, and the historic city of Lincoln is only a short car journey away.
Offers:	Stay Friday and Saturday night and get Sunday night at half price.
Facilities:	

LONDON

HARROW

Grim's Dyke Hotel ★★★ Hotel
Old Redding, Harrow, HA3 6SH
SILVER AWARD

T:	+44 (0) 20 8385 3100
E:	reservations@grimsdyke.com
W:	grimsdyke.com
Rooms:	46 • B&B per room per night (single) £75-£300; (double) £90-£320 • Credit/debit cards; cash/cheques accepted
Open:	Year round except Christmas
Description:	Once home to W S Gilbert of Gilbert and Sullivan fame. Excellent food, fine wines, cream teas, guided tours, Murder Mystery dinners, Gilbert and Sullivan operettas. Set in acres of woodland and gardens.
Offers:	Special weekend breaks.
Facilities:	

LONDON

Cardiff Hotel ♦♦♦ Guest Accommodation
5-9 Norfolk Square, London, W2 1RU

T:	+44 (0) 20 7723 9068
E:	stay@cardiff-hotel.com
W:	cardiff-hotel.com
Rooms:	61 • B&B per room per night (single) £49-£59; (double) £68-£85 • Credit/debit cards; cash/cheques accepted
Open:	Year round except Christmas
Description:	Run by the Davies family since 1958, the Cardiff Hotel overlooks a quiet garden square. Located one minute from the Heathrow Express, three minutes' walk from Hyde Park and 10 minutes from Oxford Street. We offer comfortable, en suite rooms with TV, telephone, tea-making facilities, hairdryer and central heating.
Offers:	Five nights for the price of four on selected dates/rooms. Winter offer: doubles from £55. See website for details.
Facilities:	

LONDON

Crescent Hotel ★★★ Guest Accommodation
49-50 Cartwright Gardens, Bloomsbury, London, WC1H 9EL

T:	+44 (0) 20 7387 1515
E:	General.Enquiries@CrescentHotelofLondon.com
W:	CrescentHotelofLondon.com
Rooms:	27 • B&B per room per night (single) £45-£79; (double) £89-£95 • Credit/debit cards; cash/cheques accepted
Open:	Year round
Description:	Founded 1956. Comfortable, elegant, family-run hotel in quiet Georgian crescent, with private garden square and tennis courts. All bedrooms are non-smoking and have colour TV, tea/coffee tray and direct-dial telephone; most are en suite. English breakfast is individually prepared.
Offers:	10% discount on stays of three nights, to include Sunday and Monday (excluding Christmas and New Year).
Facilities:	

LONDON

Crown Moran
★★★★ Hotel
SILVER AWARD

142-152 Cricklewood Broadway, Cricklewood, NW2 3ED

T:	+44 (0) 20 8452 4175
E:	crownres@moranhotels.com
W:	crownmoranhotels.co.uk
Rooms:	116 • B&B per room per night (single) £105-£145; (double) £125-£165 • Credit/debit cards; cash/cheques, euros accepted
Open:	Year round except Christmas
Description:	Strategically located between Marble Arch and the M1 with superb facilities: leisure centre, restaurant, five bars, on-site parking and meeting facilities.
Offers:	Check website for third-night-free promotions and discounted packages.
Facilities:	

LONDON

Dillons Hotel
♦♦ Guest Accommodation

21 Belsize Park, London, NW3 4DU

T:	+44 (0) 20 7794 3360
E:	desk@dillonshotel.com
W:	dillonshotel.com
Rooms:	15 • B&B per room per night (single) £35-£49; (double) £54-£68 • Credit/debit cards; cash/cheques, euros accepted
Open:	Year round
Description:	Located just six minutes' walk from either Swiss Cottage or Belsize Park underground stations, close to the Royal Free Hospital and convenient for Camden Market and central London. Dillons Hotel provides comfortable, reasonably priced bed and breakfast accommodation. All rooms have colour TV and many have private shower/wc.
Offers:	Discounts available for stays of seven or more nights. Ask at the time of booking.
Facilities:	

LONDON

Hamlet UK
★★★ Self Catering

Booking address: Hamlet UK, 47 Willian Way, Letchworth, SG6 2HJ

T:	+44 (0) 20 8883 0024
W:	hamletuk.com
Units:	4 • Sleeps from 4-6 • Low season £540-£720; high season £595-£775 • Credit/debit cards; cash/cheques, euros accepted
Open:	Year round
Description:	Friendly and personal service. Very attractive surroundings. Comfortable and clean accommodation close to public transport, supermarket, the Tower of London, Tower Bridge and the ExCeL exhibition centre. Fully fitted kitchen, full bathroom, linen and towels provided, TV, direct-dial phone, wireless broadband connection, washer/dryer, off-street parking. See guests' feedback on our website.
Offers:	Discounted last-minute and long-term lets.
Facilities:	

LONDON

Kandara Guesthouse ♦♦♦ Guest Accommodation
68 Ockendon Road, Islington, London, N1 3NW

T:	+44 (0) 20 7226 5721
E:	admin@kandara.co.uk
W:	kandara.co.uk
Rooms:	11 • B&B per room per night (single) £43-£49; (double) £54-£68 • Credit/debit cards; cash/cheques, euros accepted
Open:	Year round except Christmas
Description:	A family-run guesthouse near the Angel, Islington. Quietly situated in a conservation area. All bedrooms and bathrooms have recently been decorated and fitted to a high standard. Ten bus routes and two underground stations provide excellent public transport services. Free overnight street parking and free cycle storage.
Offers:	Book for three nights or more and save up to 15%.
Facilities:	

LONDON

Lincoln House Hotel ★★ Guest Accommodation
33 Gloucester Place, London, W1U 8HY

T:	+44 (0) 20 7486 7630
E:	reservations@lincoln-house-hotel.co.uk
W:	lincoln-house-hotel.co.uk
Rooms:	23 • B&B per room per night (single) £55-£75; (double) £75-£89 • Credit/debit cards; cash/cheques accepted
Open:	Year round
Description:	Built in the days of King George III, this hotel offers Georgian townhouse charm and character with en suite rooms and modern comforts. Ideally located in the heart of London's West End, next to Oxford Street shopping. Within easy reach of most theatres, museums and exhibitions. Suitable for business and leisure.
Offers:	Long-stay discounts on request. Most Sundays discounted. For latest long-stay and other special offers visit our website.
Facilities:	

LONDON

London Lodge Hotel ★★★ Hotel
134-136 Lexham Gardens, London, W8 6JE

T:	+44 (0) 20 7244 8444
E:	info@londonlodgehotel.com
W:	londonlodgehotel.com
Rooms:	28 • B&B per room per night (single) £96-£137; (double) £126-£201 • Credit/debit cards; cash/cheques accepted
Open:	Year round
Description:	Beautifully refurbished townhouse hotel in a quiet street in the heart of Kensington. All rooms individually designed and air-conditioned. Satellite TV, PC modem lines, wireless Internet, mini-bar. Executive rooms have whirlpool bath and private safe. Car parking available, bookings essential.
Offers:	Double rooms at £99 per room per night including breakfast, minimum two nights. Other offers available – please enquire.
Facilities:	

LONDON

Vandon House Hotel ♦♦♦ Guest Accommodation
1 Vandon Street, London, SW1H 0AH

T:	+44 (0) 20 7799 6780
E:	info@vandonhouse.com
W:	vandonhouse.com
Rooms:	32 • B&B per room per night (single) £44 • Credit/debit cards; cash/cheques accepted
Open:	Mid-May to end of August and two weeks over New Year.
Description:	Excellent-value, friendly hotel in superb location. Buckingham Palace, St James's Park and Westminster Abbey lie only a few minutes away. We pride ourselves on our family atmosphere. A terrific base for exploring London.
Offers:	10% discount on stays of seven nights or more.
Facilities:	

LONDON

Barry House Hotel ♦♦♦ Guest Accommodation
12 Sussex Place, London, W2 2TP

T:	+44 (0) 20 7723 7340
E:	hotel@barryhouse.co.uk
W:	barryhouse.co.uk
Rooms:	18 • B&B per room per night (single) £39-£60; (double) £70-£80 • Credit/debit cards; cash/cheques accepted
Open:	Year round
Description:	The family-run Barry House offers warm hospitality in a Victorian townhouse. Comfortable en suite rooms with English breakfast served each morning. Located close to the West End – Paddington Station and Hyde Park are just three minutes' walk away.
Offers:	Stay seven nights, get one night free.
Facilities:	

OLD TRAFFORD

Old Trafford Lodge Travel Accommodation
Lancashire County Cricket Club, Old Trafford, Manchester, M16 0PX

T:	+44 (0) 161 874 3333
E:	lodge@lccc.co.uk
W:	lccc.co.uk
Units:	Rooms: 68 • B&B per room per night from £49-£74 • Credit/debit cards; cash/cheques accepted
Open:	Year round except Christmas and New Year
Description:	Located at the Lancashire County Cricket ground, the hotel has executive bedrooms overlooking the pitch. Comfortable bar and lounge area, free parking. Broadband at reasonable rates and free match-day tickets on selected dates.
Offers:	Two-night weekend break, only £44 per room per night Friday-Sunday, up to two adults and two children, includes continental breakfast.
Facilities:	

MANCHESTER

SALE

Lennox Lea Hotel ♦Hotel
Irlam Road, Sale, Cheshire, M33 2BH

T:	+44 (0) 161 973 1764
E:	info@lennoxlea.co.uk
W:	lennoxlea.co.uk
Rooms:	28 • B&B per room per night (single) £35.95-£55.95; (double) £55.95-£75.95 • Credit/debit cards; cash/cheques accepted
Open:	Year round
Description:	An attractive Victorian building set in its own grounds with ample free parking. Privately run, offering a warm welcome, comfortable accommodation and excellent food. Situated on a peaceful, tree-lined road while conveniently located for many North West attractions. One mile from the motorway network and 0.3 miles from the tram.
Offers:	Friday and Saturday DB&B for two, £90 per room (sharing a double or twin).
Facilities:	

MERSEYSIDE

LIVERPOOL

Radisson SAS Hotel Liverpool ★★★★Hotel
107 Old Hall Street, Liverpool, Merseyside, L3 9BD
SILVER AWARD

T:	+44 (0) 151 966 1500
E:	info.liverpool@radissonsas.com
W:	radissonsas.com
Rooms:	194 • B&B per room per night (single) £99-£180; (double) £109-£190 • Credit/debit cards; cash/cheques, euros accepted
Open:	Year round
Description:	In the heart of Liverpool's city centre with breathtaking views over the River Mersey and an interior with its own style and artistic flair. Liverpool's premier de luxe hotel combines stylishly designed bedrooms, an exquisite award-winning restaurant Filini, The White Bar and extensive leisure facilities making it the perfect place to relax and have fun.
Offers:	£49.50 per person per night room only, plus a bottle of wine, based on two sharing. Golf can be organised.
Facilities:	

SOUTHPORT

Martin Lane Farmhouse Holiday Cottages
★★★★Self Catering
Martin Lane Farmhouse Holiday Cottages, Ormskirk, L40 8JH

T:	+44 (0) 151 966 1500
W:	martinlanefarmhouse.btinternet.co.uk
Units:	2 • Sleeps from 1-6 • Low season £285-£350; high season £325-£410 • Cash/cheques, euros accepted
Open:	Year round
Description:	Beautiful, award-winning country cottages, nestling in the rich arable farmland of West Lancashire and just four miles from Southport and the seaside. Our cottages have a friendly, relaxed, family atmosphere. The ideal base for visiting all the North West's major attractions.
Offers:	10% discount on two-week bookings.
Facilities:	

BRANCASTER STAITHE

Vista and Carpenters Cottage   ★★★Self Catering
Booking address: Dale View, Main Road, Brancaster Staithe, King's Lynn, PE31 8BY

T:	+44 (0) 151 966 1500
Units:	2 • Sleeps from 2-6 • Low season £210-£300; high season £300-£750 • Cash/cheques accepted
Open:	Year round
Description:	These lovely cottages enjoy one of the best views along the Norfolk coast. Walking down the cottage gardens you meet the saltmarsh and the Norfolk coastal path. The cottages have exposed beams and open fires as well as central heating throughout. Close to amenities. Pets welcome.
Offers:	Short breaks (weekend and mid-week) available during low season or at short notice; minimum three nights.
Facilities:	

COLTISHALL

Hedges Guesthouse   ♦♦♦♦Guest Accommodation
Tunstead Road, Coltishall, Norfolk, NR12 7AL

T:	+44 (0) 1603 738361
E:	info@hedgesbandb.co.uk
W:	hedgesbandb.co.uk
Rooms:	5 • B&B per room per night (single) £27.50-£40; (double) £47-£49 • Credit/debit cards; cash/cheques accepted
Open:	Year round except Christmas
Description:	Hear evening owlsong and the dawn chorus at this friendly, family-run guesthouse. Set in large, peaceful gardens surrounded by open countryside, yet convenient for local amenities. Ideal base for exploring the Norfolk Broads, Norwich and Norfolk coast. Families welcome, spacious lounge with log fire, licensed, plenty of parking.
Offers:	Three nights for the price of two November-April.
Facilities:	

CROMER

Elderton Lodge Hotel/Langtry Restaurant   ★★Hotel
Gunton Park, Cromer, Norwich, Norfolk, NR11 8TZ   SILVER AWARD

T:	+44 (0) 1263 833547
E:	enquiries@eldertonlodge.co.uk
W:	eldertonlodge.co.uk
Rooms:	11 • B&B per room per night (single) £65; (double) £100-£120 • Credit/debit cards; cash/cheques accepted
Open:	Year round
Description:	A former Georgian shooting lodge enjoying a truly relaxed atmosphere and stunning surroundings. Eleven individually decorated rooms and excellent fayre using fresh local produce. Elderton Lodge is ideally situated for visiting all North Norfolk attractions, including National Trust properties, the Norfolk Broads and the famous Blakeney Marshes.
Offers:	Three nights for the price of two B&B quoting Enjoy England.
Facilities:	

NORFOLK

NORFOLK

CROMER

Poppyland Holiday Cottages ★★★★Self Catering
Booking address: 21 Regent Street, Wickmere, Norwich, NR11 7ND

T:	+44 (0) 1263 833547
Units:	7 • Sleeps from 2-6 • Low season £165-£255; high season £285-£599 • Credit/debit cards accepted
Open:	Year round
Description:	Individual, award-winning properties, five of which are in Overstrand, a fishing village with safe sandy beaches, one mile east of Cromer. The remaining properties are in the rural hamlet of Wickmere, surrounded by open countryside within a conservation area seven miles south of Sheringham. Ideal for walking, cycling and bird-watching.
Offers:	Short breaks available September-May. Senior citizens: 10% discount low season. Phone for late-availability reduced rates.
Facilities:	

DISS

Old Rectory Hopton ★★★★★B&B
High Street, Hopton, Diss, Norfolk, IP22 2QX

GOLD AWARD

T:	+44 (0) 1953 688135
E:	llewellyn.hopton@btinternet.com
W:	theoldrectoryhopton.com
Rooms:	3 • B&B per room per night (single) £60-£70; (double) £90-£100 • Cash/cheques accepted
Open:	Year round except Christmas and New Year
Description:	The Old Rectory is a Listed building, dating from the 16thC, standing in walled grounds. The house is well situated to explore East Anglia, being on the Norfolk/Suffolk border. The house is beautifully furnished, and many period features add to the charm of this lovely home. A non-smoking house.
Offers:	10% discount on B&B rate for three or more nights November to March.
Facilities:	

ERPINGHAM

Grange Farm ★★★Self Catering
Grange Farm Holidays, Scarrow Beck Farm, Erpingham, Norwich, NR11 7QU

T:	+44 (0) 1953 688135
W:	grangefarmholidays.co.uk
Units:	4 • Sleeps from 2-7 • Low season £200-£400; high season £380-£650 • Cash/cheques accepted
Open:	Year round
Description:	A 17thC farmhouse and converted period farm buildings around a courtyard, all in a large garden, in the middle of an 80-acre farm beside a river. Heated, indoor swimming pool. Open Christmas and New Year.
Offers:	Weekends (up to four nights) from £150 in low season.
Facilities:	

NORFOLK

FAKENHAM

Fakenham Racecourse ★★★Touring Park
The Racecourse, Fakenham, Norfolk, NR21 7NY

T:	+44 (0) 1328 862388
E:	caravan@fakenhamracecourse.co.uk
W:	fakenhamracecourse.co.uk
Pitches:	Touring: 120; touring caravans: 120; motor caravans: 30; tents: 30 • Per night (caravan, motor caravan) £12-£25; (tent) £7-£25 • Credit/debit cards; cash/cheques accepted
Open:	Year round
Description:	Fakenham Racecourse is the ideal base for caravanning and camping holidays in Norfolk. Just 10 miles from a magnificent coastline and on the edge of the market town, the site is in beautiful countryside and sheltered by conifers. The grounds and modern facilities are excellently maintained.
Offers:	Open to all but with discounts for Caravan Club members. Special rates for rally groups. Check website for events.
Facilities:	

FOXLEY

Moor Farm Stable Cottages ★★★★Self Catering
Moor Farm, Foxley, Dereham, NR20 4QP

T:	+44 (0) 1328 862388
W:	moorfarmstablecottages.co.uk
Units:	12 • Sleeps from 3-10 • Low season £200-£550; high season £350-£860 • Cash/cheques accepted
Open:	Year round
Description:	Located on working farm, a courtyard of two- and three-bedroomed self-catering cottages, all fully equipped and centrally heated, two specially adapted for disabled. Ideally situated for coast, Broads, Norwich, Sandringham. 365 acres of mature woodland adjoining owners' farm in which to walk. Fishing available in owners' lake close by. Pets welcome.
Offers:	Two-/three-night breaks available (mid-week or weekend) October-May, five nights Christmas/New Year.
Facilities:	

HINGHAM

The Granary ★★★Self Catering
Booking address: College Farm, Hingham, Norwich, NR9 4PP

T:	+44 (0) 1953 851311
Units:	1 • Sleeps 4 • Low season £190-£295; high season £295-£345 • Cash/cheques accepted
Open:	Year round
Description:	Tastefully converted 18thC granary. Peaceful location on small stud farm with pets galore. Very attractive, well-equipped accommodation with original oak beams throughout. Warm and cosy in winter. Perfect location to explore Norfolk.
Offers:	Three-night low season breaks available for only £120.
Facilities:	

NORFOLK

HOLME NEXT THE SEA

Broadwater Cottage ★★★★Self Catering
Booking address: Vine Farm, 38 Church Street, Cambridge, CB2 5DS

T:	+44 (0) 1953 851311
W:	broadwatercottage.co.uk
Units:	1 • Sleeps 6 • Low season £240-£300; high season £400-£680 • Cash/cheques accepted
Open:	Year round
Description:	Comfortable flint, chalk and carrstone cottage in the village centre close to an excellent pub/restaurant with garden. The beach is a short walk across open fields and sand dunes with salt marshes beyond. Enclosed garden overlooking fields, conservatory and woodburner. One double, two twins, shower room and bathroom. Off-road parking.
Offers:	Discounts for off-season short breaks, long weekends and two-person occupancy. Pets by arrangement at additional cost.
Facilities:	

HUNSTANTON

Searles Leisure Resort
★★★★★Holiday, Touring & Camping Park

South Beach Road, Hunstanton, Norfolk, PE36 5BB

T:	+44 (0) 1485 534211
E:	bookings@searles.co.uk
W:	searles.co.uk
Pitches:	Touring: 332; touring caravans: 157; motor caravans: 50; tents: 125; caravan holiday homes: 156 • Per night (caravan, motor caravan) £11-£33; (tent) £10-£32; (caravan holiday home) £189-£1,188 • Credit/debit cards; cash/cheques accepted
Open:	Year round except Christmas and New Year
Description:	Family run, and established for 50 years – excellent pitches and hook-ups, bars, restaurants, entertainment, pools, nine-hole golf-course, fishing lake and more.
Offers:	Superb themed breaks every autumn. Kids' breaks, music weekends, Turkey and Tinsel breaks. Please check website.
Facilities:	

HUNSTANTON

The King William IV Country Inn ★★★★Inn
Heacham Road, Sedgeford, Hunstanton, Norfolk, PE36 5LU

T:	+44 (0) 1485 571765
E:	info@thekingwilliamsedgeford.co.uk
W:	thekingwilliamsedgeford.co.uk
Rooms:	4 • B&B per room per night (single) £50-£60; (double) £85-£90 • Credit/debit cards; cash/cheques accepted
Open:	Year round
Description:	Popular and busy traditional country inn, close to North Norfolk's beautiful coastline, Peddars Way, RSPB bird reserves and golf. High-standard, comfortable en suite accommodation with king-size beds. Extensive menu and daily specials served in two non-smoking restaurants, bar and garden. A delightful escape – whatever the season.
Offers:	Mid-week offer – third night half price (Sunday-Thursday).
Facilities:	

114

NORFOLK

NORWICH

Spixworth Hall Cottages ★★★★Self Catering
Spixworth Hall Cottages, Buxton Road, Spixworth, Norwich, NR10 3PR

T:	+44 (0) 1603 893013
W:	hallcottages.co.uk
Units:	8 • Sleeps from 3-10 • Low season £250-£490; high season £330-£990 • Credit/debit cards; cash/cheques, euros accepted
Open:	Year round
Description:	These delightful cottages, situated in seclusion on a farm, are ideal for exploring Norwich, the Broads and coast. They have quality furnishings and equipment, log fires and attractive gardens. Farm and woodland walks, swimming, tennis, fishing, a games barn and space to relax and unwind.
Offers:	Three-night breaks October-March from £150. Four nights for the price of three, Monday-Thursday. Snowdrop and bluebell walks.
Facilities:	

OVERSTRAND

Sea Marge Hotel ★★★Hotel
16 High Street, Overstrand, Norfolk, NR27 0AB
GOLD AWARD

T:	+44 (0) 1263 579579
E:	reservations@mackenziehotels.com
W:	mackenziehotels.com
Rooms:	24 • B&B per room per night (single) £83-£126; (double) £126-£158 • Credit/debit cards; cash/cheques accepted
Open:	Year round
Description:	Perched on the cliffs of the beautiful North Norfolk coast, you will find the Sea Marge, an elegant Edwardian mansion steeped in history. First-class, comfortable accommodation, magnificent sea views and access to an unspoilt beach. Exquisite food and impeccable service provided by in-house Frazer's Restaurant. You will want to return time and time again.
Offers:	Christmas four-night break. New Year two-night break. Murder Mystery weekend. Romantic Valentine two-night escape.
Facilities:	

SEDGEFORD

Cobble Cottage ★★★★Self Catering
Booking address: Norfolk Country Cottages, Carlton House, Market Place, Reepham, Norwich, NR10 4JJ

T:	+44 (0) 1263 579579
W:	norfolkcottages.co.uk/properties/841
Units:	1 • Sleeps 8 • Low season £414-£511; high season £556-£673 • Credit/debit cards; cash/cheques, euros accepted
Open:	Year round
Description:	Sedgeford is close to both the sandy beaches of the North Norfolk Heritage Coast and the west-facing coastline of the Wash, and the RSPB reserves of Titchwell Marsh and Snettisham. Recently refurbished with two car-parking bays, parts of the cottage are thought to date from the late 1700s.
Offers:	Three- to six-night stays available October-April (excluding bank holidays, half-terms) and sometimes from April-October.
Facilities:	

NORFOLK

SWANTON ABBOTT

Pheasant Cottage ★★★★★ Guest Accommodation
Long Common Lane, North Walsham, NR10 5BH

T:	+44 (0) 1692 538169
E:	melanie@pheasantcottage.freeserve.co.uk
W:	pheasantcottage.com
Rooms:	3 • B&B per room per night (single) £45-£50; (double) £60-£90 • Cash/cheques, euros accepted
Open:	Year round except Christmas and New Year
Description:	In a beautiful corner of North Norfolk, on the edge of a quiet village, this 17thC cottage has been lovingly transformed to create a home of exceptional quality. Boasting oak beams, attractive furnishings, stunning views across fields and two market towns close by. Pretty gardens with orchard, sitting-out areas, and log cabin for afternoon teas.
Offers:	Mid-week specials – three nights for the price of two, or four nights for the price of three (Monday-Friday).
Facilities:	

TITCHWELL

Briarfields Hotel ★★ Hotel
Main Road, Titchwell, King's Lynn, PE31 8BB

T:	+44 (0) 1485 210742
E:	briarfields@norfolk-hotels.co.uk
W:	norfolk-hotels.co.uk
Rooms:	22 • B&B per room per night (single) £55-£75; (double) £70-£110 • Credit/debit cards; cash/cheques accepted
Open:	Year round
Description:	Briarfields is a renovated barn perfectly situated for visiting the North Norfolk coast. Old beams and oak floor, log fire, excellent bar and restaurant dishes, afternoon teas, real ales and four poster beds. Exceptional views from decking area of the sea over the RSPB marshes. Large garden and children's play area.
Offers:	Special discount rates for groups of more than 10. Reduced winter tariff from November-April.
Facilities:	

UPPER SHERINGHAM

The Dales Hotel ★★★★ Hotel
Lodge Hill, Upper Sheringham, Norfolk, NR26 8TJ

T:	+44 (0) 1263 824555
E:	dales@mackenziehotels.com
W:	mackenziehotels.com
Rooms:	17 • B&B per room per night (single) £87-£134; (double) £134-£156 • Credit/debit cards; cash/cheques accepted
Open:	Year round
Description:	Nestled in National Trust parkland, close to the North Norfolk coast, you will find a quintessentially English, Grade II Listed country house. Bedrooms furnished with traditional oak and beautiful fabrics. Mullioned windows, original fireplaces and a fine oak staircase. A place to relax!
Offers:	Christmas four-night break. New Year two-night break. Romantic Valentine two-night escape. Summer jazz weekend.
Facilities:	

WELLS-NEXT-THE-SEA

Harbour Cottage ★★★Self Catering
Booking address: 233 Melton Road, Edwalton, NG12 4DB

| T: | +44 (0) 1263 824555 |
| W: | harbourcottagewells.co.uk |

| Units: | 1 • Sleeps 7 • Low season £360-£490; high season £410-£500 • Cash/cheques, euros accepted |

| Open: | Year round |

| Description: | Charming, traditional, 180-year-old three-bedroom luxury home, sensitively refurbished to a high standard. Lounge with log-burner, cloakroom off, modern oak dining kitchen. Rear bedrooms and bathroom have fabulous sea views. Attractive south-facing patio garden. Close to all amenities. Ideal for families wishing to walk, bird-watch or just relax. |

| Offers: | Short stays available October-February (excluding Christmas and New Year). Last-minute bookings sometimes available – contact owners for details. |

| Facilities: | |

WEST RUNTON

The Links Country Park Hotel & Golf Club ★★★Hotel
Sandy Lane, West Runton, Norfolk, NR27 9QH

T:	+44 (0) 1263 838383
E:	sales@links-hotel.co.uk
W:	links-hotel.co.uk

| Rooms: | 49 • B&B per room per night (single) £60-£85; (double) £120-£180 • Credit/debit cards; cash/cheques, euros accepted |

| Open: | Year round |

| Description: | Norfolk's oldest and longest-established leisure, conference and golfing hotel, The Links combines modern comforts with reassuringly traditional levels of personal service and attention. Situated on the stunningly peaceful North Norfolk coast, but close to the lively towns and cities of Cromer, Sheringham and Norwich, it's the ideal base for all. |

| Offers: | Short getaways, golf breaks and a wide variety of offers and special-interest breaks available all year round-call us! |

| Facilities: | |

CORBY

Moat Cottage ♦♦♦♦Guest Accommodation
18 Little Oakley, Corby, Northamptonshire, NN18 8HA

T:	+44 (0) 1536 745013
E:	moatcott@aol.com
W:	moat-cottage.com

| Rooms: | 2 • B&B per room per night (single) £35-£37.50; (double) £45-£50 • Cash/cheques accepted |

| Open: | Year round except Christmas |

| Description: | 16thC beamed, thatched cottage in the centre of a quiet conservation village, yet only four miles from Rockingham speedway. Private ground-floor suites opening onto a beautiful south-facing garden with secluded seating. Secure private parking. Organic produce used wherever possible. |

| Offers: | Weekly breaks – self-catering in the Lavender Barn £195 October-April; £245 May-September. |

| Facilities: | |

NORFOLK

NORTHAMPTONSHIRE

117

NORTHAMPTONSHIRE

EAST HADDON

East Haddon Grange Country Cottages
★★★★ Self Catering

East Haddon Grange, East Haddon, NN6 8DR

T:	+44 (0) 1604 770368
E:	enquiries@easthaddongrange.co.uk
W:	easthaddongrange.co.uk

Rooms:	4 • Sleeps from 2-5 • Low season £245-£415; high season £275-£560 • Cash/cheques accepted
Open:	Year round
Description:	Relax in these traditional stone cottages converted from an old barn on a family farm surrounded by open countryside. The cottages offer spacious accommodation in an idyllic rural setting only six miles from Northampton.
Offers:	Discounts available for longer stays. Special rates for mid-week/weekend breaks.
Facilities:	

SILVERSTONE

Whittlebury Hall Hotel and Spa
★★★★ Hotel
SILVER AWARD

Whittlebury, Towcester, Northamptonshire, NN12 8QH

T:	+44 (0) 1327 857857
E:	sales@whittleburyhall.co.uk
W:	whittleburyhall.co.uk

Rooms:	211 • B&B per room per night (single) £100-£0; (double) £125-£0 • Credit/debit cards; cash/cheques, euros accepted
Open:	Year round
Description:	Whittlebury Hall blends classical Georgian architecture with rich furnishings and fabrics, creating a truly impressive hotel. Motor-racing enthusiasts enjoy its proximity to Silverstone circuit, while others relax at The Spa – the ultimate health and leisure experience.
Offers:	Residential and day Pamper Packages including beauty treatments. Birthday and Anniversary packages, Christmas and New Year celebrations. Silverstone event packages.
Facilities:	

WELLINGBOROUGH

Friendly Lodge Cottage
★★★★ Self Catering

Friendly Lodge Farm, Station Road, Raunds, Wellingborough, NN9 6BT

| T: | +44 (0) 1327 857857 |

Units:	1 • Sleeps from 6+ • Low season from £350 • Cash/cheques accepted
Open:	Year round
Description:	New, spacious, luxury self-catering cottage on arable farm in rolling countryside. Lounge/diner, fully equipped kitchen and utility room, three bedrooms, including ground-floor double with en suite disabled facilities. Ideally situated for many attractions and places of interest in the Heart of England.
Offers:	Three-night weekend breaks – £150.
Facilities:	

NORTHUMBERLAND

ALNWICK

Village Farm ★★★ Self Catering
Booking address: Town Foot Farm, Shilbottle, Alnwick, NE66 2HG

T:	+44 (0) 1327 857857
W:	villagefarmcottages.co.uk
Units:	12 • Sleeps from 1-12 • Low season £150-£510; high season £270-£1650 • Credit/debit cards; cash/cheques accepted
Open:	Year round
Description:	17thC farmhouse, cottages and beautifully appointed chalets complemented by excellent facilities – indoor heated swimming pool, health club, steam room, sauna, sunshower, beauty therapist, games room, tennis, riding, fishing and adventure playground. Situated between Alnwick and Heritage Coast. A warm, personal welcome.
Offers:	Two-/three-night stays available November-Easter (excluding Christmas, New Year and half-terms).
Facilities:	

BAMBURGH

Waren House Hotel ★★★ Country House Hotel
SILVER AWARD
Waren Mill, Belford, Northumberland, NE70 7EE

T:	+44 (0) 1668 214581
E:	enquiries@warenhousehotel.co.uk
W:	warenhousehotel.co.uk
Rooms:	13 • B&B per room per night (double) £103-£185 • Credit/debit cards; cash/cheques, euros accepted
Open:	Year round
Description:	Traditional, beautifully restored and renovated, award-winning country-house hotel in six acres of wooded grounds and walled garden on edge of Budle Bay overlooking Holy Island. Superb accommodation, excellent food, choice of over 250 reasonably priced wines. Two miles Bamburgh Castle, five miles Farne Islands. Children over 14 welcome. Ground-floor suite with wheelchair access.
Offers:	Short breaks – DB&B from £76 per person per night.
Facilities:	

BAMBURGH

Waren Lea Hall ★★★★★ Self Catering
Booking address: Abbotsholme, Hervines Road, Amersham, HP6 5HS

T:	+44 (0) 1668 214581
W:	selfcateringluxury.co.uk
Units:	3 • Sleeps from 2-28 • Low season £221-£1,666; high season £394-£2,362 • Cash/cheques accepted
Open:	Year round
Description:	Imposing, spacious country house on shore of Budle Bay at Waren Mill near Bamburgh in two acres of water's edge parkland. Breathtaking, panoramic views of Lindisfarne and the Cheviots. Waren Lea Hall enjoys an unrivalled location with easy access for walking, golf, fishing etc.
Offers:	Short breaks available from November-March. Weekend breaks, three nights, Friday-Monday. Mid-week breaks, four nights, Monday-Friday.
Facilities:	

NORTHUMBERLAND

BARDON MILL

Twice Brewed Inn ♦♦♦ Guest Accommodation
Bardon Mill, Hexham, Northumberland, NE47 7AN

T:	+44 (0) 1434 344534
E:	info@twicebrewedinn.co.uk
W:	twicebrewedinn.co.uk
Rooms:	14 • B&B per room per night (single) £25-£28; (double) £48-£70 • Credit/debit cards; cash/cheques accepted
Open:	Year round except Christmas
Description:	Family-run inn 0.5 miles from Hadrian's Wall offering accommodation, a warm welcome, good food, real ales, breathtaking views and wide-open spaces. Centrally placed for visits to Scotland, Cumbria and the North East (all within one hour's drive).
Offers:	Bi-annual bridge weekend held first weekend in March and first weekend in November.
Facilities:	

BERWICK-UPON-TWEED

King's Arms Hotel ★★★ Hotel
43 Hide Hill, Berwick-upon-Tweed, TD15 1EJ

T:	+44 (0) 1289 307454
E:	enquiries@kingsarms-hotel.com
W:	kingsarms-hotel.com
Rooms:	28 • B&B per room per night (single) £84-£95; (double) £129-£149 • Credit/debit cards; cash/cheques, euros accepted
Open:	Year round
Description:	18thC Georgian coaching inn with beautiful en suite bedrooms, medieval walled garden and Il Porto di Mare seafood restaurant. An ideal centre for touring the Borders, Lindisfarne, Farne islands, Holy Island etc. Weekend breaks within medieval town walls. A step back in history.
Offers:	Short breaks to include visits to all major historical sites. Fishing arranged on Tweed tributaries. Golfing packages – choice of four courses.
Facilities:	

BERWICK-UPON-TWEED

Marshall Meadows Country House Hotel ★★★ Hotel
Marshall Meadows, Berwick-upon-Tweed, TD15 1UT

T:	+44 (0) 1289 331133
E:	stay@marshallmeadows.co.uk
W:	marshallmeadows.co.uk
Rooms:	19 • B&B per room per night (single) £85-£95; (double) £120-£150 • Credit/debit cards; cash/cheques accepted
Open:	Year round except Christmas
Description:	Georgian mansion in woodland gardens off the A1, two minutes' drive north of Berwick. Magnificent public rooms, comfortable, well-equipped bedrooms, excellent service and menus drawing on local produce. Rosette dining award. A favourite with golfers, fishermen and Borders explorers.
Offers:	Inclusive breaks available throughout the year. Weddings are a speciality. Non-residents always welcome.
Facilities:	

CORNHILL-ON-TWEED

Coach House at Crookham ♦♦♦♦ Guest Accommodation
Crookham, Cornhill-on-Tweed, Northumberland, TD12 4TD   SILVER AWARD

T:	+44 (0) 1890 820293
E:	stay@coachhousecrookham.com
W:	coachhousecrookham.com
Rooms:	10 • B&B per room per night (single) £35-£60; (double) £70-£90 • Credit/debit cards; cash/cheques accepted
Open:	Year round except Christmas
Description:	17thC dower house with spacious, fully equipped, en suite bedrooms set in a rustic courtyard. The perfect location to explore the Scottish Borders, Northumberland coast and Alnwick. Offering unsurpassed hospitality in comfortable surroundings. Fresh, home-cooked food with afternoon tea served. Fully licensed. Your home in the country.
Offers:	Three nights for price of two, November-March.
Facilities:	

CORNHILL-ON-TWEED

Tillmouth Park Country House Hotel ★★★ Hotel
Cornhill-on-Tweed, Northumberland, TD12 4UU   SILVER AWARD

T:	+44 (0) 1890 882255
E:	reception@tillmouthpark.f9.co.uk
W:	tillmouthpark.co.uk
Rooms:	14 • B&B per room per night (single) £90-£140; (double) £125-£180 • Credit/debit cards; cash/cheques accepted
Open:	Year round except Christmas
Description:	This magnificent Victorian mansion stands in 15 acres of secluded parkland. Public rooms are graced with comfy sofas, antiques and oil paintings, while all bedrooms are individually designed with period furniture and fine fabrics. The four-poster rooms are very special indeed. The Library Dining Room deserves its two Rosettes. A true country retreat.
Offers:	Summer – three nights' DB&B for two in luxury four-poster bedroom with champagne, flowers and chocolates – £595.
Facilities:	

CRAMLINGTON

Burradon Farm Houses/Cottages ★★★★ Self Catering
Burradon Farm, Cramlington, NE23 7ND

T:	+44 (0) 1890 882255
W:	burradonfarm.co.uk
Units:	9 • Sleeps from 2-36 • Low season £270-£520; high season £430-£840 • Credit/debit cards; cash/cheques accepted
Open:	Year round
Description:	Burradon Farm is only a few miles from the spectacular Northumbrian coastline and within easy reach of the cultural heritage and dynamic centre which is Newcastle-upon-Tyne. The new barn conversions have become characterful, high-quality houses and cottages boasting every amenity and facility to ensure an enjoyable visit. Dishwasher in houses.
Offers:	Three-four night stays welcomed, all year round.
Facilities:	

NORTHUMBERLAND

NORTHUMBERLAND

FORD

Ford Castle
★★★★ Self Catering
Ford Castle, Ford Village, Berwick-upon-Tweed, TD15 2PX

T:	+44 (0) 1890 882255
W:	fordcastle.org.uk
Units:	2 • Sleeps from 2-13 • Low season £336-£594; high season £448-£931 • Credit/debit cards; cash/cheques accepted
Open:	Year round
Description:	Ford Castle is a residential activity centre, dating back to the 14thC, with two self-catering properties within the grounds. The Flag Tower has been refurbished to a very high standard. The Clock Tower cottage has three bedrooms, one with en suite facilities.
Offers:	Weekend and short breaks, minimum two nights, available throughout the year.
Facilities:	

HAYDON BRIDGE

Grindon Cartshed
♦ Guest Accommodation
Haydon Bridge, Hexham, NE47 6NQ

T:	+44 (0) 1434 684273
E:	cartshed@grindon.force9.co.uk
W:	grindon-cartshed.co.uk
Rooms:	3 • B&B per room per night (single) £30-£33; (double) £60-£66 • Credit/debit cards; cash/cheques accepted
Open:	Year round
Description:	A warm welcome awaits at the beautifully converted cartshed, within walking distance of Hadrian's Wall. Ideal location for touring. Licensed and offering delicious meals prepared from local produce.
Offers:	Three or more nights – £27.50 per person per night.
Facilities:	

HEXHAM

Langley Castle
★★★★ Hotel
SILVER AWARD
Langley-on-Tyne, Hexham, Northumberland, NE47 5LU

T:	+44 (0) 1434 688888
E:	manager@langleycastle.com
W:	langleycastle.com
Rooms:	19 • B&B per room per night (single) £99.50-£184.50; (double) £119-£239 • Credit/debit cards; cash/cheques accepted
Open:	Year round
Description:	A genuine 14thC castle set in woodland estate. All en suite rooms with facilities, some with window seats set into seven-foot-thick walls. Sauna, four-poster beds. The magnificent drawing room, with blazing log fire, complements the intimate Josephine Restaurant.
Offers:	Reserve a castle-view room and we will offer a 'feature' room in the main castle (if available) at check-in, at no extra charge.
Facilities:	

NORTHUMBERLAND

KIELDER WATER

The Pheasant Inn (by Kielder Water) ★★★★Inn
Stannersburn, Hexham, Northumberland, NE48 1DD SILVER AWARD

T:	+44 (0) 1434 240382
E:	enquiries@thepheasantinn.com
W:	thepheasantinn.com
Rooms:	8 • B&B per room per night (single) £45-£50; (double) £75-£80 • Credit/debit cards; cash/cheques accepted
Open:	Year round except Christmas and New Year
Description:	Charming 16thC inn, retaining its character while providing comfortable, modern, en suite accommodation. Features include stone walls and low-beamed ceilings in the bars, antique artefacts and open fires. Emphasis on traditional home cooking, using fresh vegetables, served in bar or dining room. Sunday roasts are renowned for their quality.
Offers:	Reduced rates 1 November-30 April, DB&B £60 per person per night.
Facilities:	

MATFEN

Matfen Hall ★★★★Hotel
Matfen, Newcastle upon Tyne, NE20 0RH

T:	+44 (0) 1661 886500
E:	info@matfenhall.com
W:	matfenhall.com
Rooms:	53 • B&B per room per night (single) £115-£190; (double) £170-£265 • Credit/debit cards; cash/cheques accepted
Open:	Year round
Description:	Voted Large Hotel of the Year 2006 in the Excellence in England Awards, Matfen Hall, in Northumberland's beautiful countryside, is only 25 minutes from Newcastle's centre and 15 minutes from its international airport. The hotel offers luxurious bedrooms, award-winning restaurant, conference suites, golf and acclaimed spa and leisure club.
Offers:	Mid-week breaks from £180 per person for two nights' DB&B. Special anniversary packages available.
Facilities:	

MORPETH

Longhirst Hall ★★★Hotel
Longhirst, Morpeth, Northumberland, NE61 3LL

T:	+44 (0) 1670 791348
E:	enquiries@longhirst.co.uk
W:	longhirst.co.uk
Rooms:	77 • B&B per room per night (single) £45-£85; (double) £50-£108 • Credit/debit cards; cash/cheques accepted
Open:	Year round
Description:	Longhirst Hall is an early 19thC, John Dobson-designed building set in 75 acres of woodland and landscaped gardens. All en suite bedrooms in the hall, and 34 dormy houses, each able to accommodate up to eight guests. The perfect blend of business, adventure and tranquillity.
Offers:	Exclusive Alnwick Garden breaks, including tickets and brochure, £118 (£59 per person).
Facilities:	

NORTHUMBERLAND

NEWBIGGIN-BY-THE-SEA

Tahfay House ★★★★Self Catering
Booking address: 4 Fawdon House Farm, Longhirst, Morpeth, NE61 3LQ

T:	+44 (0) 1670 791348
W:	cozydays.co.uk
Units:	1 • Sleeps from 10 • Low season £350-£650; high season £650-£900 • Cash/cheques accepted
Open:	Year round
Description:	Tahfay House offers spacious accommodation just 50m from the sea, 30 minutes from Newcastle and is ideally located for exploring Northumberland. This refurbished, tastefully appointed Victorian town house has five bedrooms. Northumberland's Heritage Trail boasts wonderful castles and miles of exquisite beaches, bays and lovely seaside villages.
Offers:	Three-night stays available October-March (excluding Christmas and New Year). Last-minute discounts available. Reduction for parties of up to five people.
Facilities:	

OTTERBURN

Butterchurn Guesthouse ★★★★Guesthouse
Otterburn, NE19 1NP

T:	+44 (0) 1830 520585
E:	keith@butterchurn.freeserve.co.uk
W:	butterchurnguesthouse.co.uk
Rooms:	7 • B&B per room per night (single) £33-£38; (double) £55-£60 • Cash/cheques accepted
Open:	Year round
Description:	Excellent family-run guesthouse in quiet village location, renowned for its welcome, quality of service and ambience. Situated in Northumberland National Park, on the scenic route to Scotland. Central for Hadrian's Wall, Kielder Water, coast and castles. Everyone welcome in the county known as the 'Land of Far Horizons'.
Offers:	Discount of 10% for stays of three or more nights.
Facilities:	

ROTHBURY

Burnfoot Guesthouse ♦♦♦♦Guest Accommodation
Netherton, Rothbury, Morpeth, NE65 7EY

T:	+44 (0) 1669 631061
E:	burnfootbb@aol.com
W:	burnfoothouse.co.uk
Rooms:	4 • B&B per room per night (single) £35-£50; (double) £50-£56 • Credit/debit cards; cash/cheques, euros accepted
Open:	Year round
Description:	A warm, friendly welcome awaits guests. Enjoy a relaxing and informal visit in our 250-year-old house. Set in the scenic valley of Netherton, just north of Rothbury. The location is ideal for touring the heart of Northumberland. We welcome families and pets.
Offers:	Winter Special October-March: £40 per room. Christmas/New Year breaks: from £65 per person.
Facilities:	

NORTHUMBERLAND

ROTHBURY

Low Alwinton Cottages ★★★★Self Catering
Booking address: 12 Parkshiel, South Shields, NE34 8BU

T:	+44 (0) 1669 631061
W:	lowalwinton.co.uk
Units:	4 • Sleeps from 4-21 • Low season £200-£300; high season £320-£495 • Credit/debit cards; cash/cheques, euros accepted
Open:	Year round
Description:	Luxury cottages nestling in a spectacular wooded valley, amid the glorious National Park. Located beside the River Coquet and 10 minutes from Caistron trout fishery. Stunning panoramic views. Otters, birds, squirrel and deer are just some of the wildlife found here. Ideal for nature lovers, walkers, fishermen, cyclists and families.
Offers:	If four people or fewer in Byre Cottage (sleeps eight), £50 off.
Facilities:	

SEAHOUSES

Seafield Caravan Park ★★★★★Holiday & Touring Park
Seafield Road, Seahouses, Northumberland, NE68 7SP

T:	+44 (0) 1665 720628
E:	info@seafieldpark.co.uk
W:	seafieldpark.co.uk
Pitches:	Touring: 18; touring caravans: 18; motor caravans: 18; caravan holiday homes: 37 • Per night (caravan, motor caravan) £18-£35; caravan holiday home £ 295-£620 • Credit/debit cards; cash/cheques accepted
Open:	Year round except Christmas and New Year
Description:	Luxurious holiday homes for hire on Northumberland's premier park. Fully appointed caravans. Superior, fully serviced touring pitches. Prices include full use of Ocean Club facilities (ocean-club.co.uk).
Offers:	Seasonal discounts available on three-, four- and seven-day breaks.
Facilities:	

WARK

Battlesteads Hotel ♦Hotel
Wark, Hexham, NE48 3LS

T:	+44 (0) 1434 230209
E:	info@battlesteads.com
W:	battlesteads.com
Rooms:	14 • B&B per room per night (single) £40-£45; (double) £80-£80 • Credit/debit cards; cash/cheques accepted
Open:	Year round
Description:	18thC inn, formerly a farmhouse close to the Roman Wall and Kielder Water. An ideal centre for exploring Border country and for relaxing, walking or cycling. Ground-floor bedrooms available. Excellent restaurant using fresh, local produce. Three cask ales.
Offers:	November-March – two nights' B&B – 20% off, three nights' B&B – 30% off. Please see website.
Facilities:	

NOTTINGHAMSHIRE

LANGAR

Langar Hall
Langar, Nottingham, NG13 9HG

★★★ Hotel
SILVER AWARD

T:	+44 (0) 1949 860559
E:	imogen@langarhall.co.uk
W:	langarhall.com
Rooms:	12 • B&B per room per night (single) £75-£110; (double) £90-£210 • Credit/debit cards; cash/cheques accepted
Open:	Year round
Description:	This charming hotel near Nottingham offers a haven of tranquillity away from city life. This country house stands in quiet seclusion overlooking carp ponds and ancient trees in the park. Langar enjoys the reputation for exceptional hospitality, efficient, friendly service, comfortable bedrooms, award-winning food and an interesting wine list.
Offers:	For one-night stay on Sunday, double occupancy at single rate. Weekend discounts available on standard rooms only.
Facilities:	

MANSFIELD

Watson Avenue
★★★★ Self Catering

Booking address: David Blount Ltd, 44 Station Street, Kirkby-in-Ashfield, Mansfield, NG17 7AS

T:	+44 (0) 1949 860559
W:	nottshouse.co.uk
Units:	2 • Sleeps from 6 • £80-£180 all year • Cash/cheques, euros accepted
Open:	Year round
Description:	High-quality living in 2004-built houses. Ideal for visiting Sherwood Forest, numerous nearby historic houses, cycling, golfing, walks. Few minutes' walk to town's cultural quarter. Three double bedrooms (one en suite), lounge, dining room, kitchen, bathroom, contemporary furnishings, multi media to all main rooms, security, parking, gardens, patio.
Offers:	Book for just a day or a week. Discounts for stays of a week or more.
Facilities:	

NEWARK

The Grange Hotel
73 London Road, Newark, Nottinghamshire, NG24 1RZ

★★★ Hotel
SILVER AWARD

T:	+44 (0) 1636 703399
E:	info@grangenewark.co.uk
W:	grangenewark.co.uk
Rooms:	19 • B&B per room per night (single) £72-£100; (double) £96-£150 • Credit/debit cards; cash/cheques accepted
Open:	Year round except Christmas and New Year
Description:	This stylish Victorian hotel with tranquil, landscaped gardens has been sympathetically refurbished, retaining many of its original features. Located in a quiet, residential area less than one mile from the town centre.
Offers:	Weekend breaks: DB&B £65-£92 per person per night, minimum two nights, based on sharing twin/double bedroom. Subject to availability.
Facilities:	

OXFORDSHIRE

ABINGDON

The Upper Reaches ★★★ Hotel
Thames Street, Abingdon, Oxfordshire, OX14 3JA

T:	+44 (0) 1235 522536
E:	info@upperreaches-abingdon.co.uk
W:	upperreaches-abingdon.co.uk
Rooms:	31 • B&B per room per night (single) £60-£160; (double) £60-£180 • Credit/debit cards; cash/cheques, euros accepted
Open:	Year round except Christmas
Description:	Built from Abingdon Abbey's old corn mill (millwheel still working). Most of the bedrooms have a view of either the Thames or gardens. Moorings for up to six boats. Choice of brasserie and fine-dining restaurant. Riverside dining.
Offers:	Free moorings for patrons and special weekend rates. Daily boat hire.
Facilities:	

BURFORD

Bay Tree Hotel ★★★ Hotel
Sheep Street, Burford, Oxfordshire, OX18 4LW

T:	+44 (0) 1993 822791
E:	info@baytreehotel.info
W:	cotswold-inns-hotels.co.uk/baytree
Rooms:	21 • B&B per room per night (single) £119-£129; (double) £165-£250 • Credit/debit cards; cash/cheques accepted
Open:	Year round
Description:	The hotel is steeped in history, with stone walls and woven tapestries. It has welcomed visitors since 1565. The award-winning candlelit restaurant serves local, seasonal produce complemented by an extensive wine list.
Offers:	Mid-week special offer (Sunday-Thursday). Stay three nights for the price of two in a garden room and receive: free upgrade, free champagne and two nights' dinner, £89 per person per night.
Facilities:	

BURFORD

The Lamb Inn ★★★ Hotel
Sheep Street, Burford, OX18 4LR
SILVER AWARD

T:	+44 (0) 1993 823155
E:	info@lambinn-burford.co.uk
W:	cotswold-inns-hotels.co.uk/lamb
Rooms:	15 • B&B per room per night (single) £115-£115; (double) £145-£235 • Credit/debit cards; cash/cheques accepted
Open:	Year round
Description:	The Lamb dates to the 15th century. To step inside is to step back in history. Flagstone floors, gleaming copper, brass and silver reflecting the flicker of log fires, and antiques that glow with age. Outside there is a stunning courtyard and walled garden, ideal for dining alfresco in the warmer months.
Offers:	Three nights for the price of two B&B.
Facilities:	

RUTLAND

CALDECOTT

Wisteria Cottage ★★★Self Catering
Booking address: 22 Main Street, Caldecott, LE16 8RS

T:	+44 (0) 1993 823155
W:	rutland-cottages.co.uk
Rooms:	2 • Sleeps from 1-8 • Low season £190-£385; high season £215-£550 • Cash/cheques, euros accepted
Open:	Year round
Description:	Charming stone-built cottage in historic Rutland, overlooking the rolling hills of the Welland valley. The cottage can be used as one or two dwellings, offering high-quality accommodation, a secluded garden and secure parking – an ideal location for watersports, walking, cycling, fishing and bird-watching.
Offers:	Open Christmas and New Year. Two-, three-night weekend breaks. Special rates for long-term stays.
Facilities:	

COTTESMORE

Tithe Barn ★★★★Guest Accommodation
Clatterpot Lane, Cottesmore, Oakham, LE15 7DW

T:	+44 (0) 1572 813591
E:	jp@thetithebarn.co.uk
W:	tithebarn-rutland.co.uk
Rooms:	7 • B&B per room per night (single) £35-£40; (double) £55-£70 • Credit/debit cards; cash/cheques accepted
Open:	Year round
Description:	An attractive 17thC converted tithe barn. Spacious, comfortable, en suite rooms. Two superior rooms have power showers and king-size beds. Five minutes from Rutland Water, Barnsdale Gardens and A1. A warm and friendly home with a panelled dining room, striking hall and a wealth of original features. All rooms have tea/coffee facilities.
Offers:	Discounts on stays of five or more days.
Facilities:	

OAKHAM

The Old Wisteria Hotel ★★★Hotel
4 Catmos Street, Oakham, LE15 6HW

T:	+44 (0) 1572 722844
E:	enquiries@wisteriahotel.co.uk
W:	wisteriahotel.co.uk
Rooms:	25 • B&B per room per night (single) £55-£75; (double) £80-£100 • Credit/debit cards; cash/cheques accepted
Open:	Year round
Description:	Ideal base for touring with rolling countryside, picturesque villages and a variety of attractions including Barnsdale Gardens and Rutland Water. A welcoming country-house ambience and 'The Cottage' (c1604) lounge bar and restaurant provide an intimate setting for relaxation.
Offers:	Special offers, including Wine and Dine breaks. Please visit our website for our special on-line bookings.
Facilities:	

SHROPSHIRE

BITTERLEY

Angel House
★★★★ B&B
SILVER AWARD

Angel Bank, Bitterley, Ludlow, Shropshire, SY8 3HT

T:	+44 (0) 1584 891377
E:	stay@angelhousecleehill.co.uk
W:	angelhousecleehill.co.uk
Rooms:	2 • B&B per room per night (single) £40-£65; (double) £65 • Cash/cheques accepted
Open:	Year round
Description:	Formerly The Angel Inn, this converted pub offers comfortable, en suite rooms. Guests can enjoy the view of four counties from the conservatory or warm themselves by the log-burning stove in the lounge. Enjoy home-cooked local produce before setting out to explore this beautiful county.
Offers:	Discounts on four days or more (excluding Saturday) see website.
Facilities:	

BRIDGNORTH

The Old Vicarage Hotel
★★★ Hotel

Hallon, Worfield, Bridgnorth, Shropshire, WV15 5JZ

T:	+44 (0) 1746 716497
E:	admin@the-old-vicarage.demon.co.uk
W:	oldvicarageworfield.com
Rooms:	14 • B&B per room per night (single) £75-£110; (double) £99.50-£175 • Credit/debit cards; cash/cheques accepted
Open:	Year round except Christmas
Description:	Family-run country-house hotel in the peaceful hamlet of Worfield. The restaurant boasts many awards with menus sourcing fresh, local ingredients. Ideal location for business or pleasure. Within easy reach of motorway routes. Local attractions include Severn Valley Railway and Ironbridge Gorge. Half-board prices based on two-night stay.
Offers:	Third night free (B&B) for two or more nights on our DB&B rate, don't miss out. Sunday night saver – £99 per room B&B.
Facilities:	

CLUN

Pooh Hall Cottages
★★★★★ Self Catering

Booking address: Woodside, Clun, Craven Arms, SY7 0JB

T:	+44 (0) 1746 716497
W:	pooh-hallcottages.co.uk
Units:	3 • Sleeps 2 • Low season £275-£340; high season £360-£425 • Cash/cheques accepted
Open:	Year round
Description:	Beautifully designed stone cottage retreats, each having outdoor seating with wonderful views across the Clun Valley. One mile from town centre for pubs and shops; many other places of interest within easy reach. Wood-burning stoves, walks from the door and a fresh-meal service.
Offers:	Three-/four-night breaks available. Kennel available for occasional use (no charge).
Facilities:	

SHROPSHIRE

IRONBRIDGE

Bird In Hand Inn ★★★Inn
Waterloo Street, Ironbridge, Telford, TF8 7HG

T:	+44 (0) 1952 432226
Rooms:	3 • B&B per room per night (single) £30-£45; (double) £50-£60 • Credit/debit cards; cash/cheques accepted
Open:	Year round except Christmas and New Year
Description:	Family-run inn, c1774, situated in the centre of Ironbridge Gorge. En suite accommodation, extensive menu with traditional Sunday roast. Winner of four-star catering award from the *Shropshire Star*.
Offers:	November-March – book three nights' DB&B and receive third night free. From £175 per couple.
Facilities:	

IRONBRIDGE

Eleys of Ironbridge ★★★★Self Catering
Eleys of Ironbridge, 13 Tontine Hill, Ironbridge, TF8 7AL

T:	+44 (0) 1952 432030
E:	info@eleys-ironbridge.co.uk
W:	eleys-ironbridge.co.uk
Units:	6 • Sleeps from 2-7 • Low season £180-£385; high season £210-£435 • Credit/debit cards; cash/cheques accepted
Open:	Year round
Description:	One of Ironbridge's premier holiday/letting companies offering a wide range of accommodation to suit all. Central Ironbridge, riverside or rural locations. Some with views of the 'iron bridge' itself, all with private parking. 3/4/7 night breaks available all year round. Holiday or business lets. Free colour brochure and fantastic new website.
Offers:	Weekend and mid-week breaks available. Check out our website for special offers and free museum tickets.
Facilities:	

LUDLOW

Bromley Court B&B ★★★★★Guest Accommodation
73 Lower Broad Street, Ludlow, Shropshire, SY8 1PH   GOLD AWARD

T:	+44 (0) 1584 876996
E:	phil@ludlowhotels.com
W:	ludlowhotels.com
Rooms:	3 • B&B per room per night (single) £75-£105; (double) £95-£115 • Credit/debit cards accepted
Open:	Year round
Description:	Tudor cottages of great charm, in old Ludlow town. Each forms a delightful, individually furnished suite for privacy and relaxation. Within walking distance of everything in Ludlow, including the Michelins! Come, therefore, to Ludlow to eat like lords and to Bromley Court to stay like them!
Offers:	Three nights' B&B for the price of two available periodically (excluding weekends and bank holidays).
Facilities:	

SHROPSHIRE

LUDLOW

Sutton Court Farm Cottages ★★★★ Self Catering
Sutton Court Farm, Little Sutton, Stanton Lacy, Ludlow, SY8 2AJ

T:	+44 (0) 1584 876996
W:	suttoncourtfarm.co.uk
Units:	6 • Sleeps from 2-6 • Low season £208-£430; high season £345-£500 • Cash/cheques accepted
Open:	Year round
Description:	Comfortable cottages set around a peaceful courtyard in the beautiful Corvedale, just five miles from historic Ludlow. World Heritage Ironbridge Gorge, Shrewsbury, Hereford and the Welsh borders all within easy reach. Short breaks available all year. Cream teas and evening meals can be ordered in advance.
Offers:	Short breaks from October-March (excluding bank holidays). Three nights for price of two, four nights for three.
Facilities:	

LUDLOW

The Clive Restaurant with Rooms
◆◆◆◆ Guest Accommodation
SILVER AWARD

Bromfield, Ludlow, Shropshire, SY8 2JR

T:	+44 (0) 1584 856565
E:	info@theclive.co.uk
W:	theclive.co.uk
Rooms:	15 • B&B per room per night (single) £50-£80; (double) £70-£100 • Credit/debit cards; cash/cheques accepted
Open:	Year round except Christmas
Description:	The Clive offers en suite bedrooms in period outbuildings that have been tastefully converted to provide contemporary accommodation. On the main A49 road in the village of Bromfield just two miles north of Ludlow with ample parking.
Offers:	Three nights for the price of two, Sunday-Thursday (excluding Christmas, New Year and bank holidays). October-May only.
Facilities:	

LUDLOW

The Feathers at Ludlow ★★★ Hotel
Bull Ring, Ludlow, Shropshire, SY8 1AA

T:	+44 (0) 1584 875261
E:	enquiries@feathersatludlow.co.uk
W:	feathersatludlow.co.uk
Rooms:	40 • B&B per room per night (single) £70-£90; (double) £95-£150 • Credit/debit cards; cash/cheques accepted
Open:	Year round
Description:	Situated at the heart of the ancient market town of Ludlow. The hotel is internationally recognised for its Jacobean architecture and medieval heritage.
Offers:	Special weekend leisure breaks from £45 per person per night B&B based on two people sharing a twin/double room for two nights.
Facilities:	

SHROPSHIRE

MUCH WENLOCK

Gaskell Arms Hotel ★★Hotel
High Street, Much Wenlock, TF13 6AQ

T:	+44 (0) 1952 727212
E:	maxine@gaskellarms.co.uk
W:	gaskellarms.co.uk
Rooms:	19 • B&B per room per night (single) £60-£70; (double) £76-£95 • Credit/debit cards; cash/cheques accepted
Open:	Year round
Description:	A charming, 17thC coaching inn in the historic town of Much Wenlock, central for the World Heritage site of Ironbridge, Shrewsbury, Bridgnorth and Ludlow. A family-owned freehouse provides an extensive bar and restaurant menu. All bedrooms are delightfully decorated and en suite. Log fires, beer garden, private car park. Luxurious, galleried bedrooms.
Offers:	Weekend breaks £100-£120 per person DB&B (March-October). 10% discount for five nights or more.
Facilities:	

SOMERSET

BATH

Athole Guesthouse ★★★★★B&B
33 Upper Oldfield Park, Bath, BA2 3JX

GOLD AWARD

T:	+44 (0) 1225 334307
E:	info@atholehouse.co.uk
W:	atholehouse.co.uk
Rooms:	4 • B&B per room per night (single) £48-£58; (double) £68-£78 • Credit/debit cards; cash/cheques, euros accepted
Open:	Year round
Description:	Large Victorian home restored to give bright, inviting, quiet bedrooms, sleek furniture, sparkling bathrooms, digital TV, safe. Hospitality is old style. Award-winning breakfasts. Parking behind remote-control gates or in garage. Twelve minutes' walk from centre. Free transfer from/to station.
Offers:	Three nights for 2/50% off second night, November-February. Four nights for 3/50% off third night, March-May and September-October.
Facilities:	

BATH

Carfax Hotel ◆◆◆◆◆Guest Accommodation
13-15 Great Pulteney Street, Bath, BA2 4BS

T:	+44 (0) 1225 462089
E:	reservations@carfaxhotel.co.uk
W:	carfaxhotel.co.uk
Rooms:	31 • B&B per room per night (single) £69-£79; (double) £96-£145 • Credit/debit cards; cash/cheques accepted
Open:	Year round
Description:	A trio of Georgian houses overlooking Henrietta Park with a view to the surrounding hills. A stroll to the Pump Rooms, Roman baths, canal and river. Recently restored and refurbished, well-appointed rooms. Lift to all floors. Car park for 13 cars. Senior citizens' rates all year.
Offers:	Four nights for the price of three, mid-week booking Sunday to Thursday inclusive.
Facilities:	

SOMERSET

BATH

Church Farm Country Cottages ★★★★Self Catering
Booking address: Church Farm, Winsley, Bradford-on-Avon, BA15 2JH

T:	+44 (0) 1225 462089
W:	churchfarmcottages.com
Units:	7 • Sleeps from 2-4 • Low season £275-£645; high season £465-£875 • Credit/debit cards; cash/cheques, euros accepted
Open:	Year round
Description:	Well-equipped, single-storey, traditional cow byres. Bath four miles. Working farm with sheep, free-range hens and horses. Swim in our luxurious, heated indoor pool (12m x 5m), whatever the weather! Pub/shop 500m. Kennet & Avon Canal nearby for boating, cycling and walking. Regular buses.
Offers:	Four-night mid-week break (Monday-Thursday) available at same price as three-night weekend break (Friday-Sunday), excluding school holidays.
Facilities:	

BATH

Greyfield Farm Cottages ★★★★★Self Catering
Booking address: Greyfield Road, High Littleton, Bristol, BS39 6YQ

T:	+44 (0) 1225 462089
W:	greyfieldfarm.com
Units:	5 • Sleeps from 2-4 • Low season £211-£311; high season £341-£462 • Cash/cheques, euros accepted
Open:	Year round
Description:	Attractive stone cottages in peaceful, private, 3.5-acre setting overlooking the Mendips. The cottages are spacious, fully equipped and very comfortable. Each enjoys its own garden/patio and adjacent safe parking. Free facilities include hot tub, sauna, fitness and barbecue centres plus video/DVD library.
Offers:	Fully flexible bookings and short breaks available all year round. Availability calendar and full details on website.
Facilities:	

BATH

Lindisfarne Guesthouse ★★★★B&B
41a Warminster Road, Bath, BA2 6XJ

T:	+44 (0) 1225 466342
E:	lindisfarne-bath@talk21.com
W:	bath.org/hotel/lindisfarne.htm
Rooms:	4 • B&B per room per night (single) £35-£39; (double) £55-£65 • Credit/debit cards; cash/cheques accepted
Open:	Year round except Christmas
Description:	Comfortable, en suite rooms, good-quality full English breakfast and friendly proprietors. Within walking distance of pub/restaurants. About 1.50 miles from Bath city centre on regular bus route. Near walks along the Kennet & Avon canal. Easy drive to university. Large car park.
Offers:	10% discount for stays of four or more nights.
Facilities:	

SOMERSET

BATH

Newton Mill Camping ★★★★ Touring & Camping Park
Newton Road, Bath, BA2 9JF

T:	+44 (0) 1225 333909
E:	newtonmill@hotmail.com
W:	campinginbath.co.uk
Pitches:	Touring: 195; touring caravans: 90; motor caravans: 90; tents: 105 • Per night (caravan, motor caravan) £17.50-£19.50; (tent) £14.50-£17 • Credit/debit cards; cash/cheques accepted
Open:	Year round
Description:	In an idyllic hidden valley close to the city centre with easy access. Superb heated amenities (5-star Loo of the Year 2006) including showers, bathrooms and private facilities. Old Mill bar/restaurant year round. David Bellamy Gold Award for Conservation. ADAC Campingplatz Auszeichnung 2006.
Offers:	5% discount on stays of seven days (selected periods). New Year package.
Facilities:	

BATH

Royal Hotel ♦♦♦♦ Guest Accommodation
Manvers Street, Bath, BA1 1JP
SILVER AWARD

T:	+44 (0) 1225 463134
E:	royal@rhotel.freeserve.co.uk
W:	royalhotelbath.co.uk
Rooms:	31 • B&B per room per night (single) £59-£69; (double) £80-£120 • Credit/debit cards; cash/cheques, euros accepted
Open:	Year round
Description:	An attractive Georgian-style building designed by Brunel more than 150 years ago. Wonderful central position, close to all attractions and the railway station. All rooms recently redecorated and en suite. Air-conditioned restaurant and bar. Excellent reputation for freshly prepared food, served in intimate atmosphere. Excellent-value menus.
Offers:	November-February: DB&B from £35 per person per night (excluding Christmas/New Year), minimum two-night stay.
Facilities:	

BATH

The Hollies ★★★★ Guest Accommodation
Hatfield Road, Bath, BA2 2BD
SILVER AWARD

T:	+44 (0) 1225 313366
E:	davcartwright@lineone.net
Rooms:	3 • B&B per room per night (single) £55-£65; (double) £65-£75 • Credit/debit cards; cash/cheques accepted
Open:	Year round except Christmas and New Year
Description:	The Hollies was built in 1851 and stands in its own award-winning garden just 15 minutes' walk from Bath centre. Offering peace and quiet, the owners have upgraded and redecorated the guest rooms, all with bathrooms. The house is furnished with antiques, and a library is available for guests.
Offers:	Four nights or more, 10% discount.
Facilities:	

SOMERSET

BATH

The Old Mill Hotel ♦♦♦♦ Guest Accommodation
Toll Bridge Road, Bath, BA1 7DE
SILVER AWARD

T:	+44 (0) 1225 858476
E:	info@oldmillbath.co.uk
W:	oldmillbath.co.uk
Rooms:	27 • B&B per room per night (single) £57-£62; (double) £64-£138 • Credit/debit cards; cash/cheques, euros accepted
Open:	Year round
Description:	Beautifully located by the River Avon alongside the historic toll bridge with breathtaking, panoramic views. Lovely glass-surrounded restaurant overlooking the gardens and river. Most rooms with river views. Only five minutes from the centre of Bath. Free car parking. Excellent reputation for quality of food and personal service.
Offers:	November-February: DB&B rate from £35 per person per night with minimum two-night stay (excluding Christmas/New Year).
Facilities:	

BRATTON

Woodcombe Lodges ★★★★ Self Catering
Woodcombe Lodges, Bratton Lane, Minehead, TA24 8SQ

T:	+44 (0) 1225 858476
W:	woodcombelodge.co.uk
Units:	8 • Sleeps from 2-11 • Low season £170-£700; high season £270-£1,250 • Credit/debit cards; cash/cheques accepted
Open:	Year round
Description:	Timber lodges and stone cottages in a tranquil, rural setting on the edge of Exmoor National Park. Standing in a beautiful, 2.50-acre garden with wonderful views towards the wooded slopes of Exmoor. Minehead's seafront, harbour, shops etc. 1.50 miles. Close to Dunster, Selworthy, Porlock and many local beauty spots.
Offers:	Short breaks available November-Easter, minimum three nights.
Facilities:	

BRIDGWATER

Fairways International Touring Caravan and Camping
★★ Touring & Camping Park

Bath Road, Bawdrip, Bridgwater, Somerset, TA7 8PP

T:	+44 (0) 1278 685569
E:	fairwaysint@btinternet.com
W:	fairwaysint.btinternet.co.uk
Pitches:	Touring: 200 • Per night (caravan, motor caravan) £9-£16.50; (tent) £6-£55 • Credit/debit cards; cash/cheques, euros accepted
Open:	1 March to mid-November.
Description:	International touring park in countryside. On-site accessory centre for tents, caravans and motor homes. Storage, store and stay, storage on pitch, seasonals and rallies welcomed. Fishing one mile; seaside six.
Offers:	Seven nights for six.
Facilities:	

SOMERSET

DUNSTER

Yarn Market Hotel (Exmoor) ★★★Hotel
25 High Street, Dunster, Minehead, Somerset, TA24 6SF

T:	+44 (0) 1643 821425
E:	yarnmarket.hotel@virgin.net
W:	yarnmarkethotel.co.uk
Rooms:	15 • B&B per room per night (single) £40-£65; (double) £60-£110 • Credit/debit cards; cash/cheques accepted
Open:	Year round
Description:	Within Exmoor National Park, this hotel is ideal for walking, riding, fishing etc. Family run with a friendly atmosphere. All rooms en suite with colour TV etc. Four-poster and Superior rooms available. Totally non-smoking. Home-cooked dishes to cater for all tastes. Group bookings welcomed. Conference facilities. Special Christmas and New Year breaks.
Offers:	Discounted rates for longer stays and mid-week bookings. Ring for newsletter on special events.
Facilities:	

MILVERTON

Wellisford Manor Barn ★★★★★Self Catering
Wellisford Manor Barn, Wellington, TA21 0SB

T:	+44 (0) 1643 821425
W:	wellisfordmanorbarn.com
Units:	1 • Sleeps 14 • Low season £1,243 • Cash/cheques, euros accepted
Open:	Year round
Description:	Luxury, contemporary, converted barn/coach house set around private landscaped garden with eight-seater hot tub and barbecue. Sleeps 14, three bathrooms (two en suite) and wet room, media room with four-foot plasma screen, well-equipped kitchen and utility room. Dining and garden table seat 14. All bedrooms have real linen bedding and plasma TVs. City luxury in peaceful countryside.
Offers:	Discounted rates available throughout the year for bookings two weeks prior to arrival date.
Facilities:	

MINEHEAD

Wyndcott Hotel ★★Small Hotel
Martlet Road, Minehead, TA24 5QE

T:	+44 (0) 1643 704522
E:	thwyndcott@fsmail.net
W:	wyndcotthotel.co.uk
Rooms:	9 • B&B per room per night (single) £40-£45; (double) £75-£80 • Credit/debit cards; cash/cheques, euros accepted
Open:	Year round
Description:	Enjoy the comfort and hospitality of this country house hotel and let the Wyndcott be your home from home while you explore the beautiful West Somerset coast and the splendour of Exmoor. Licensed restaurant offers a sumptuous selection of local produce prepared on the premises by resident chef.
Offers:	Three-, four- or seven-day HB breaks. Reductions for children sharing with two adults. Christmas and New Year packages.
Facilities:	

SOMERSET

STOGUMBER

Wick House ♦♦♦ Guest Accommodation
2 Brook Street, Stogumber, Taunton, Somerset, TA4 3SZ

T:	+44 (0) 1984 656422
E:	sheila@wickhouse.fsbusiness.co.uk
W:	wickhouse.fsbusiness.co.uk
Rooms:	5 • B&B per room per night (single) £28-£38; (double) £56-£64 • Credit/debit cards; cash/cheques accepted
Open:	Year round
Description:	A listed family home in the picturesque village of Stogumber, situated in a designated Area of Outstanding Natural Beauty. The village nestles between hills in Exmoor National Park. Offering a friendly, informal atmosphere – perfect for escaping the stresses of the modern world.
Offers:	Special rates for full week and mid-week breaks of two-five nights. Residential upholstery and art courses. Honeymoon room available.
Facilities:	

TAUNTON

Rydon Farm ★★★★ B&B
West Newton, Bridgwater, Somerset, TA7 0BZ

T:	+44 (0) 1278 663472
E:	info@rydonfarm.com
W:	rydonfarm.com
Rooms:	2 • B&B per room per night (single) £35-£40; (double) £50-£60 • Cash/cheques, euros accepted
Open:	Year round except Christmas
Description:	16thC beamed farmhouse set in beautiful landscaped gardens. Situated midway between Taunton and Bridgwater. Double and twin rooms have the option of a private bathroom, are all fully furnished and include many period features. Ideal for walkers, cyclists and general holidaymakers.
Offers:	Discounts on stays of three or more days.
Facilities:	

WELLS

The Crown at Wells ★★ Hotel
Market Place, Wells, Somerset, BA5 2RP

T:	+44 (0) 1749 673457
E:	stay@crownatwells.co.uk
W:	crownatwells.co.uk
Rooms:	15 • B&B per room per night (single) £60-£70; (double) £90-£110 • Credit/debit cards; cash/cheques accepted
Open:	Year round
Description:	The 15thC Crown is situated in the heart of Wells, overlooked by the cathedral and Bishop's Palace. Affordable, en suite accommodation. A variety of delicious meals, snacks and refreshments are served throughout the day. The Crown provides a friendly service in comfortable surroundings.
Offers:	Stay Friday and Saturday night and get 50% off Sunday night's stay (excluding bank holiday weekends).
Facilities:	

SOMERSET

WESTONZOYLAND

Hill View ♦♦♦♦ Guest Accommodation
55 Liney Road, Westonzoyland, Bridgwater, TA7 0EU   SILVER AWARD

T:	+44 (0) 1278 699027
E:	hillview@westonzoyland.fsbusiness.co.uk
W:	visit-hillview.co.uk
Rooms:	2 • B&B per room per night (single) £35-£48; (double) £55-£68 • Cash/cheques, euros accepted
Open:	Year round except Christmas
Description:	Stylish, en suite non-smoking accommodation with excellent standard of service, comfort and hospitality. Peaceful, rural location with unspoilt views at edge of historic village. Hospitality trays, TV/video available. Traditional breakfasts using local produce whenever available. Good food in local pubs. Perfectly placed for touring, country pursuits or relaxing!
Offers:	Seasonal discounts available for four nights or more/double occupancy. Please call us for details.
Facilities:	

WINSFORD

Halse Farm Caravan & Tent Park
★★★★ Touring & Camping Park

Winsford, Minehead, Somerset, TA24 7JL

T:	+44 (0) 1643 851259
E:	brit@halsefarm.co.uk
W:	halsefarm.co.uk
Pitches:	Touring: 44; touring caravans: 22; motor caravans: 22; tents: 22 • Per night (caravan, motor caravan, tent) £9.50-£11.50 • Credit/debit cards; cash/cheques accepted
Open:	Mid-March to end of October
Description:	Exmoor National Park, small, peaceful, working farm with spectacular views. Paradise for walkers and country lovers. David Bellamy Gold Conservation Award.
Offers:	10% discount for one week or more, paid 10 days in advance.
Facilities:	

STAFFORDSHIRE

ALSTONEFIELD

Dove Cottage Fishing Lodge ★★★★★ Self Catering
Dove Cottage Fishing Lodge, c/o 112 High Street, Burford, OX18 4QJ

T:	+44 (0) 1993 825900
W:	dovecottages.co.uk
Units:	1 • Sleeps from 5-6 • Low season £345-£540; high season £750-£1,305 • Cash/cheques accepted
Open:	Year round
Description:	Situated in a beautiful and idyllic part of Wolfscote Dale, enjoying stunning views along the River Dove. Relax in a comfortable and highly maintained family home. Let us spoil you with fires laid daily, welcome grocery basket, electric blankets and hand cream! Large gardens, toys, videos.
Offers:	Two-rods fishing on River Dove (April-October). Short breaks available October-April (including Christmas and New Year).
Facilities:	

STAFFORDSHIRE

ALTON

Bulls Head Inn ♦♦♦ Guest Accommodation
High Street, Alton, Stoke-on-Trent, ST10 4AQ

T:	+44 (0) 1538 702307
E:	janet@alton.freeserve.co.uk
W:	thebullsheadinn.freeserve.co.uk
Rooms:	7 • B&B per room per night (single) £35-£45 • (double) £55-£65 • Credit/debit cards; cash/cheques accepted
Open:	Year round
Description:	This family-owned business is in the village of Alton, close to Alton Towers. An 18thC inn offering traditional cask ales and home cooking, with a real log fire and a friendly atmosphere. All rooms en suite, separate restaurant.
Offers:	Group bookings welcome if over 18 years of age. Birthday celebrations and hen parties accommodated. Small-conference facilities available.
Facilities:	

ALTON

Windy Arbour ♦♦♦♦ Guest Accommodation
Hollis Lane, Denstone, Uttoxeter, ST14 5HP

T:	+44 (0) 1889 591013
E:	stay@windyarbour.co.uk
W:	windyarbour.co.uk
Rooms:	5 • B&B per room per night (single) £30 • (double) £45 • Cash/cheques accepted
Open:	Year round except Christmas and New Year
Description:	Windy Arbour is a peaceful haven graced with superb views and big skies. A warm country welcome is guaranteed. The farmhouse and converted outbuildings can accommodate up to 24. Alton Towers, Peak District and Derbyshire Dales all within easy reach.
Offers:	Family rooms: £60 (four sharing); £80 (five sharing), £100 (eight sharing). Four nights for three; seven nights for five.
Facilities:	

LEEK

Foxtwood Cottages ★★★★ Self Catering
Booking address: Foxt Road, Foxt, Stoke-on-Trent, ST10 2HJ

T:	+44 (0) 1889 591013
W:	foxtwood.co.uk
Units:	3 • Sleeps from 4-10 • Low season £233-£538; high from £381-£939 • Cash/cheques; euros accepted
Open:	Year round
Description:	Orchids in the flower meadow, a kingfisher flashing by, a fleeting glimpse of a deer in the woods. Relax and watch canal boats chug past, hear the steam trains whistle along the valley. Come and explore this fascinating area.
Offers:	Special winter breaks for the retired. Four nights mid-week for less than a three-night weekend.
Facilities:	

STAFFORDSHIRE

STOKE-ON-TRENT

The Star Caravan and Camping Park
★★★★★ Holiday, Touring & Camping Park
Star Road, Cotton, Stoke-on-Trent, Staffordshire, ST10 3DW

T:	+44 (0) 1538 702219
W:	starcaravanpark.co.uk
Pitches:	Touring: 120; touring caravans: 60; motor caravans: 30; tents: 30; caravan holiday homes: 9 • Per night (caravan, motor caravan, tent) £12-£14; caravan holiday home £280-£400 • Cash/cheques accepted
Open:	March to October.
Description:	Closest touring park to Alton Towers. Strict 11pm-all-quiet rule. No single-sex groups. Ten miles from four market towns; four miles from the Peak District National Park.
Offers:	Early-season discounts on caravan holiday homes. Free second-day admission to Alton Towers for two.
Facilities:	

STONE

Fox Hollow
★★★★ Self Catering
Booking address: Cresswell Road, Hilderstone, Stone, ST15 8SL

T:	+44 (0) 1538 702219
W:	foxhollowbarnes.co.uk
Units:	1 • Sleeps from 4 • Low season £300-£350; high season £300-£350 • Cash/cheques accepted
Open:	Year round
Description:	A converted cowshed, comprising two double bedrooms, upstairs family bathroom, farmhouse-style kitchen, lounge, through dining room and downstairs wc. Central heating. Set in eight acres. Manicured gardens, stream. We have chickens, goats and rabbits – lovely for children.
Offers:	Discounts available for senior citizens.
Facilities:	

SUFFOLK

ALDEBURGH

Mile Hill Barn
★★★★★ Guest Accommodation
Main Road, Kelsale, Saxmundham, IP17 2RG — GOLD AWARD

T:	+44 (0) 1728 668519
E:	mail@mile-hill-barn.co.uk
W:	mile-hill-barn.co.uk
Rooms:	3 • B&B per room per night (double) £90-£110 • Cash/cheques; euros accepted
Open:	Year round except Christmas
Description:	Superbly converted Suffolk oak barn. Delightful, ground-floor, en suite, luxury double rooms. Separate access. Private parking. Landscaped gardens. Beamed and vaulted guest lounge. Aga breakfasts with many choices. Child, pet and smoke-free zone!
Offers:	Celebration Package of Cava (Spanish bubbly), flowers and chocolates – just £25.
Facilities:	

SUFFOLK

CAVENDISH

Embleton House ★★★★ Guest Accommodation
Melford Road, Cavendish, Sudbury, Suffolk, CO10 8AA   SILVER AWARD

T:	+44 (0) 1787 280447
E:	silverned@aol.com
W:	embletonhouse.co.uk
Rooms:	5 • B&B per room per night (single) £40-£50 • (double) £58-£75 • Cash/cheques accepted
Open:	Year round
Description:	A large, family-run, 1930s house set well back from the road within its own secluded, mature gardens at the eastern edge of Cavendish village. Spacious, recently appointed en suite bedrooms. Stour Valley views. Suffolk breakfast. Good pub within eight minutes' walk. Ideal base for exploring Long Melford, Clare, Lavenham and beyond.
Offers:	Special rates for three nights or more. Holistic therapies on site, heated pool (May-September) and tennis court.
Facilities:	

EYE

The White Horse Inn ♦♦♦♦ Guest Accommodation
Stoke Ash, Eye, Suffolk, IP23 7ET

T:	+44 (0) 1379 678222
E:	mail@whitehorse-suffolk.co.uk
W:	whitehorse-suffolk.co.uk
Rooms:	11 • B&B per room per night (single) £47.5-£0 • (double) £57.5-£0 • Credit/debit cards; cash/cheques accepted
Open:	Year round
Description:	Easy to find on the A140, midway between Ipswich and Norwich, the inn has been a landmark on this road since 1647 and is heaped with history and character. The accommodation is modern and comfortable, tucked away in the grounds to the rear of the property. Home-cooked food is served all day.
Offers:	Stay two nights, get third night free! (subject to availability) Friday/Saturday/Sunday. £57.50 per double.
Facilities:	

HADLEIGH

Wattisham Hall ★★★★ Self Catering
Wattisham Hall, Wattisham, Ipswich, IP7 7JX

T:	+44 (0) 1379 678222
W:	wattishamhall.co.uk
Units:	3 • Sleeps from 1-8 • Low season £350-£470; high season £580-£1,000 • Cash/cheques accepted
Open:	Year round
Description:	Charming barn conversion within an ancient moat, surrounded by tranquil countryside. The cottages are beautifully furnished, having exposed beams, oak floors, wood-burning stoves and plenty of character. Enclosed patio gardens, shared games room and outdoor play area. Within easy reach of Constable Country.
Offers:	Short breaks available all year excluding May and October half-terms, school summer holidays, Christmas and New Year.
Facilities:	

SUFFOLK

IPSWICH

Best Western Ufford Park, Golf and Leisure ★★★Hotel
Yarmouth Road, Ufford, Woodbridge, Suffolk, IP12 1QW

T:	0844 477 3737
E:	mail@uffordpark.co.uk
W:	uffordpark.co.uk

Rooms:	87 • B&B per room per night (single) £100-£120 • (double) £120-£170 • Credit/debit cards; cash/cheques accepted
Open:	Year round
Description:	This Best Western Connoisseur hotel is set in 120 acres of historic parkland, with an 18-hole, par-71 golf course, 32-bay (two-storey) floodlit driving range, golf academy and shop, deck-level pool, spa etc, beauty and hair salons.
Offers:	One night beauty breaks from £125 per person. Sunday night golf special from £75 per person (DB&B and golf). Two-night golf tuition breaks from £275 per person DB&B plus 4 hours' tuition (minimum two people).
Facilities:	

KELSALE

East Green Farm Cottages ★★★★Self Catering
East Green Farm Cottages, Kelsale, IP17 2PH

T:	0844 477 3737
W:	eastgreencottages.co.uk

Units:	4 • Sleeps from 4-6 • Low season £225-£355; high season £345-£665 • Cash/cheques accepted
Open:	Year round
Description:	Between Southwold and Aldeburgh and only two miles from the beautiful Heritage Coast. The Granary, The Old Stables, The Hayloft and The Dairy are charming, spacious, fully equipped, converted barns set in the grounds of a 500-year-old farmhouse. Thirteen acres of paddocks, tennis court and outdoor swimming pool. Tennis coaching available.
Offers:	Short breaks and weekends available from £165. Tennis weekends for groups.
Facilities:	

LAVENHAM

Blaize Cottages ★★★★★Self Catering
Blaize Cottages, Blaize House, Church Street, Sudbury, CO10 9QT

T:	0844 477 3737
W:	blaizecottages.com

Units:	2 • Sleeps from 2-4 • Low season £350-£460; high season £550-£740 • Credit/debit cards; cash/cheques accepted
Open:	Year round
Description:	Enjoy England Excellence Awards 2005/2006: Top three Self-Catering Holiday of the Year. Blaize Barn and Lady Cottage are luxury cottages in the heart of Lavenham, England's finest medieval village. Within 200m of excellent pubs, restaurants and village shops. Sky TV, DVD library, large beds, baths, landscaped private gardens and luxury furnishings.
Offers:	Three-day weekend breaks or four-day mid-week breaks all year. Romantic breaks and gift vouchers available.
Facilities:	

SUFFOLK

LAVENHAM

Lavenham Great House ♦♦♦♦ Guest Accommodation
Market Place, Lavenham, Sudbury, Suffolk, CO10 9QZ   SILVER AWARD

T:	+44 (0) 1787 247431
E:	info@greathouse.co.uk
W:	greathouse.co.uk
Rooms:	5 • B&B per room per night (single) £70-£99 • (double) £80-£160 • Credit/debit cards; cash/cheques accepted
Open:	Year round except January
Description:	'English country charm and wonderful French food – what could be a better combination?' 'One of the six best British country-house hotels' – *GHM*. Delightful country house with award-winning restaurant overlooking the magnificent market place. Beautifully decorated, individual, en suite bedrooms, most with sitting areas, one with four-poster.
Offers:	Two-/three-night stay from £75 per person per night including DB&B (full English breakfast). Tuesday-Thursday inclusive.
Facilities:	

LAVENHAM

The Rector's Retreat ★★★ Self Catering
The Old Convent, The Street, Kettlebaston, Ipswich, IP7 7QA

T:	+44 (0) 1787 247431
W:	kettlebaston.fsnet.co.uk
Units:	1 • Sleeps from 2 • Low season £294-£322; high season £326-£364 • Cash/cheques accepted
Open:	Year round
Description:	Timber building within the curtilage of a Grade II Listed thatched cottage. Recently refurbished and renovated to provide wheelchair access. Complimentary basic provisions (milk/beverages and toiletries). The Retreat comprises a double bedroom with en suite shower, lounge/diner, kitchen, electric storage heaters. Electricity and linen included. Brochure available.
Offers:	June and September: Seven nights for £294. Minimum three nights' stay from £44 per couple, per night.
Facilities:	

LAXFIELD

Meadow Cottage ★★★★ Self Catering
Meadow Cottage Leisure, Quinton House, Laxfield, IP13 8DN

T:	+44 (0) 1787 247431
Units:	1 • Sleeps from 1-5 • Low season £200-£350; high season £360-£525 • Cash/cheques accepted
Open:	Year round
Description:	Pretty Victorian cottage offering spacious accommodation in the centre of Laxfield. Ideal base for exploring Suffolk's Heritage Coast. Extremely well appointed, the cottage is cosy and comfortable all year round and overlooks peaceful meadowland. Two pubs/restaurants within 100 yards.
Offers:	First basket of logs for woodburner free from 1 October 2006 to 1 April 2007; further logs available from owner.
Facilities:	

SUFFOLK

NAYLAND

Gladwins Farm ★★★★ Self Catering
Gladwins Farm, Harpers Hill, Colchester, CO6 4NU

T:	+44 (0) 1787 247431
W:	gladwinsfarm.co.uk
Units:	9 • Sleeps from 2-8 • Low season £260-£875; high season £570-£1800 • Credit/debit cards; cash/cheques accepted
Open:	Year round
Description:	Extensive wooded grounds in Suffolk's rolling Constable Country with marvellous views make ours a wonderful location. Charming villages and gardens to explore - not far from the sea. Heated indoor pool, sauna, hot tub, tennis, fishing, animals and playground. Pets welcome. Chelsworth and Melford cottages have private hot tubs.
Offers:	Short breaks October-Easter. Three-night weekends or four-night mid-week breaks at 70% full-week rate.
Facilities:	

SUSSEX – EAST

BRIGHTON & HOVE

Ambassador Hotel ◆◆◆◆ Guest Accommodation
23 New Steine, Marine Parade, Brighton, BN2 1PD

T:	+44 (0) 1273 676869
E:	info@ambassadorbrighton.co.uk
W:	ambassadorbrighton.co.uk
Rooms:	24 • B&B per room per night (single) £36-£65 • (double) £55-£120 • Credit/debit cards; cash/cheques, euros accepted
Open:	Year round
Description:	Centrally located in Georgian garden square overlooking the sea, 24-hour reception and security, residents' bar. Local Sussex farm and organic produce. Gold Award Green Tourism Scheme member. A few minutes' walk to Brighton Centre, Dome, theatres, restaurants, nightlife, Royal Pavilion.
Offers:	Mid-week breaks Sunday-Thursday £35 per person per night November-May and £40 per person per night June-October, minimum two nights.
Facilities:	

BRIGHTON & HOVE

Kilcolgan Bungalow ★★★★★ Self Catering
Booking address: 22 Baches Street, London, N1 6DL

T:	+44 (0) 1273 676869
W:	holidaybungalowsbrightonuk.com
Units:	1 • Sleeps from 2 - 6 • Low season £500-£650; high season £700-£850 • Cash/cheques; euros accepted
Open:	Year round
Description:	Welcome to excellence in self-catering accommodation. Exceptional, detached, three-bedroomed bungalow comprehensively equipped, with emphasis on comfort. Secluded, landscaped garden overlooking farmland. Garage parking for two vehicles. Accessible to the disabled. Pets by arrangement (small charge).
Offers:	Short breaks (minimum three nights) possible during low season (excluding Christmas and New Year). Terms on request.
Facilities:	

SUSSEX – EAST

EASTBOURNE

Best Western Lansdowne Hotel ★★★Hotel
King Edwards Parade, Eastbourne, East Sussex, BN21 4EE SILVER AWARD

T:	+44 (0) 1323 725174
E:	reception@lansdowne-hotel.co.uk
W:	bw-lansdownehotel.co.uk
Rooms:	101 • B&B per room per night (single) £50-£75 • (double) £92-£168 • Credit/debit cards; cash/cheques accepted
Open:	Year round except 2-12 January
Description:	Traditional, privately owned seafront hotel. Theatres, shops and conference centre nearby. En suite bedrooms, including executive/superior rooms. Snooker and games rooms. Sky Sports TV. Lunchtime bar and lounge menu. Traditional lunch on Sunday. Christmas, New Year and Easter programme.
Offers:	Golfing holidays all year. Arrangements with 13 local clubs. Duplicate/social bridge weekends winter and spring with residential hosts.
Facilities:	

EASTBOURNE

Birling Gap Hotel ♦♦♦Guest Accommodation
Birling Gap, Seven Sisters Cliffs, Eastbourne, BN20 0AB

T:	+44 (0) 1323 423197
E:	reception@birlinggaphotel.co.uk
W:	birlinggaphotel.co.uk
Rooms:	9 • B&B per room per night (single) £35-£65 • (double) £60-£80 • Credit/debit cards; cash/cheques, euros accepted
Open:	Year round
Description:	Magnificent cliff-top position on Seven Sisters cliffs with views of country, sea and beach. Superb downland and beach walks. Old-world Thatched Bar and Oak Room Restaurant. Coffee shop and games room, function and conference suite. Off A259 coast road at East Dean, 1.5 miles west of Beachy Head.
Offers:	Three nights for the price of two, October-March (excluding bank holidays, Christmas and New Year). Pre-booked only.
Facilities:	

EASTBOURNE

Fairfields Farm Caravan & Camping Park
★★★★Touring & Camping Park
Eastbourne Road, Westham, Pevensey, East Sussex, BN24 5NG

T:	+44 (0) 1323 763165
E:	enquiries@fairfieldsfarm.com
W:	fairfieldsfarm.com
Pitches:	Touring: 60; touring caravans: 60; motor caravans: 60; tents: 60 • Per night (caravan, motor caravan, tent) £11-£16 • Credit/debit cards; cash/cheques accepted
Open:	April to October
Description:	A quiet country touring site on a working farm. Close to the beautiful seaside resort of Eastbourne, and a good base from which to explore the attractions of south east England.
Offers:	Special low season, mid-week offer – three nights for the price of two. Contact for more details.
Facilities:	

SUSSEX – EAST

EASTBOURNE

The Grand Hotel ★★★★★Hotel
King Edwards Parade, Eastbourne, East Sussex, BN21 4EQ GOLD AWARD

T:	+44 (0) 1323 412345
E:	reservations@grandeastbourne.com
W:	grandeastbourne.com
Rooms:	152 • B&B per room per night (single) £140-£345 • (double) £170-£375 • Credit/debit cards; cash/cheques, euros accepted
Open:	Year round
Description:	Built in 1875 and recently restored to its former glory, The Grand Hotel is a stunning example of the highest levels of service. Facilities include health club, two restaurants, kids' club and two swimming pools. Only five minutes from magnificent Sussex countryside, 55 minutes from Gatwick.
Offers:	Promotions during 2007 include gourmet evenings, musical events and seasonal promotions. See website for information.
Facilities:	

FOREST ROW

Ashdown Park Hotel ★★★★Hotel
Wych Cross, Forest Row, East Sussex, RH18 5JR GOLD AWARD

T:	+44 (0) 1342 824988
E:	sales@ashdownpark.com
W:	ashdownpark.com
Rooms:	106 • B&B per room per night (single) £140-£345 • (double) £170-£375 • Credit/debit cards; cash/cheques, euros accepted
Open:	Year round
Description:	Built in the 1860s and sympathetically restored for modern-day luxury. With 186 acres of landscaped grounds, and set in the heart of the Ashdown Forest, the hotel boasts splendid rooms and suites of character. Facilities include the award-winning Anderida Restaurant, golf course and country club with gym, pool, health and beauty salon and spa treatments.
Offers:	Promotions during 2007 include gourmet evenings, musical events and seasonal promotions. See website for details.
Facilities:	

HEATHFIELD

Iwood B&B ★★★★Guest Accommodation
Mutton Hall Lane, Heathfield, East Sussex, TN21 8NR GOLD AWARD

T:	+44 (0) 1435 863918
E:	iwoodbb@aol.com
W:	iwoodbb.com
Rooms:	4 • B&B per room per night (single) £25-£35 • (double) £50-£70 • Credit/debit cards; cash/cheques accepted
Open:	Year round except Christmas and New Year
Description:	Secluded house in lovely gardens with distant views of South Downs and sea. Within easy reach of coastal towns, including 1066 attractions around Hastings, and historic towns of Battle, Rye, Lewes and Tunbridge Wells. Excellent standards maintained to ensure a comfortable stay. Be prepared for an excellent breakfast! Suitable for partially disabled guests.
Offers:	Concessionary rates in excess of seven nights' stay.
Facilities:	

SUSSEX – EAST

LEWES

Langtons House ♦♦♦♦ Guest Accommodation
143b High Street, Lewes, East Sussex, BN7 1XT SILVER AWARD

T:	+44 (0) 1273 476644
E:	info@langtonshouse.com
W:	langtonshouse.com
Rooms:	3 • B&B per room per night (single) £70-£80 • (double) £80-£90 • Credit/debit cards; cash/cheques accepted
Open:	Year round except Christmas
Description:	Boutique-style B&B and holiday lets, situated in a landmark building in the centre of Lewes. Exquisite suites, all with en suite bathrooms. Healthy continental breakfast. WI-FI Internet, flat-screen TVs and DVD players. White Company bath products for true pampering.
Offers:	Mid-week breaks: reduced rates for four or more nights.
Facilities:	

ROTHERFIELD

Medway Farm Barn Cottage ★★★★ Self Catering
Medway Farm Barn, Catts Hill, Crowborough, TN6 3NQ

T:	+44 (0) 1273 476644
W:	medwayfarmbarn.co.uk
Units:	1 • Sleeps from 1-4 • Low season £300-£350; high season £500-£560 • Cash/cheques; euros accepted
Open:	Year round
Description:	Delightful, detached, newly converted two-bedroom cottage in the heart of Sussex, close to local amenities. London and coastal towns within easy reach. Superb woodland walks surround the property. Children and pets welcome.
Offers:	Equestrian facilities available to include stable, grazing, sand and school hacking on local bridle paths.
Facilities:	

RYE

Jeake's House ♦♦♦♦♦ Guest Accommodation
Mermaid Street, Rye, East Sussex, TN31 7ET SILVER AWARD

T:	+44 (0) 1797 222828
E:	stay@jeakeshouse.com
W:	jeakeshouse.com
Rooms:	11 • B&B per room per night (single) £70-£79 • (double) £90-£122 • Credit/debit cards; cash/cheques accepted
Open:	Year round
Description:	Ideally located historic house on winding, cobbled street in the heart of ancient medieval town. Individually restored rooms provide traditional luxury combined with all modern facilities. Book-lined bar, cosy parlours, extensive breakfast menu to suit all tastes. Easy walk to restaurants and shops.
Offers:	Reductions for a stay of four or more nights. Mid-week winter breaks.
Facilities:	

147

SUSSEX – EAST

RYE

Manor Farm Oast ♦♦♦♦♦ Guest Accommodation
Windmill Lane, Icklesham, East Sussex, TN36 4WL — GOLD AWARD

T:	+44 (0) 1424 813787
E:	manor.farm.oast@lineone.net
W:	manorfarmoast.co.uk
Rooms:	3 • B&B per room per night (single) £54-£63 • (double) £84-£94 • Credit/debit cards; cash/cheques, euros accepted
Open:	Year round except Christmas and New Year
Description:	Three-roundel oast house in the heart of 1066 country. Quiet and secluded in orchards, close to Rye, Battle and Hastings. Ideal for romantic breaks. All rooms are tastefully furnished, and home-cooked dinners exceptionally good using local produce. Tourism South East winner of B&B of the Year 2004. Wedding licence.
Offers:	Group Murder Mystery dinners. Honeymoon breaks. Romantic dinners.
Facilities:	

RYE

Rye Lodge Hotel ★★★ Hotel
Hilders Cliff, Rye, East Sussex, TN31 7LD — GOLD AWARD

T:	+44 (0) 1797 223838
E:	info@ryelodge.co.uk
W:	ryelodge.co.uk
Rooms:	18 • B&B per room per night (single) £75-£125 • (double) £100-£200 • Credit/debit cards; cash/cheques, euros accepted
Open:	Year round
Description:	Stunning estuary views yet adjacent to town centre. Dine by candlelight in the elegant, marble-floored Terrace Restaurant serving delicious food and fine wines. Full room service – enjoy breakfast in bed. Heated indoor pool and sauna, private car park, plus all the delights of Rye.
Offers:	Wine and food breaks: gourmet meals, wine tastings, talks, visits to vineyards. Historic interludes include special visits to historic stately homes etc.
Facilities:	

STONEGATE

Coopers Farm Cottage ★★★★★ Self Catering
Coopers Farm Cottage, Bardown Road, Stonegate, Wadhurst, TN5 7EH

T:	+44 (0) 1797 223838
W:	coopersfarmstonegate.co.uk
Units:	1 • Sleeps from 4 • Low season £380-£480; high season £480-£680 • Cash/cheques; euros accepted
Open:	Year round except Christmas
Description:	Coopers Cottage combines the charm of an ancient building – huge inglenook fireplace and a wealth of beams – with the comfort of five-star accommodation. Enjoy the peace and seclusion of this traditional working farm situated in the High Weald Area of Outstanding Natural Beauty. Horses welcome.
Offers:	From November-March: £300 for the weekend or a four-night, mid-week break.
Facilities:	

SUSSEX – EAST

TICEHURST

Dale Hill Hotel & Golf Club
★★★★Hotel
SILVER AWARD
Dale Hill, Ticehurst, Wadhurst, TN5 7DQ

T:	+44 (0) 1580 200112
Rooms:	35 • B&B per room per night (single) £80-£90 • (double) £124-£160 • Credit/debit cards; cash/cheques accepted
Open:	Year round
Description:	Situated in beautiful, historic 1066 Country high on the Kentish Weald. All rooms furnished to the highest standard. The award-winning Wealden Restaurant provides outstanding cuisine. Two 18-hole golf courses, one designed by Ian Woosnam to USGA-Championship specifications. Nearby are Scotney Castle, Sissinghurst (a moated Tudor castle with gardens) and Bewl Water.
Offers:	DB&B packages from £90 per person per night. Includes three-course menu, accommodation and full English buffet breakfast. Golf packages also available.
Facilities:	

SUSSEX – WEST

CHICHESTER

Cornerstones
★★★★Self Catering
Booking address: Goodwood Gardens, Chichester, PO20 1SP

T:	+44 (0) 1580 200112
W:	cornercottages.com
Units:	1 • Sleeps from 1-6 • Low season £385-£555; high season £555-£645 • Cash/cheques accepted
Open:	Year round
Description:	Sussex-style house. Two bedrooms upstairs, one downstairs. Bathroom. Separate shower room. Equipped to high standard. Double garage. Enclosed gardens. Village between Chichester and coast. Easy walks to pub/restaurant, post office/shop, church and Pagham nature reserve. Five-minute drive to Chichester. Ten minutes to Goodwood Racecourse.
Offers:	Short breaks available October-May. Reduced rates for couples October-May.
Facilities:	

CHICHESTER

Millstream Hotel
★★★Hotel
GOLD AWARD
Bosham Lane, Bosham, Chichester, West Sussex, PO18 8HL

T:	+44 (0) 1243 573234
E:	info@millstream-hotel.co.uk
W:	millstream-hotel.co.uk
Rooms:	35 • B&B per room per night (single) £79-£89 • (double) £138-£158 • Credit/debit cards; cash/cheques accepted
Open:	Year round
Description:	Country house dating from 1701, set in a picturesque quayside village four miles west of Chichester. All bedrooms are individually furnished with every modern facility. The millstream, from which the hotel takes its name, flows through the gardens on its way to the sea 300 yards away.
Offers:	Hibernation breaks available from November-April. Sunday or Thursday nights half price if part of a three-night break.
Facilities:	

SUSSEX – WEST

EAST GRINSTEAD

Saxons ♦♦♦♦ Guest Accommodation
Horsted Lane, Sharpthorne, East Grinstead, West Sussex, RH19 4HY

T:	+44 (0) 1342 810821
E:	aliexcol@aol.com
W:	saxons.freeuk.com
Rooms:	3 • B&B per room per night (single) £35-£50 • (double) £55-£0 • Cash/cheques; euros accepted
Open:	Year round
Description:	Saxons is a large, detached country house situated in a beautiful, quiet rural area with stunning views over surrounding countryside. Close to many National Trust gardens, stately homes and Bluebell Railway. Convenient for Brighton, central London (45 minutes by train) and Gatwick Airport (10 miles). Close to Ashdown Forest.
Offers:	Three nights for the price of two on request, 1 November-Easter.
Facilities:	

GATWICK

The Corner House ♦♦♦♦ Guest Accommodation
Massetts Road, Horley, RH6 7ED

T:	+44 (0) 1293 784574
E:	info@thecornerhouse.co.uk
W:	thecornerhouse.co.uk
Rooms:	26 • B&B per room per night (single) £29-£45 • (double) £49-£69 • Credit/debit cards; cash/cheques accepted
Open:	Year round except Christmas and New Year
Description:	Family-run guesthouse offering quality accommodation. Bar/restaurant, en suite rooms with tea/coffee facilities. Holiday parking, 24-hour transfers to and from Gatwick. Let us take the strain out of getting you to the plane.
Offers:	Lingfield racecourse nearby. Accommodation and transfers arranged for race meetings. Book online through our website.
Facilities:	

HENFIELD

New Hall Cottage/Holiday Flat ★★★ Self Catering
New Hall Cottage/Holiday Flat, New Hall Lane, Small Dole, Henfield, BN5 9YJ

T:	+44 (0) 1293 784574
Units:	2 • Sleeps from 3-5 • Low season £260-£320; high season £320-£440 • Cash/cheques accepted
Open:	Year round
Description:	Self-contained flat and 17thC cottage attached to manor house. Set in 3.5 acres of mature gardens and surrounded by farmland. Within easy reach of famous Sussex gardens – Nymans, High Beeches, Wakehurst Place, Leonardslee – and less than an hour from Wisley. Or visit the towns of Brighton, Arundel, Lewes and Chichester.
Offers:	Short breaks available: £150 for two nights, each extra night £45.
Facilities:	

SUSSEX – WEST

HORSHAM

Honeybridge Park ★★★★ Holiday Park
Honeybridge Lane, Dial Post, Nr Horsham, West Sussex, RH13 8NX

T:	+44 (0) 1403 710923
E:	enquiries@honeybridgepark.co.uk
W:	honeybridgepark.co.uk
Pitches:	Touring: 200; touring caravans: 200; motor caravans: 100; tents: 80 • Per night (caravan, motor caravan) £15-£23; tent from £15-£19 • Credit/debit cards; cash/cheques, euros accepted
Open:	Year round
Description:	Delightfully situated within an Area of Outstanding Natural Beauty. A rural retreat with relaxed atmosphere providing exclusive holiday lodges for sale. Ideal touring base.
Offers:	10% discount on pitch fees for senior citizens, foreign Camping Carnet holders and seven nights or more. Mid-week special: £6 off (including Tuesday).
Facilities:	

SELSEY

St Andrews Lodge Hotel ◆◆◆◆ Guest Accommodation
Chichester Road, Selsey, Chichester, West Sussex, PO20 0LX

T:	+44 (0) 1243 606899
E:	info@standrewslodge.co.uk
W:	standrewslodge.co.uk
Rooms:	10 • B&B per room per night (single) £36-£50 • (double) £62.5-£85 • Credit/debit cards; cash/cheques accepted
Open:	Year round except Christmas and New Year
Description:	Situated in the small seaside town of Selsey close to unspoilt beaches and five minutes from Pagham Harbour. Enjoy our delicious breakfast and stay in one of our pretty refurbished rooms, five of which are ground floor and open directly onto our large south-facing garden. Dogs welcome, licensed bar, ample parking.
Offers:	Special winter offers available October-February. 25% discount for stay of three or more nights. Phone for details.
Facilities:	

WORTHING

Chatsworth Hotel ★★★ Hotel
SILVER AWARD
Steyne, Worthing, West Sussex, BN11 3DU

T:	+44 (0) 1903 236103
E:	hotel@chatsworthworthing.co.uk
W:	chatsworthworthing.co.uk
Rooms:	98 • B&B per room per night (single) £75-£100 • (double) £99-£140 • Credit/debit cards; cash/cheques accepted
Open:	Year round
Description:	The Chatsworth offers a unique and prestigious venue for accommodation, functions and conferences. All conference and function rooms and many bedrooms are air-conditioned. The attractive Georgian frontage overlooks Steyne Gardens and the sea. Licensed to hold civil wedding ceremonies.
Offers:	Breaks from £65 per person per night DB&B based on two sharing a twin/double for two nights (subject to availability).
Facilities:	

WARWICKSHIRE

KENILWORTH

Best Western Peacock Hotel ★★★Hotel
149 Warwick Road, Kenilworth, Warwickshire, CV8 1HY

T:	+44 (0) 1926 851156
E:	reservations@peacockhotel.com
W:	peacockhotel.com
Rooms:	29 • B&B per room per night (single) £39-£100 • (double) £49-£160 • Credit/debit cards; cash/cheques, euros accepted
Open:	Year round
Description:	Award-winning hotel providing outstanding quality with first-class service. Luxurious accommodation, four-poster room, choice of three restaurants ranked 'Best UK Restaurant Group 2005', and cocktail bar. Ideal for short breaks, conferences and weddings. Accessible to all major routes.
Offers:	Weekend leisure break – stay Friday and Saturday night and get Sunday night free, £49 per person per night including dinner based on two sharing.
Facilities:	

LEAMINGTON SPA

Barn Owl Cottage ★★★★Self Catering
Booking address: Fosseway Barns, Fosse Way, Leamington Spa, CV33 9BQ

T:	+44 (0) 1926 851156
W:	barnowlcottage.co.uk
Units:	1 • Sleeps from 1-2 • Low season £250-£280; high season £280-£300 • Cash/cheques; euros accepted
Open:	Year round
Description:	Superbly appointed luxury cottage in delightful rural setting close to Warwick, Stratford and the Cotswolds. Tastefully decorated living/dining room, modern, well-equipped fitted kitchen and attractive twin-bedded room. Delightful, landscaped cottage garden with patio. Open views and nearby public right of way.
Offers:	Short breaks available. 10% discount if booking two weeks.
Facilities:	

STRATFORD-UPON-AVON

Avonlea ◆◆◆◆Guest Accommodation
47 Shipston Road, Stratford-upon-Avon, Warwickshire, CV37 7LN

T:	+44 (0) 1789 205940
E:	avonlea-stratford@lineone.net
W:	avonlea-stratford.co.uk
Rooms:	8 • B&B per room per night (single) £30-£45 • (double) £54-£78 • Credit/debit cards; cash/cheques, euros accepted
Open:	Year round except Christmas
Description:	Stylish Victorian townhouse situated only five minutes' walk from the theatre and town centre. All rooms are en suite and furnished to the highest quality. Our guests are assured of a warm welcome and friendly atmosphere.
Offers:	Three nights for the price of two from October-March.
Facilities:	

STRATFORD-UPON-AVON

Ravenhurst ♦♦♦ Guest Accommodation
2 Broad Walk, Stratford-upon-Avon, CV37 6HS

T:	+44 (0) 1789 292515
Rooms:	5 • B&B per room per night (single) £30-£35 • (double) £50-£60 • Credit/debit cards; cash/cheques accepted
Open:	Year round except Christmas
Description:	Victorian townhouse built in 1865, quiet location, a few minutes' walk from town centre, historical buildings and Royal Shakespeare Theatre. Comfortable home. Breakfasts a speciality. Off-street parking available. All bedrooms en suite, non-smoking. Richard Workman and family offer you a warm welcome and a vast amount of local knowledge.
Offers:	Three nights for price of two, Sunday-Thursday, November-March inclusive.
Facilities:	

STRATFORD-UPON-AVON

Stratford Manor ★★★★ Hotel
Warwick Road, Stratford-upon-Avon, Warwickshire, CV37 0PY

T:	+44 (0) 1789 731173
E:	stratfordmanor@marstonhotels.com
W:	marstonhotels.com
Rooms:	104 • B&B per room per night (single) £118-£147.50 • (double) £141-£196 • Credit/debit cards; cash/cheques accepted
Open:	Year round
Description:	The Stratford Manor is a modern hotel with excellent leisure facilities, only four miles from Stratford. There's a new bar and restaurant, and the Reflections Leisure Club invites guests to indulge in a sauna, swim in the pool, work out in the gym or use the tennis courts.
Offers:	Save 20% on our two-night HB break in July and August and November to February (excluding bank holidays, 23 December-1 January and Valentines).
Facilities:	

WARWICK

Shrewley Pools Farm ★★★★ Guest Accommodation
Haseley, Warwick, CV35 7HB
SILVER AWARD

T:	+44 (0) 1926 484315
W:	s-h-systems.co.uk/hotels/shrewley.html
Rooms:	2 • B&B per room per night (single) £40-£50 • (double) £55-£65 • Cash/cheques accepted
Open:	Year round except Christmas
Description:	Glorious 17thC traditional family farmhouse with log fires, oak floors, beams etc, set in an acre of outstanding garden featuring herbaceous borders and unusual trees and shrubs. Two spacious en suite bedrooms and own sitting room with books and games. Perfectly situated for numerous attractions. Surrounded by picturesque farmland. Private fishing.
Offers:	Four-acre lake stocked with carp and tench: £7 per day.
Facilities:	

WARWICKSHIRE

WILTSHIRE

COLLINGBOURNE KINGSTON

Manor Farm B&B ★★★★Farmhouse
Collingbourne Kingston, Marlborough, Wiltshire, SN8 3SD

T:	+44 (0) 1264 850859
E:	stay@manorfm.com
W:	manorfm.com

Rooms: 3 • B&B per room per night (single) £38-£42 • (double) £55-£60 • Credit/debit cards; cash/cheques, euros accepted

Open: Year round

Description: An attractive, Grade II Listed, period village farmhouse with comfortable and spacious rooms (all en suite/private) on a working family farm. Sumptuous traditional, vegetarian, gluten-free and other special-diet breakfasts. Beautiful countryside with superb walking and cycling from the farm.

Offers: Pleasure flights from our private airstrip over Wiltshire's ancient places, white horses and crop circles by balloon, aeroplane and helicopter.

Facilities:

DEVIZES

Eastcott Manor ★★★B&B
Easterton, Devizes, Wiltshire, SN10 4PH

| T: | +44 (0) 1380 813313 |
| E: | janetInfirth@aol.com |

Rooms: 4 • B&B per room per night (single) £28-£30 • (double) £60-£64 • Cash/cheques accepted

Open: Year round except Christmas and New Year

Description: Comfortable Grade II Elizabethan manor house on north edge of Salisbury Plain. Wonderful walking and cycling, convenient for Kennet and Avon Canal, Bath, Salisbury, Stonehenge, Avebury, National Trust properties and other beautiful houses. Large garden, set in own 20-acre grounds. Tranquil setting. Nearest road B3098.

Offers: 10% discount for stays of three or more nights subject to availability

Facilities:

LACOCK

Cyder House/Cheese House ★★★★Self Catering
Booking address: Wick Farm, Wick Lane, Chippenham, SN15 2LU

| T: | +44 (0) 1380 813313 |
| W: | cheeseandcyderhouses.co.uk |

Units: 2 • Sleeps from 2-5 • Low season £290-£440; high season £445-£615 • Credit/debit cards; cash/cheques accepted

Open: Year round

Description: Tastefully converted, beamed farm building with many original features, 1.5 miles from National Trust village. Garden with furniture and barbecue. Good for Bath (12 miles), Stonehenge, Stourhead, Longleat and Wiltshire chalk horses.

Offers: Anglers welcome at our coarse fishing lake. Short breaks low season.

Facilities:

SALISBURY

Alabare Guesthouse ★★★Guesthouse
15 Tollgate Road, Salisbury, Wiltshire, SP1 2JA

T:	+44 (0) 1722 340206
E:	bookings@alabare.org
W:	alabare.org
Rooms:	10 • B&B per room per night (single) £30-£45 • (double) £50-£70 • Credit/debit cards; cash/cheques accepted
Open:	Year round except Christmas
Description:	This is a small oasis in the heart of Salisbury with ample off-road parking. Established as a small retreat centre, the venue is a good choice for a holiday break. There are many local places of interest, and Salisbury offers a wide variety of restaurants and shops. Online booking available.
Offers:	Special rates for extended stays of three weeks or more out of season. Also four nights for the price of three October-April.
Facilities:	

SALISBURY

Burcombe Manor ♦♦♦♦Guest Accommodation
Burcombe Lane, Burcombe, Salisbury, SP2 0EJ

T:	+44 (0) 1722 744288
E:	nick@burcombemanor.fsnet.co.uk
W:	burcombemanor.co.uk
Rooms:	3 • B&B per room per night (single) £40-£45 • (double) £55-£60 • Credit/debit cards; cash/cheques accepted
Open:	Year round
Description:	Burcombe Manor is set in the Nadder Valley four miles west of Salisbury. The house, built in 1865, has large, oak-floor hall, oak banisters, centrally heated bedrooms, most en suite. Guests have their own sitting room in which to plan their day. Local base to explore Wilton, Salisbury and surrounding area.
Offers:	Reduction for stays of three or more nights.
Facilities:	

SALISBURY

Manor Farm ♦♦♦♦Guest Accommodation
Burcombe Lane, Burcombe, Salisbury, SP2 0EJ

T:	+44 (0) 1722 742177
E:	suecombes@manorfarmburcombe.fsnet.co.uk
W:	manorfarmburcombebandb.com
Rooms:	2 • B&B per room per night (double) £50-£52 • Credit/debit cards; cash/cheques accepted
Open:	1 March to 1 December.
Description:	A comfortable farmhouse, warm and attractively furnished, on 1,400-acre mixed farm in a quiet, pretty village 0.25 miles off A30, west of Salisbury. Ideal base for touring this lovely area. Nearby attractions include Wilton House, Salisbury and Stonehenge. Wonderful walks, good riding. Pub with good food nearby.
Offers:	Reduction for stays of three or more nights.
Facilities:	

WILTSHIRE

WILTSHIRE

SALISBURY

The Hayloft, Ebblesway Courtyard ★★★★Self Catering
Booking address: High Road, Broad Chalke, Salisbury, SP5 5EF

T:	+44 (0) 1722 742177
W:	ebbleswaycourtyard.co.uk
Units:	1 • Sleeps from 1-2 • Low season £300-£350; high season £450-£495 • Credit/debit cards; cash/cheques, euros accepted
Open:	Year round
Description:	Luxury cottage in award-winning courtyard. Beautiful location seven miles from Salisbury. Retaining the charm and character of the original farm building, yet providing the latest luxury fittings. Spa bath, digital TV, DVD, WI-FI. Private gardens. Excellent walking, cycling, pubs, restaurants and tourist attractions, including Stonehenge and Salisbury Cathedral.
Offers:	Short breaks all year – four nights mid-week, three nights weekend. Gift vouchers available. Special romantic breaks – see website.
Facilities:	

WINTERBOURNE STOKE

Scotland Lodge Farm ★★★★B&B
Winterbourne Stoke, Salisbury, SP3 4TF

T:	+44 (0) 1980 621199
E:	william.lockwood@bigwig.net
W:	smoothhound.co.uk/hotels/scotlandl.html
Rooms:	3 • B&B per room per night (single) £30-£35 • (double) £55-£60 • Credit/debit cards; cash/cheques accepted
Open:	Year round except Christmas
Description:	Warm welcome at family-run competition yard set in 46 acres of grassland. Lovely views and walks, Stonehenge/Salisbury nearby. Dogs, children and horses welcomed - stabling available on shavings. Conservatory for guests' use. French, German, Italian spoken. Easy access off A303 with entry through automatic gate. Excellent local pubs. Salisbury Tourism Customer Service award winner 2004.
Offers:	Discounts for stays of three or more nights.
Facilities:	

WORCESTERSHIRE

BROADWAY

Southwold Guesthouse ★★★Guesthouse
Station Road, Broadway, Worcestershire, WR12 7DE

T:	+44 (0) 1386 853681
E:	elvira@cotswolds-broadway-southwold.co.uk
W:	cotswolds-broadway-southwold.co.uk
Rooms:	8 • B&B per room per night (single) £38-£42 • (double) £65-£85 • Credit/debit cards; cash/cheques, euros accepted
Open:	Year round
Description:	Southwold Guesthouse is a non-smoking property three minutes' walk from the centre of Broadway, an ideal base for touring the Cotswolds. A wonderful, peaceful atmosphere is created by a mixture of a classic Russian culture and a traditional English home.
Offers:	Discounts available for walking and cycling groups, wedding parties, large families – whatever the occasion.
Facilities:	

WORCESTERSHIRE

BROADWAY

The Broadway Hotel
★★★ Hotel
SILVER AWARD

The Green, Broadway, Worcestershire, WR12 7AA

T:	+44 (0) 1386 852401
E:	info@broadwayhotel.info
W:	cotswold-inns-hotels.co.uk/broadway
Rooms:	20 • B&B per room per night (single) £80-£135 • (double) £135-£175 • Credit/debit cards; cash/cheques accepted
Open:	Year round
Description:	The 16thC Broadway Hotel stands proudly in the picturesque Cotswold village of Broadway, where every stone evokes memories of Elizabethan England. Guests can relax in the cosy lounge and enjoy our famous afternoon tea. All bedrooms are uniquely decorated in warm colours with classic furniture that creates the perfect country-house style.
Offers:	Stay two nights (DB&B) and get a third night for £35 per person (B&B).
Facilities:	

MALVERN

Cotford Hotel & Restaurant
★★ Hotel

Graham Road, Malvern, Worcestershire, WR14 2HU

T:	+44 (0) 1684 572427
E:	reservations@cotfordhotel.co.uk
W:	cotfordhotel.co.uk
Rooms:	15 • B&B per room per night (single) £55-£69 • (double) £89-£99 • Credit/debit cards; cash/cheques accepted
Open:	Year round
Description:	Beautiful Victorian hotel built in 1851, reputedly for the Bishop of Worcester. All rooms en suite and non-smoking with satellite TV, Movie Channel, broadband connection, telephone, radio, hairdryer and tea-making facilities. Complimentary use of Malvern Splash pool and sauna. Close to town, theatre and hills, set in its own mature gardens.
Offers:	Special DB&B breaks available, minimum two nights.
Facilities:	

MALVERN

Hidelow House Cottages
★★★★ Self Catering

Hidelow House, Acton Green, Acton Beauchamp, Worcester, WR6 5AH

T:	+44 (0) 1684 572427
W:	hidelow.co.uk
Units:	6 • Sleeps from 2-9 • Low season £259-£559; high season £562-£1,272 • Credit/debit cards; cash/cheques, euros accepted
Open:	Year round
Description:	Relax and unwind in luxury for a short break or longer. A peaceful, rural retreat with exceptional views, on the edge of an Area of Outstanding Natural Beauty, yet only 2.5 hours from London and Manchester. Former hop kilns and a tithe barn, now with four-poster beds, log fires and barbecues.
Offers:	Honeymoons and romantic breaks a speciality (champagne and roses). Personal transport service.
Facilities:	

WORCESTERSHIRE

MALVERN

The Cottage in the Wood Hotel
★★★ Hotel
SILVER AWARD

Holywell Road, Malvern Wells, Malvern, WR14 4LG

T:	+44 (0) 1684 575859
E:	reception@cottageinthewood.co.uk
W:	cottageinthewood.co.uk
Rooms:	31 • B&B per room per night (single) £82-£110 • (double) £99-£180 • Credit/debit cards; cash/cheques accepted
Open:	Year round
Description:	Set high on the Malvern Hills with 30-mile views to the Cotswolds. 'The best view in England' - *Daily Mail*. All en suite. Family owned and run. Exceptional food. Daily half-board prices based on minimum two-night stay. Weekly is seven nights for price of six. Breaks available all week, all year. From the grounds, direct access to the Malvern Hills.
Offers:	DB&B rates include a full three-course choice from the a la carte menu.
Facilities:	

UPTON UPON SEVERN

Captains Retreat
★★★★ Self Catering

Booking address: White Cottage, Church End, Hanley Castle, Worcester, WR8 0BL

T:	+44 (0) 1684 575859
Units:	1 • Sleeps from 1-2 • Low season £150-£250; high season £250-£500 • Cash/cheques accepted
Open:	Year round
Description:	Converted from a 17thC inn, this fully renovated and spacious first-floor apartment offers the perfect base for exploring and relaxing in this beautiful part of the country. Two hundred yards from open countryside, just off the centre of Upton, this beautiful timber-framed accommodation offers the perfect retreat.
Offers:	Short three-day breaks available, from £120.
Facilities:	

YORKSHIRE – EAST

BARMBY MOOR

Northwood Coach House
★★★★ Self Catering

Northwood Coach House, St Helens Square, Barmby Moor, YO42 4HF

T:	+44 (0) 1759 302305
E:	annjgregory@hotmail.com
W:	northwoodcoachhouse.co.uk
Units:	1 • Sleeps from 1-6 • Low season £375-£400; high season £440-£600 • Cash/cheques; euros accepted
Open:	Year round
Description:	This pretty, three-bedroomed, converted Victorian coach house overlooks open countryside. Warm and cosy in winter, it is ideally situated in a picturesque village on the edge of the Wolds, only 12 miles from York and convenient for the coast and moors. Pubs, shops and restaurants nearby.
Offers:	Short breaks (three days), bookable 28 days in advance, 60% normal weekly rate.
Facilities:	

BRIDLINGTON

Bay View Hotel ★★Hotel
52 South Marine Drive, Bridlington, YO15 3JJ

T:	+44 (0) 1262 674225
E:	info@bay-view-hotel.com
W:	bay-view-hotel.com
Rooms:	28 • B&B per room per night (single) £30-£49 • (double) £60-£98 • Credit/debit cards; cash/cheques, euros accepted
Open:	Year round
Description:	Overlooking South Beach, this attractive, licensed seafront hotel offers all en suite bedrooms and good-quality accommodation, including family suites and specially equipped rooms for the disabled. All beds have memory foam mattresses for ultimate sleeping comfort.
Offers:	15% discount for bookings of three or more nights, 25% discount for three or more nights (excluding Friday and Saturday).
Facilities:	

HORNSEA

Wentworth House Hotel ★★★★Guesthouse
12 Seaside Road, Aldrough, Hull, HU11 4RX

T:	+44 (0) 1964 527246
E:	mteale@eduktion.co.uk
W:	wentworthhousehotel.com
Rooms:	8 • B&B per room per night (single) £35-£50 • (double) £59-£65 • Credit/debit cards; cash/cheques, euros accepted
Open:	Year round except Christmas
Description:	A family-run hotel set in spacious gardens, offering delightful accommodation in a friendly and homely atmosphere. It is ideally suited to those who are working and require first-class facilities in a peaceful environment. Close to many amenities, rural and city. Away from the crowd in a safe environment.
Offers:	Fishing, bird-watching and art-themed breaks. Stately-home tours and Murder Mystery evenings. Licensed for civil ceremonies.
Facilities:	

BEDALE

Elmfield House ♦♦♦♦Guest Accommodation
SILVER AWARD
Bedale, DL8 1NE

T:	+44 (0) 1677 450558
E:	stay@elmfieldhouse.co.uk
W:	elmfieldhouse.co.uk
Rooms:	7 • B&B per room per night (single) £45-£51 • (double) £70-£80 • Credit/debit cards; cash/cheques accepted
Open:	Year round
Description:	Family-run country house in peaceful, open countryside with long-distance views. Enjoy a drink in the garden or a walk in the grounds with fishing lake and woodland paths. All rooms are spacious and well appointed with en suite facilities. Hearty Yorkshire breakfast using local ingredients.
Offers:	Seasonal offers and discounts on stays of seven or more nights – see website. Packages for groups – please enquire.
Facilities:	

YORKSHIRE – NORTH

BURNSALL

The Devonshire Fell Hotel and Restaurant ★★Hotel
Burnsall, Skipton, North Yorkshire, BD23 6BT
SILVER AWARD

T:	+44 (0) 1756 729000
E:	res@devonshirehotels.co.uk
W:	devonshirehotels.co.uk
Rooms:	12 • B&B per room per night (single) £77-£133.25 • (double) £129-£225 • Credit/debit cards; cash/cheques, euros accepted
Open:	Year round
Description:	Unique city-chic hotel in the countryside with stunning views across the Yorkshire Dales. Bright, squishy sofas, vibrant decor, contemporary art, huge wood-burning stove, well-equipped bedrooms and bathrooms – plus free access to The Devonshire health spa and Bolton Abbey Estate.
Offers:	Sunday night sleepover in a double room, including champagne, spa entry, Yorkshire breakfast and a delicious dinner, from £155 per couple.
Facilities:	

GRINTON

Feetham Holme ★★★★Self Catering
Booking address: Plantation Business Services,
Plantation House, Chipping Road, Clitheroe, BB7 3LX

T:	+44 (0) 1756 729000
Units:	3 • Sleeps from 2-13 • Low season £305-£395; high season £415-£580 • Cash/cheques accepted
Open:	Year round
Description:	Fully renovated cottages in the heart of the National Park, beautiful secluded location. Tastefully finished and fully equipped accommodation. Wood-burning stoves and original features make the cottages a delight to enjoy. Design award for renovation.
Offers:	Weekend and mid-week breaks available. Discount for booking all units together.
Facilities:	

HARROGATE

Ashness Apartments ★★★★Self Catering
Ashness Apartments, 15 St Marys Avenue, Harrogate, HG2 0LP

T:	+44 (0) 1756 729000
W:	ashness.com
Units:	23 • Sleeps from 2-4 • Low season £325-£455; high season £370-£535 • Credit/debit cards; cash/cheques accepted
Open:	Year round
Description:	High-quality apartments, superbly situated in a nice, quiet road of fine Victorian townhouses very near the town centre of Harrogate. Excellent shops, restaurants and cafes are a short walk away through Montpellier Gardens with the Stray and Valley Gardens just around the corner.
Offers:	Short breaks from £60 per night, minimum two nights.
Facilities:	

HARROGATE

Rudding Holiday Park
★★★★★ Holiday, Touring & Camping Park
Follifoot, Harrogate, North Yorkshire, HG3 1JH

T:	+44 (0) 1423 870439
E:	holiday-park@ruddingpark.com
W:	ruddingpark.com
Pitches:	Touring: 141 • Per night (caravan, motor caravan, tent) £15-£29 • Credit/debit cards; cash/cheques, euros accepted
Open:	Year round except Christmas and New Year
Description:	Award-winning campsite. Just three miles south of Harrogate, in peaceful setting, offering Deer House pub, swimming pool, golf course, driving range and shop. Closed February. Self-catering timber lodges also available.
Offers:	Peak season – seven nights for the price of six. Off-peak – four nights for the price of three.
Facilities:	

HARROGATE

The Barn @ Fir Tree Farm
★★★★ Self Catering
Booking address: High Winsley, Brimham Rocks Road, Burnt Yates, Harrogate, HG3 3EP

T:	+44 (0) 1423 870439
W:	thebarninharrogate.co.uk
Units:	1 • Sleeps from 1-5 • Low season £175-£295; high season £250-£495 • Cash/cheques accepted
Open:	Year round
Description:	Recently converted, The Barn offers stylish accommodation comprising two luxurious en suite bedrooms, fully equipped kitchen, cosy lounge and dining area. Features include widescreen TV and CD player. The Barn is just 15 minutes from Harrogate and overlooks the scenic Nidderdale Valley. Children's ball pool and toys available on request.
Offers:	Complimentary welcome hamper provided on arrival.
Facilities:	

HARROGATE

The White Hart Hotel/Conference Centre ★★★ Hotel
Cold Bath Road, Harrogate, HG2 0NF

T:	+44 (0) 1423 505681
E:	reception@whitehart.net
W:	whitehart.net
Rooms:	53 • B&B per room per night (single) £70-£75 • (double) £90-£95 • Credit/debit cards; cash/cheques accepted
Open:	Year round except Christmas and New Year
Description:	The White Hart Hotel & Conference Centre is a Grade II Listed building with all en suite rooms which are well presented and decorated. There are lifts to all floors, free parking and a comfortable lounge and bar area. There are also 15 fully equipped conference suites.
Offers:	Weekend breaks £50 single B&B, £75 twin/double B&B.
Facilities:	

YORKSHIRE – NORTH

YORKSHIRE – NORTH

HELMSLEY

Feversham Arms Hotel
★★★ Hotel
SILVER AWARD

1 High Street, Helmsley, YO62 5AG

T:	+44 (0) 1439 770766
E:	info@fevershamarmshotel.com
W:	fevershamarmshotel.com
Rooms:	24 • B&B per room per night (single) £140-£245 • (double) £150-£255 • Credit/debit cards; cash/cheques accepted
Open:	Year round
Description:	Luxury hideaway hotel with an excellent restaurant, chic design, leisure facilities, open fires and welcoming service. On edge of the North Yorkshire Moors and close to York. Each room has its own character and decor, TV with integral DVD/CD and a DVD/CD library. Every bathroom pampers you with Molton Brown toiletries and big, soft bathrobes.
Offers:	Please enquire at time of booking.
Facilities:	

HELMSLEY

The Hawnby Hotel
♦♦♦♦ Guest Accommodation

Hilltop, Hawnby, York, YO62 5QS

T:	+44 (0) 1439 798202
E:	info@hawnbyhotel.co.uk
W:	hawnbyhotel.co.uk
Rooms:	9 • B&B per room per night (single) £55-£59 • (double) £70-£79 • Credit/debit cards; cash/cheques, euros accepted
Open:	Year round
Description:	In an unspoilt village in the heart of the North York Moors National Park, offering spectacular views from its hill-top location. Exceptional en suite bedrooms. A peaceful, relaxing break at any time of year. Easy access for hiking, climbing, horse-riding, hang-gliding and stately homes. York 45 miles.
Offers:	Three-night stay: £70 per room per night at any time.
Facilities:	

LEYBURN

Street Head Inn
♦♦♦♦ Guest Accommodation

Newbiggin, Leyburn, North Yorkshire, DL8 3TE

T:	+44 (0) 1969 663282
E:	joanne.fawcett@virgin.net
W:	streetheadinn.co.uk
Rooms:	5 • B&B per room per night (single) £40-£45 • (double) £64-£75 • Credit/debit cards; cash/cheques accepted
Open:	Year round
Description:	Traditional, family-run, 17thC inn surrounded by the stunning scenery of Bishopdale. Well-appointed, en suite rooms with king-size beds. The inn has a large, local following and extensive a la carte menu. These attributes combine to provide an ideal base from which to explore the Dales.
Offers:	Discounts on stays of four or more days.
Facilities:	

YORKSHIRE – NORTH

LEYBURN

Sunnyridge ★★★Farmhouse
Argill Farm, Harmby, Leyburn, DL8 5HQ

T:	+44 (0) 1969 622478
E:	richah@freenet.co.uk
Rooms:	2 • B&B per room per night (double) £50-£60 • Cash/cheques accepted
Open:	Year round except Christmas
Description:	A warm welcome awaits you at Sunnyridge – a spacious bungalow set amid beautiful countryside with magnificent views over Wensleydale – the heart of the Yorkshire Dales and Herriot Country. Guests relax in comfortable surroundings after busy days walking or touring and visiting historic sites, gardens, market towns, Dales villages and many local attractions.
Offers:	Short-break deals available – £25 per night (including bank holidays) minimum three nights.
Facilities:	

LEYBURN

The Old Vicarage ♦♦♦Guest Accommodation
West Witton, Leyburn, DL8 4LX

T:	+44 (0) 1969 622108
E:	info@dalesbreaks.co.uk
W:	dalesbreaks.co.uk
Rooms:	3 • B&B per room per night (single) £27-£30 • (double) £48-£58 • Cash/cheques; euros accepted
Open:	Year round except Christmas and New Year
Description:	Four-poster, family and double en suite rooms with all facilities provided. This charming Grade II Listed former Dales vicarage has wonderful views right across Wensleydale. Spacious private car parking. Centrally placed for visiting the Dales, Lake District, Whitby or York. Friends old and new most welcome.
Offers:	Stay four nights for the price of three, Sunday-Thursday, September-March inclusive
Facilities:	

MALTON

Walnut Garth ★★★★Self Catering
Booking address: Havendale, Main Street, Swinton, YO17 6SL

T:	+44 (0) 1969 622108
E:	cas@radfords.org
W:	radfords.org
Units:	1 • Sleeps from 1-4 • Low season £202-£246; high season £280-£440 • Cash/cheques accepted
Open:	Year round
Description:	Tastefully decorated, two-bedroom cottage furnished to a high standard with all modern conveniences. Walnut Garth is set in the grounds of owner's property at edge of village, yet only two miles from market town of Malton and excellent selection of local amenities and attractions. Easy access to York and coast.
Offers:	10% discount for stays of two weeks or longer.
Facilities:	

YORKSHIRE – NORTH

PICKERING

Keld Head Farm Cottages ★★★★Self Catering
Keld Head Farm Cottages, Keld Head, Pickering, YO18 8LL

| T: | +44 (0) 1969 622108 |
| W: | keldheadcottages.com |

| Units: | 9 • Sleeps from 2-8 • Low season £189-£380; high season £424-£1,050 • Cash/cheques; euros accepted |

| Open: | Year round |

| Description: | On the edge of Pickering, in open countryside overlooking fields where sheep and cows graze. Beautiful, spacious, character stone cottages with pantile roofs, traditional stone fireplaces and beamed ceilings, tastefully furnished with the emphasis on comfort and relaxation. Some rooms with four-poster beds. Award-winning gardens with garden house. York, moors and coast easily accessible. |

| Offers: | Senior citizen and two-person discounts. Short breaks. |

| Facilities: | |

PICKERING

Let's Holiday ★★★★Self Catering
Booking address: Let's Holiday, Pickering, YO18 8QA

| T: | +44 (0) 1969 622108 |
| W: | letsholiday.com |

| Units: | 3 • Sleeps from 4-6 • Low season £282-£346; high season £610-£790 • Credit/debit cards; cash/cheques accepted |

| Open: | Year round |

| Description: | Comfortable and fully equipped offering indoor pool, spa and sauna, and set in extensive level grounds at the heart of our National Park village. Paddocks and stabling for DIY livery. Village pub, play area and duck pond nearby. Perfect for exploring North York Moors, the coast and City of York. |

| Offers: | Low season short breaks – two or three nights over the weekend and four nights for the price of three mid-week. |

| Facilities: | |

SCARBOROUGH

Cayton Village ★★★★★Touring & Camping Park
Mill Lane, Cayton Bay, Scarborough, North Yorkshire, YO11 3NN

T:	+44 (0) 1723 583171
E:	info@caytontouring.co.uk
W:	caytontouring.co.uk

| Pitches: | Touring: 200 • Per night (caravan, motor caravan) £11.50-£24; tent from £9-£18 • Credit/debit cards; cash/cheques accepted |

| Open: | March to October |

| Description: | Luxurious facilities, adventure playground, site shop, dog walk. Seasonal pitches, supersites, hardstanding and storage. Half a mile to beach. Next to village. |

| Offers: | Low season savers: seven nights – £7 discount, any four nights Sunday-Thursday inclusive – £4 discount, senior citizen seven-night special - £10 discount. |

| Facilities: | |

SCARBOROUGH

Flower of May Holiday Parks Ltd
★★★★★ Holiday, Touring & Camping Park

Lebberston, Scarborough, North Yorkshire, YO11 3NU

T:	+44 (0) 1723 584311
E:	info@flowerofmay.com
W:	flowerofmay.com
Pitches:	Touring: 300; touring caravans: 220; motor caravans: 30; tents: 50; caravan holiday homes: 20 • Per night (caravan, motor caravan) £13.50-£18.50; Tent from £11-£18.50; caravan holiday home £190-£450 • Credit/debit cards; cash/cheques accepted
Open:	April to October
Description:	Excellent facilities on family-run park. Luxury indoor pool, adventure playground, golf course. Ideal for coast and country.
Offers:	Early-booking discount: £25 off full week's hire. 10% discount off full week's pitch fees, booked by post in advance.
Facilities:	

SCARBOROUGH

Howdale
◆◆◆◆ Guest Accommodation

121 Queen's Parade, Scarborough, North Yorkshire, YO12 7HU

T:	+44 (0) 1723 372696
E:	mail@howdalehotel.co.uk
W:	howdalehotel.co.uk
Rooms:	15 • B&B per room per night (single) £22-£25 • (double) £50-£59 • Credit/debit cards; cash/cheques accepted
Open:	Year round except Christmas and New Year
Description:	Beautifully situated overlooking North Bay and Scarborough Castle, yet close to town. Renowned for cleanliness and the friendly, efficient service provided in a comfortable atmosphere. Substantial breakfasts are deservedly famous. Thirteen of the excellent bedrooms are en suite, many have sea views. All have TV, tea/coffee facilities, hairdryer etc.
Offers:	Mini-breaks (three nights minimum) March-early July, September and October, from £23 per person per night.
Facilities:	

SKIPTON

Cononley Hall B&B
◆◆◆◆◆ Guest Accommodation

Main Street, Cononley, Skipton, BD20 8LJ   SILVER AWARD

T:	+44 (0) 1535 633923
E:	cononleyhall@madasafish.com
W:	cononleyhall.co.uk
Rooms:	3 • B&B per room per night (single) £50-£50 • (double) £70-£80 • Credit/debit cards; cash/cheques accepted
Open:	Year round except Christmas and New Year
Description:	Grade II Listed Georgian house in unspoilt village, near to Skipton. Cononley Hall is ideally located for those wishing to explore the Dales or Brontë countryside and attractions. All rooms are en suite and offer excellent facilities. Breakfast consists of local produce, including own free-range eggs.
Offers:	Stays of three nights or more only £35 per person (based on two sharing). Children aged three and under – free.
Facilities:	

YORKSHIRE – NORTH

YORKSHIRE – NORTH

STAITHES

Pennysteel Cottage ★★★Self Catering
Booking address: Waterfront Cottages, 2 Star Row, North Dalton, Driffield, YO25 9UX

T:	+44 (0) 1377 217662
E:	chris@adastra-music.co.uk
W:	waterfrontcottages.co.uk
Units:	1 • Sleeps - call for details • Low season £237-£325; high season £330-£595 • Credit/debit cards; cash/cheques accepted
Open:	Year round
Description:	Old fisherman's cottage of unique character with beamed ceilings, wood-panelled walls and wood-burning stove. All windows and terrace overlook the picturesque harbour of Staithes. Ideal for the coast and walking. Top-quality restaurant, pub serving food, cafes, art gallery and craft and local shops all within a few yards.
Offers:	5% discount for repeat booking.
Facilities:	

THIRSK

Borrowby Mill B&B ♦♦♦♦Guest Accommodation
Borrowby, Nr Thirsk, YO7 4AW
SILVER AWARD

T:	+44 (0) 1845 537717
E:	mvpborrowby@compuserve.com
W:	borrowbymill.co.uk
Rooms:	3 • B&B per room per night (single) £37.5-£60 • (double) £66-£70 • Credit/debit cards; cash/cheques accepted
Open:	Year round except Christmas and New Year
Description:	Tastefully converted 18thC flour mill in a secluded location between Thirsk and Northallerton. Convenient for touring North Yorkshire Moors and Dales. Cosy en suite rooms, excellent breakfasts and dinners prepared by chef/proprietor. Relax in our drawing room with library or explore our woodland gardens.
Offers:	In spring and autumn we run courses in all types of embroidery. Please ask for our brochure.
Facilities:	

THORALBY

The George Inn ♦♦♦♦Guest Accommodation
Thoralby, Leyburn, North Yorkshire, DL8 3SU

T:	+44 (0) 1969 663256
E:	visit@thegeorge.tv
W:	thegeorge.tv
Rooms:	2 • B&B per room per night (double) £56-£66 • Credit/debit cards; cash/cheques accepted
Open:	Year round
Description:	The George Inn is in the picturesque village of Thoralby in Bishopdale, a hidden oasis in the heart of the Dales. This is an ideal location for exploring the Yorkshire Dales National Park. We provide en suite bed and breakfast accommodation, together with excellent meals, real ales and good wines.
Offers:	Easter to end October, minimum three-night stay, Monday-Thursday – 10% discount. Winter extra 5% discount.
Facilities:	

YORKSHIRE – NORTH

WHITBY

Saxonville Hotel
★★★ Hotel
SILVER AWARD

Ladysmith Avenue, Whitby, North Yorkshire, YO21 3HX

T:	+44 (0) 1947 602631
E:	newtons@saxonville.co.uk
W:	saxonville.co.uk
Rooms:	23 • B&B per room per night (single) £60-£85 • (double) £120-£150 • Credit/debit cards; cash/cheques accepted
Open:	Year round except Christmas and New Year
Description:	Family owned and run since 1946. The hotel is situated on the West Cliff just a short stroll from Whitby's narrow streets and winding alleys. Guests are assured of a warm, friendly welcome and a high standard of service. Private car park. No supplement on single rooms.
Offers:	Three-night break (any night) during 2007 from £195 per person.
Facilities:	

YORK

23 St Marys
♦♦♦♦ Guest Accommodation
SILVER AWARD

23 St Marys, York, YO30 7DD

T:	+44 (0) 1904 622738
E:	stmarys23@hotmail.com
W:	23stmarys.co.uk
Rooms:	9 • B&B per room per night (single) £36-£45 • (double) £60-£80 • Credit/debit cards; cash/cheques, euros accepted
Open:	Year round
Description:	Large Victorian terraced house peacefully set within five minutes' stroll of city centre. Spacious rooms, antique furnishings, en suite bedrooms of different sizes and character. Extensive breakfast menu in elegant surroundings. Julie and Chris will offer you a warm welcome to their home.
Offers:	Third night at 50% reduction (excluding peak periods).
Facilities:	

YORK

Ascot Lodge
★★★★ Guest Accommodation

112 Acomb Road, York, YO24 4EY

T:	+44 (0) 1904 798234
E:	info@ascotlodge.com
W:	ascotlodge.com
Rooms:	10 • B&B per room per night (single) £30-£35 • (double) £60-£70 • Cash/cheques accepted
Open:	Year round
Description:	Receive a warm welcome at this beautiful mid-Victorian guesthouse on the west side of York. Peaceful, yet near to the city centre – 25 minutes' walk or 5-10 minutes by regular bus service. Luxurious, en suite double, family and single rooms. Non-smoking throughout. Secure, private car park. Vegetarians catered for.
Offers:	Single-night price reduction for two or more nights' stay.
Facilities:	

YORKSHIRE – NORTH

YORK

Best Western York Pavilion Hotel ★★★Hotel
45 Main Street, Fulford, York, YO10 4PJ

T:	+44 (0) 1904 622099
E:	help@yorkpavilionhotel.com
W:	yorkpavilionhotel.com
Rooms:	57 • B&B per room per night (single) £90 • (double) £130-£150 • Credit/debit cards; cash/cheques accepted
Open:	Year round
Description:	The most distinctive hotel in the area, situated just 1.5 miles from the historic city of York. An elegant, Grade II Listed building boasting spacious, en suite bedrooms, equipped to modern standards with traditional and tasteful decor. Situated close to the racecourse, it is a perfect venue for entertaining.
Offers:	Sunday night free when booking Friday and Saturday.
Facilities:	

YORK

Bishops Hotel ♦♦♦♦♦ Guest Accommodation
135 Holgate Road, York, YO24 4DF
SILVER AWARD

T:	+44 (0) 1904 628000
E:	enquiries@bishopshotel.co.uk
W:	bishopshotel.co.uk
Rooms:	13 • B&B per room per night (single) £40-£50 • (double) £70-£120 • Credit/debit cards (5% surcharge on credit cards); cash/cheques, euros accepted
Open:	Year round except Christmas
Description:	Elegant Victorian villa, peaceful yet near to the city centre. Spacious, comfortable interior with individually styled suites and bedrooms all en suite. Hearty breakfast using fresh, local produce. Non-smoking, fully licensed establishment.
Offers:	Celebration Package of flowers, chocolates and champagne. Business-traveller and off-peak, mid-week, short-break rates available Sunday-Thursday.
Facilities:	

YORK

Blakeney Hotel ★★★★Hotel
180 Stockton Lane, York, YO31 1ES

T:	+44 (0) 1904 422786
E:	reception@blakeneyhotel-york.co.uk
W:	blakeneyhotel-york.co.uk
Rooms:	17 • B&B per room per night (single) £38-£50 • (double) £56-£80 • Credit/debit cards; cash/cheques, euros accepted
Open:	Year round except Christmas
Description:	Within easy reach of the city centre. Well-appointed, en suite bedrooms with colour TV and tea-/coffee-making facilities. Comfortable lounge and licensed bar. Full English breakfasts and evening dinner – special diets catered for. Non-smoking. Large, private car park.
Offers:	10% discount for seven or more nights. Special rates for three nights' DB&B (excluding bank holidays).
Facilities:	

YORKSHIRE – NORTH

YORK

Dean Court Hotel ★★★Hotel
Duncombe Place, York, YO1 7EF

T:	+44 (0) 1904 625082
E:	info@deancourt-york.co.uk
W:	deancourt-york.co.uk
Rooms:	37 • B&B per room per night (single) £85-£120 • (double) £115-£205 • Credit/debit cards; cash/cheques accepted
Open:	Year round
Description:	Superbly appointed hotel opposite York Minster. All the historic attractions of York are within easy walking distance. All public areas have been tastefully refurbished (February 2004) along with the rosette-awarded restaurant, re-launched as DCH. The new decor is contemporary with magnificent design features. The Court Café-Bistro opened April 2006.
Offers:	Two-night, mid-week literary or wine and food breaks with top authors, wine producers.
Facilities:	

YORK

Hedley House Hotel ★★Hotel
3-4 Bootham Terrace, York, YO30 7DH
SILVER AWARD

T:	0800 583 6374
E:	greg@hedleyhouse.com
W:	hedleyhouse.com
Rooms:	24 • B&B per room per night (single) £50-£70 • (double) £80-£100 • Credit/debit cards; cash/cheques accepted
Open:	Year round except Christmas
Description:	Family-run hotel in a quiet residential area, eight minutes from city centre, near bus and rail. All rooms recently refurbished. Lounge bar and restaurant. Vegetarian and special diets catered for. Off-street car park and lock-up garages available. Garden decking with six-person outdoor aqua spa Jacuzzi.
Offers:	Winter break – book two nights, get third half price. Chocolates, champagne and flowers in your room on arrival – £45.
Facilities:	

YORK

The Grange Hotel ★★★Hotel
1 Clifton, York, YO30 6AA
GOLD AWARD

T:	+44 (0) 1904 644744
E:	info@grangehotel.co.uk
W:	grangehotel.co.uk
Rooms:	30 • B&B per room per night (single) £115-£180 • (double) £150-£260 • Credit/debit cards; cash/cheques accepted
Open:	Year round
Description:	Country house elegance in heart of the city is the hallmark of this stylish, award-winning hotel and rosette-awarded restaurant situated just a short walk from the minster and city-centre shops. Luxury accommodation and free car parking.
Offers:	Two-night breaks from £80 per person per night (two sharing) including full Yorkshire breakfast, dinner and VAT. Christmas and New Year packages available.
Facilities:	

YORKSHIRE – NORTH

YORK

The Hazelwood ♦♦♦♦ Guest Accommodation
24-25 Portland Street, York, YO31 7EH
SILVER AWARD

T:	+44 (0) 1904 626548
E:	Reservations@thehazelwoodyork.com
W:	thehazelwoodyork.com
Rooms:	13 • B&B per room per night (single) £50-£95 • (double) £80-£110 • Credit/debit cards; cash/cheques accepted
Open:	Year round
Description:	Situated in the very heart of York only 400 yards from York Minster in an extremely quiet residential area. An elegant Victorian townhouse with private car park providing high-quality accommodation in individually designed en suite bedrooms. Extensive breakfast menu catering for all tastes including vegetarian. Completely non-smoking.
Offers:	Three nights for the price of two, Sunday-Thursday, November-Easter (excluding school holidays).
Facilities:	

YORK

York House ★★★★ Guest Accommodation
62 Heworth Green, York, YO31 7TQ

T:	+44 (0) 1904 427070
E:	yorkhouse.bandb@tiscali.co.uk
W:	yorkhouseyork.com
Rooms:	8 • B&B per room per night (single) £27.5-£33 • (double) £55-£66 • Credit/debit cards; cash/cheques accepted
Open:	Year round except Christmas and New Year
Description:	Located a short stroll from the heart of one of Europe's most historic cities. York House is the perfect base for a visit to beautiful York or the surrounding area. A Georgian house with later additions, rooms feature all the modern conveniences you could possibly need for a relaxing, enjoyable stay.
Offers:	Four-poster rooms £33-£38 per person per night.
Facilities:	

YORK

York Touring Caravan Site ★★★★ Touring & Camping Park
Towthorpe Lane, Towthorpe, York, YO32 9ST

T:	+44 (0) 1904 499275
E:	info@yorkcaravansite.co.uk
W:	yorkcaravansite.co.uk
Pitches:	Touring: 40; touring caravans: 20; motor caravans: 20; tents: 10 • Per night (caravan, motor caravan, tent) £10-£18.50 • Credit/debit cards; cash/cheques accepted
Open:	Year round
Description:	Small, family-run, secluded park in an idyllic countryside setting, only five miles from York centre. Spacious pitches and superior facilities. New shower and toilet facilities. Bar open Friday and Saturday nights.
Offers:	Book seven nights in advance and only pay for six (excluding bank holidays).
Facilities:	

BARNSLEY

Brooklands Hotel ★★★★Hotel
Barnsley Road, Dodworth, Barnsley, South Yorkshire, S75 3JT

T:	+44 (0) 1226 299571
E:	enquiries@brooklandshotel.com
W:	brooklandshotel.com
Rooms:	77 • B&B per room per night (single) £85-£0 • (double) £95-£0 • Credit/debit cards; cash/cheques accepted
Open:	Year round
Description:	Winner of the Yorkshire Tourist Board's Best Hotel 2005, Brooklands offers elegance and luxury, with all en suite bedrooms. The Grill serves the best quality and choice of dishes and wines to suit all tastes. The Living Well Health Club is available for guests staying at the hotel.
Offers:	Special weekend leisure breaks from £57.50 per person per night DB&B based on two sharing a twin/double room for two nights (subject to availability).
Facilities:	

BARNSLEY

Tankersley Manor ★★★★Hotel
Church Lane, Tankersley, Barnsley, S75 3DQ SILVER AWARD

T:	+44 (0) 1226 744700
E:	tankersley@marstonhotels.com
W:	marstonhotels.com
Rooms:	100 • B&B per room per night (single) £99-£232.50 • (double) £130-£230 • Credit/debit cards; cash/cheques accepted
Open:	Year round except Christmas and New Year
Description:	Tankersley Manor sensitively incorporates a 17thC building with a modern hotel, with many original features retained. Guests are invited to enjoy the indoor pool, gym, steam and sauna rooms and indulge in body treatments. Room options include suites and executive rooms.
Offers:	Save 20% on our two-night HB break in July and August and November to February (excluding bank holidays, 23 December-1 January and Valentines).
Facilities:	

YORKSHIRE – SOUTH

BRIGHOUSE

Waterfront Lodge ★★Hotel
Huddersfield Road, Brighouse, West Yorkshire, HD6 1JZ

T:	+44 (0) 1484 715566
E:	info@waterfrontlodge.co.uk
W:	waterfrontlodge.co.uk
Rooms:	58 • B&B per room per night (single) £34.95-£50.95 • (double) £44.50-£90 • Credit/debit cards; cash/cheques accepted
Open:	Year round except Christmas and New Year
Description:	Quality designer accommodation at realistic prices, on the banks of the picturesque Calder and Hebble canal in the heart of West Yorkshire Pennines. The Waterfront is ideally located off the M62, giving access to all of Yorkshire's attractions. Dine in our contemporary continental restaurant, 'Prego'.
Offers:	Weekend breaks: double and twin rooms £40.
Facilities:	

YORKSHIRE – WEST

YORKSHIRE – WEST

HUDDERSFIELD

Healds Hall Hotel ★★★ Hotel
Leeds Road, Liversedge, West Yorkshire, WF15 6JA

T:	+44 (0) 1924 409112
E:	enquire@healdshall.co.uk
W:	healdshall.co.uk
Rooms:	24 • B&B per room per night (single) £40-£63 • (double) £60-£75 • Credit/debit cards; cash/cheques, euros accepted
Open:	Year round except Christmas and New Year
Description:	18thC, family-run hotel, with nationally acclaimed, award-winning restaurant, set in large, established gardens. All en suites have bath and shower. Ideal venue for wedding receptions and conferences. Our successful bistro is a great attraction. Licensed for civil wedding ceremonies.
Offers:	Special weekend breaks available from £100 per person, including meals. That's £200 for the whole weekend. Friday and Saturday evening includes DB&B on both evenings.
Facilities:	

OTLEY

Best Western Chevin Country Park Hotel ★★★ Hotel
Yorkgate, Otley, West Yorkshire, LS21 3NU

T:	+44 (0) 1943 467818
E:	reception@chevinhotel.com
W:	chevinhotel.com
Rooms:	49 • B&B per room per night (single) £105-£139 • (double) £115-£220 • Credit/debit cards; cash/cheques accepted
Open:	Year round
Description:	An outstanding country retreat. This extraordinary hotel quietly nestles in 50 acres of woodland with lakes and gardens. Full leisure facilities. Award-winning Lakeside Restaurant. Individually designed rooms either in the main building or exclusive woodland lodges. Open fires in winter.
Offers:	50% discount on Sunday nights (excluding bank holidays). See website for bargain offers.
Facilities:	

WENTBRIDGE

Wentbridge House Hotel ★★★ Hotel
Wentbridge, Pontefract, West Yorkshire, WF8 3JJ — SILVER AWARD

T:	+44 (0) 1977 620444
E:	info@wentbridgehouse.co.uk
W:	wentbridgehouse.co.uk
Rooms:	18 • B&B per room per night (single) £85-£130 • (double) £115-£165 • Credit/debit cards; cash/cheques accepted
Open:	Year round
Description:	Dating from 1700, 11 miles from Doncaster and situated in 20 acres of the beautiful Went Valley among century-old trees, Wentbridge House is famous for its special hospitality. Delicious, award-winning food and wines, first-rate service and individually furnished bedrooms. Wireless broadband.
Offers:	Weekend breaks available. Phone for further information. Regular special offers in the Brasserie for lunch and dinner.
Facilities:	